BYRON'S *DON JUAN*

Byron's
Don Juan

BERNARD BEATTY

BARNES & NOBLE BOOKS
Totowa, New Jersey

©1985 Bernard Beatty
First published in the USA 1985 by
Barnes & Noble Books,
81 Adams Drive,
Totowa, New Jersey, 07512

Library of Congress Cataloging in Publication Data

Beatty, B.G. (Bernard G.)
   Byron's Don Juan.

   Bibliography: p.
   Includes Index.
   1. Byron, George Gordon Byron, Baron, 1788-1824.
Don Juan. 2. Don Juan in Literature. I. Title.
PR4359.B43   1985   821'.7   85-13436
ISBN 0-389-20589-3

Printed and bound in Great Britain

CONTENTS

for

Anne, Guy, Emma, James and Sebastian

ILLUSTRATIONS

PREFACE

This study is not intended to be a general introduction to *Don Juan* nor does it claim to be comprehensive. There are other useful things for critics to do with *Don Juan* than pose and try to answer the governing questions of these chapters. However, the questions are central ones and this is not simply 'an approach' to the poem. It is by no means directed exclusively to Byron specialists or to scholars of Romantic literature. It is intended to be of some interest to all those concerned with literature in general and poetry in particular.

There are four chapters which, together, form a single argument. The terms of this argument are set up in the first chapter. Chapters 2 and 3 are the body of the argument and Chapter 4 is its terminus. The book exists in order to persuade readers of the truth of its conclusion. The last chapter, 'Aurora Raby', is the most important one in the book but it is designed to be reached after the others. The four chapters could be crudely subtitled *Death, Thought, Sex* and *Holiness* in *Don Juan* – that is what they are concerned with – but this would mislead for the book is about literary procedures not concepts.

For reasons which are explained in the first chapter, I am mainly concerned with the end of *Don Juan* but one of the objects of this concentrated attention is to sustain focus on the poem as a whole. The reader will find that all of *Don Juan* is discussed and other poems of Byron, especially *Cain* and *The Island*, are examined in so far as they throw light on Byron's masterpiece. I have found it useful to refer frequently to the original version of the Don Juan story.

There would be no point in writing a book on a well-known poem unless it called attention to something important in itself and insufficiently regarded. However, my own developing sense of *Don Juan*, and much else besides, has been wholly formed by insights, patterns of thought and a vocabulary derived from other scholars, critics and colleagues. I have also learnt a great deal from books with which I finally disagree such as G.M. Ridenour's rightly influential study *The Style of Don Juan*. What this book tries to do is indeed most economically indicated by the significant omission of two great critics. M.H. Abrams, in *Natural Supernaturalism* and elsewhere, is concerned with the survival and transmission in adapted form of religious concepts and structures in Romantic poetry. Northrop Frye, in *Secular Scripture* and throughout his remarkable career, has postulated the religious basis, authenticity and perennial vitality of Romance and comedy. Both writers largely ignore or exempt Byron's poetry from their investigations.[1] Such an exception is natural enough, for the inclusion of Byron would necessitate the modification and partial reversal of these approaches. If we read *Don Juan* with much the same interests as Abrams and Frye, do we emend the poem or dismantle some of the critical superstructure which has been erected around the imagination, secularisation, and Romantic poetry? To do the latter is not to subvert the enterprise of these great scholars but to place it in a different, even enhancing, perspective.

It would be impossible to acknowledge fully or even to track down my numerous debts but I should mention Professor G. Wilson Knight and the late Professor T.J.R. Spencer, both of whom were warm in their encouragement of the long process which led to this book. The germ of my reading of *Don Juan* is contained in a few sentences of Wilson Knight's early essay in 'The Burning Oracle'. Terence Spencer's quiet scholarship and huge delight in Byron's poetry permanently impressed me. The work of Professor Jerome McGann now occupies a major place in Byron criticism and is, I hope, sufficiently saluted in my text and endnotes. I am also indebted to a series of conversations about various stumbling-blocks in this inquiry with patient and knowledgeable colleagues, especially Vincent Newey, Tony Barley, Geoffrey Ward, David Seed, Edward Burns, John O'Brien, A.V. Knowles among many others. I owe far more than I can say to my friend and colleague at Liverpool University, Brian Nellist, who has meticulously read all my various drafts, mollified my self-doubt, endured my vanity and made innumerable, valuable suggestions. I have had the benefit not only of his incomparable erudition but also his skills as a photographer which are evident in this book.

I am grateful to the Vice-Chancellor and Senate of Liverpool University and to Professors Keith McWatters, Philip Edwards and James Cross for allowing me a term's study-leave. Joan Welford, Cathy Rees, Jacqui Dunne, Lorraine Campbell and Tina Benson deserve my thanks for their indefatigable labours with a variety of word machines. Croom Helm, and Richard Stoneman in particular, have been exemplary in their courtesy and efficiency.

All those who engage in Byron studies use with immense gratitude the splendid collection of Byron's letters edited by Leslie Marchand and the same author's indispensable biographies of the poet. Unfortunately, only two volumes of Professor McGann's eagerly awaited definitive edition of Byron's poetry are at hand as I write. This means that I quote from a variety of editions as follows:

All quotations from *Don Juan* are taken from *Byron's Don Juan: A Variorum Edition*, T.G. Steffan and W.W. Pratt (eds.) (4 vols., Austin, Texas, 1957).

All quotations from Byron's early poems and from *Childe Harold's Pilgrimage* are taken, respectively, from Volumes 1 and 2 of Lord Byron, *The Complete Poetical Works*, J.J. McGann (ed.) (Oxford, 1980).

All quotations from *Cain* are from *Lord Byron's Cain*, T.G. Steffan (ed.) (Austin, Texas, 1968).

All other quotations from Byron's poetry are from *The Works of Lord Byron*, E.H. Coleridge (ed.) (7 vols., London, 1898-1904).

Some material is quoted from the notes to the Penguin edition of *Lord Byron: Don Juan*, T.G. Steffan, E. Steffan and W.W. Pratt (eds.) (Harmondsworth, 1973).

All quotations from Byron's letters and journals are taken from *Byron's Letters and Journals*, Leslie Marchand (ed.) (12 vols., London, 1973-81).

Translations, unless otherwise stated, are my own. Where a quotation remains untranslated, the context always supplies sufficient paraphrase of its meaning.

Where quotations are given without acknowledgement, the following editions have been used:

The Authorised Version of the Bible; William Shakespeare, *The Complete Works*, Peter Alexander (ed.) (London, 1951); the Oxford Standard Authors edition of *Shelley's Poetical Works*, T. Hutchinson (ed.), (London, 1935); *Dryden's Poetical Works*, J. Sargeant (ed.) (London, 1913); the Oxford Standard Authors edition of *Spenser's Poetical Works*, J.C. Smith and E. de Selincourt (eds.) (London, 1912); and William Wordsworth, *Poetical Works*, T. Hutchinson (ed.), revised E. de Selincourt (London, 1904, 1936, paperback edn, 1969); the Twickenham edition in one volume of *The Poems of Alexander Pope*, J. Butt (ed.) (London, 1963).

Notes

1. M.H. Abrams in *Natural Supernaturalism* (New York, 1971) specifically exempts Byron from his investigation. Northrop Frye's references to Byron suggest dislike or indifference.

1 COMMANDANT AND COMMENDATORE

In a long poem, problems of procedure are central. How do we get from one part of the poem to the next? If the transitions are continually obvious at a first reading, we may come to resent the consequent reduction of poetic devices to an ancillary and local role in a work which may be poetic in all its parts but is never a poetic whole. If, on the other hand, the transitions cannot be described rationally at all, only intuited after several readings, as T.S. Eliot claimed after reading St John Perse's *Anabase*, then we may be troubled by fears that such usurpation of the wholeness brought about by intelligibility undermines the long poem altogether:

> I may, I trust, borrow from Mr Fabre two notions which may be of use to the English reader. The first is that any obscurity of the poem, on first readings, is due to the suppression of 'links in the chain', of explanatory and connecting matter, and not to incoherence or the love of cryptogram . . . The reader has to allow the images to fall into his memory successively without questioning the reasonableness of each at the moment; so that, at the end, a total effect is produced.
>
> Such selection of images and ideas has nothing chaotic about it. There is a logic of the imagination as well as a logic of concepts. People who do not appreciate poetry always find it difficult to distinguish between order and chaos in the arrangement of images; and even those who are capable of appreciating poetry cannot depend upon first impressions. I was not convinced of Mr Perse's imaginative order until I had read the poem five or six times.[1]

As always T.S. Eliot is persuasive but he is so in the manner of a barrister brilliantly arguing a case in which he cannot quite believe himself. For a successful long poem, however responsive to elusive particularities and the inspection of private eyes and ears, must inhabit and inform some much more confessedly public space than Eliot, here at any rate, seems to presume. The larger the building, the more we detect self-contradiction if it is quite unavailable to the public at large. It should be possible, though not necessarily easy, to say *why* 'a total effect is produced' and not merely *that* 'a total effect is produced'

1

when we read a long poem. It should be possible also to characterise the 'total effect' produced.

Bryon's *Don Juan* would seem to yield answers to such questions more readily than *Anabase*. It depends upon narrative and takes many a side-swipe at the unintelligibility of contemporary poetry. If then we go on to to ask more specifically 'How does *Don Juan* proceed?' and 'What kind of poem is it?', these would seem to be reasonable questions to which helpful answers could be found. It is not clear, however, that we have found them despite the substantial and impressive critical and scholarly labours that have so much illuminated Byron's masterpiece since the appearance of the Variorum *Don Juan* in 1957.

Of course, the poem itself is determined to evade critical capture. It stands still or prattles on and, in any event, avoids 'proceeding'. Correspondingly it evades specific category but invokes such diverse categories as epic, comedy, satire, romance, burlesque and novel. In any event, it disconcerts the categoriser. Hence, for practical purposes, we tend to slip over these questions. Where we might try to hold the poem to some defining procedure, we may instead simply commend its unceasing invention. The problem of category can be glanced at by noting the self-proclaimed 'medley' character of *Don Juan* and observing its undoubted manipulation of different generic devices. A reference to the eighteenth-century novel may conclude the case, but the case comes to no conclusion.

These questions nevertheless continue to puzzle the reader. For when we read *Don Juan*, we cannot avoid noticing the bizarre but recognisable devices by which it is sustained. Moreover, as the obstacles to the poem's course and survival thicken and deepen so the poem's abilities to incorporate, withstand, bypass or repel alien life-forms increases. Of course, the use of an organic metaphor such as this can scarcely be neutral but the appeal to a reader's undoubted acknowledgement of process and kind may be admitted for it is given definition by pain.

Don Juan, like any narrative, depends upon continuity. Like farce or 'great adventure' (Spenser's *Faerie Queene*, 1, 19), however, it is necessarily marked by extreme crises of continuity. Such crises provoke anxiety or uneasy laughter. Normally the surmounting of these impediments to narrative progress appeases anxieties. Suppose, for instance, that we imposed unnatural breaks in a reading performance of *Don Juan* at such awkward moments as Don Alfonso's stumbling over adulterous Juan's shoes, casting lots for cannibalism in the longboat, the return of Lambro, the Sultana's order for Juan's execution, the footpad's brandished knife on Shooter's HIll, or Juan's attempt to clutch the ghostly Black Friar — the resumption of narrative would then become as pressing and welcome as a newly changed reel in a Buster Keaton movie or resuming the thread of Moll Flanders's escapades. This comic model, however, fails to account for the persistence of a different kind of anxiety. There is a real sense in which the anxieties of the reader of *Don Juan* are deepened as well as appeased by reading on. We begin to feel emotions analogous to those associated with bereavement, the guilt peculiar to survivors.

Such guilt always fascinated Byron; here, for the first time, he makes his readers suffer it too. Because of it, elsewhere in his poetry, Lara, Alp, Azo, Manfred, Cain, even Sardanapalus, are haunted and immobilised by a past which they can never forget. But the 'forgetfulness' which Manfred vainly seeks (*Manfred* I, 1, 136) is Juan's permanent possession. Nor does Juan make Lara's mistake who 'half mistook for fate the act of will' (*Lara*, 1, 336) since Juan, at least until his 'service' with Catherine the Great, is rarely given choices. His co-operation with a comic fate is accomplished rather than requested.

Yet the reader is often at a loss to find appropriate comic response to this fate. Juan, we feel, should not desert the beautiful memory of Donna Julia's eyes for the retching movements of his sea-sick stomach, should not survive with silly, sexy opera singers whilst Haidée lies dead in her Cycladean isle. Nor can we be happy with Juan's insouciant success in the bloody Siege of Ismail nor with the narrator's[2] sick jokes about 'widows of forty' who survived that siege but were so unfortunate as to miss their wished-for rape (VIII, 132). We come to be at least as anxious that our hero *will* surmount each obstacle to comic continuity as that he will not.

A glance at two necessary precedents for Byron's poem will make this anxiety more specific.

Byron refers far more frequently to Homer's *Iliad* than to his *Odyssey* in *Don Juan* but, if Homer's two works do provide, like Plato and Aristotle for Western philosophy, dual archetypes for European poetry then Byron's wandering hero is manifestly heir to Ulysses and features of the wily Greek ancestor may still be discerned in his naïve Spanish avatar.[3] In the *Odyssey*, the hero, like Juan, sole survivor of a shipwreck, is washed up on an island inhabited by an attractive nymph. We do not begrudge his survival here any more than, finally, we regret the massacre of Penelope's suitors. This is in part because both suitors and sailors have transgressed (the latter by destroying the oxen of the sun), and thus stand in need of punishment, whilst Ulysses himself did not participate in these transgressions. Further Ulysses, as a hero, is clearly superior in cunning, skill and luck to his companions and therefore merits that survival normally accorded to the fittest by both Nature and Art. Less apparent but as real, Ulysses is a home-comer. He is not motivated by Eros, for Eros, in the paralysing shape of Circe, Calypso, Sirens or even Nausicaa, is likely to be an opponent of his safe return.

Hence Ulysses' skills as a wanderer and individual survivor in no way threaten customary moral and social values centred in community, continuity and quiet.

Byron's Don Juan, on the other hand, is inspired by Eros, does participate in the transgression but not the punishment of those who suffer, and journeys always away from his Spanish home even though he ends up in Byron's English one (Newstead/Norman Abbey). Despite his hero's luck and looks, he is more anti-hero than hero. The only society built round him is the love-feast over which he and Haidée preside in Canto IV. This 'forgetful' society usurps those very rights of returning fathers (Lambro's) which Ulysses's return restores to Ithaca.[4]

It is no wonder then that the reader is anxious. But if we go from Byron's major pagan precedent to his major Christian one we may have to revise our estimate of Juan's responsibility for this disquiet.

Tirso de Molina's *El burlador de Sevilla y convidado de Piedra* is a much less direct precedent for Byron than *The Odyssey* even though Tirso's hero is also Byron's. Byron must have seen and read plays based on the Spanish work but there is no detailed resemblance between the Spanish play and Byron's poem. Tirso's early seventeenth-century play is the prototype of Don Juan literature, of Molière's *Don Juan*, Shadwell's *The Libertine* and Mozart's *Don Giovanni*. In it, Don Juan Tenorio slays the Commander of Seville in a duel when the latter interrupts Don Juan's seduction of his daughter. Juan escapes from this, from shipwreck and further cold-hearted seductions to take sanctuary eventually in the church where the murdered commander is buried. Juan jestingly invites the stone statue of his dead adversary to a banquet. The statue comes, grasps Juan's hand, and takes him to hell forever. Not much of this finds place in Byron's poem. As everyone knows, Byron's Don Juan is seduced rather than seducing and there is no stone guest to carry Juan off to hell. It is possible, however, that much of the material[5] which Byron had at the back of his mind for inclusion in *Don Juan* found its way into that great burst of activity in 1821 when Byron left a gap between writing Canto V and Canto VI of some 16 months. *Cain* (1821), for example, provides in Act II 'A pan-

oramic view of hell' (*Don Juan*, 1, 200) which Byron had flippantly
promised his readers at the beginning of *Don Juan*. And if there are no
stone guests, there are some striking equivalents. In *Marino Faliero*,
for instance, written in 1820 but clearly associated with the plays of
the following year, we have the stone statue of the doge's ancestors
which appears to threaten him with eventual judgement for his revolutionary transgressions:

> *Doge*. Think you that he looks down on us or no?
> *Israel Bertuccio*. My Lord, these are mere fantasies; there are
>   No eyes in marble.
> *Doge*. But there are in Death.
>   I tell thee, man, there is a spirit in
>   such things that acts and sees, unseen though felt.
>
> (III, 1, 92-6)

In *Sardanapalus* (1821), the hero encounters in a dream a whole row of
stone-like ancestors seated at table. The ghastly meal recalls that to
which the Commendatore[6] invites Don Juan Tenorio in Tirso's play.
When Sardanapalus awakes, he feels his mistress's hand with some
relief:

> *Sardanapalus*. Thy hand – so – 'tis thy hand;
>   'Tis flesh; grasp – clasp – yet closer, till I feel
>   Myself that which I was.
>
> (*Sardanapalus*, IV, 1, 42-4)

The alternative present to his mind is, presumably, that it is the hand of
Nimrod, his offended ancestor, a hand-grasp analogous to that of
Tirso's Commendatore. Such contrasts between living, warm and
capable hands and the icy hands of death may well suggest and recall
the Terror fiction of Byron's days. They do not prove that Byron was
consciously recalling his Spanish precedent. The force of *Sardanapalus*
nevertheless has much greater affinity with Tirso's essential concerns
than with those of Monk Lewis *et al.*[7] The reader of Byron's play,
more sympathetic to Sardanapalus's woman-centred delight in present
existence than he is to Don Juan Tenorio's relentless abandonment of
all attachment, is certainly forced to share Sardanapalus's horror and
enlightenment when he is compelled to meet his remote ancestors who
represent some secret kinship of vitality and Death. This is Sardanapalus's description of the Commendatore experience to his mistress:

Sardanapalus. It was so palpable, I could have touched them.
I turned from one face to another, in
The hope to find at last one which I knew
Ere I saw theirs: but no — all turned upon me,
And stared, but neither ate nor drank, but stared,
Till I grew stone, as they seemed half to be,
Yet breathing stone, for I felt life in them,
And life in me: there was a horrid kind
Of sympathy between us, as if they
Had lost a part of death to come to me,
And I the half of life to sit by them.

(*Sardanapalus*, IV, 1, 117-27)

Sardanapalus does not in fact come to this damnation. It is a true vision but not the end-vision of the play. Byron's *Don Juan*, on the other hand, not only does not have these details but, as an unfinished poem, would not appear to have an end-vision of any kind.

It is just at this point, strongly tempted to give up any further exploration of the connections between Byron's Don Juan and Don Juan Tenorio,[8] that we should hold firm, for Byron's originality normally consists in finding surprising equivalents for inherited motifs. His *Don Juan is* a new version of the old European story. For the moment, it is worth considering what the audience's reaction to Don Juan Tenorio is supposed to be.

There is no reason, internal or external, to doubt the religious motivation of Tirso de Molina's play. He was a Mercedarian friar and his drama in general is consonant with this profession. In *El burlador de Sevilla* Tirso is, far more straightforwardly than Marlowe in *Dr Faustus*, writing a powerfully orthodox play of damnation and, at the same time, satirically exposing the behaviour codes of young Spanish nobles. However, to criticise convincingly, it is necessary to delineate carefully. Yet to delinate carefully invokes a close attention to what is being criticised dangerously similar to love. It is not altogether surprising that the Council of Castile rebuked Tirso for the frankness with which he represented vice in his comedies. After this warning, he seems to have written no more plays. More worryingly, it is difficult for any drama, as such, to condemn a character who possesses considerable dramatic abilities such as 'the trickster of Seville's'. Whatever we may do outside the theatre, inside it we laugh with Volpone, or even Richard III, because they are masters of those acting skills upon which our pleasure in the theatre relies. It seems likely that this is one of the reasons for the durability of Tirso de Molina's dramatic conception. For his 'hero' can fully utilise theatrical tricks for our entertainment whilst provoking a dénouement which is simultaneously a marvellous *coup de théâtre* and dependent upon a system of endings (Divine judgement) which lie quite beyond the scope of theatrical art. The actual process of the play thus relieves us from the anxieties which our uneasy relation with its hero is likely to induce. When Don Juan Tenorio, in his final short speech, loses his customary ability to talk and trick his way out of an awkward situation, we neither gloat nor sympathise. His damnation is the best possible dramatic conclusion to the play and, at the same time, releases us from the theatre's enclosure to a future reassuringly open to the other possibility of salvation.

Readers of Byron's *Don Juan* are quite differently placed. We sympathise with Juan until the Siege. From then onwards we are instructed by the narrator and by the introduction of symbolic counterparts to Juan (Leila) to have reservations about him. We remain sympathetic, however, because his character is formed by 'fate' rather than by 'acts of will'. What troubles us is not Juan himself, nor what he may become, but simply his survival. He may and, we learn, always will live to love another day. Behind him, however, stretches a trail of destruction far more considerable than that left behind Don Juan Tenorio. It includes not only an immured Julia, a dead Haidée and her father, but also a battlefield with thousands slaughtered.

It is not Juan's career with which (as with Don Juan Tenorio's) we gleefully identify and wholly condemn so much as the whole forward movement of the poem. The reader survives with Juan, uneasily complicit in his necessary zest, as the poem stretches endlessly before us for we are trapped inside this freedom more decisively than in the theatre's enclosure. Our only remedy is to read on in the hope of discovering what sort of (poetic) world it is that enforces such paradoxes and what resources may be available to us in order to endure or, even, find value in it. We would not have the patience to persist in this long-term remedy throughout 17 cantos unless the poem suggested some answers to these questions. But it will be the poem's process rather than incidental lines and themes, however important, which will yield such answers.

This is not to underestimate the charms of narrative line in the poem, the attraction of Byron's voice, nor the real helpfulness of those major analyses of *Don Juan* which have sought to account for its unity by the persistence of certain devices (such as the continuous adjustment of contexts) or certain themes (such as appearance versus reality, the

Fall, etc.). Such accounts help to explain how the poem is kept in being. But *Don Juan* is not only 'kept in being'. It grows. Certainly if Juan himself manages to leave growing pains behind him in Seville (I, 87-96), the reader experiences them ever more acutely as the poem proceeds. Even J.J. McGann, who argues cogently and with much substance for the inappropriateness of the organic metaphor to *Don Juan*, slips into personification when he has to account for its development: 'The English Cantos are the result of Byron's response to the pressure of his own poem. *Don Juan* demanded an alteration of its procedure, and Byron met the demand.'[9] Is it possible though for criticism to exhibit the process of a poem? It seems unlikely, for a poem's procedure is manifestly designed to be uncovered by an actual reading rather than by analysis yet any critical examination, however glossed as 'a reading', must be analytical or hypothetical in form. The gap between 'active' Juan and 'reflective' narrator spectacularly mirrors the gap between reading the poem and thinking about it. The most that we can do, it seems, is to acknowledge the gap.

This familiar critical problem alters character and may find some solution when referred to *Don Juan*. Readers after all somehow bridge as well as experience the gap between Juan and narrator, otherwise they would be reading two poems rather than one. Further, *Don Juan* is — and not merely because modern critical taste would like it to be — preoccupied with its own incessant process away from its point of origin. Reflexive consciousness is more agent than opponent of its forward movement. More important still, the poem is inherently unfinished. We learn with Juan that we will extricate ourselves from the enclosure of each episode. No full stop placed by the author can be final, but a full stop must finally be placed on the author himself. It is with *Don Juan* as with *Arabian Nights*, tales and episodes can be spun indefinitely. It is only the narrator (under sentence of death) who risks final termination.[10] Indeed since the openness of *Don Juan* to its future is shown to be dependent upon Byron's relation to his, we can see why organic metaphors are both appropriate and yet, as Professor McGann argues, inadmissible. Appropriate, because we must therefore talk about the 'life' of the poem, inadmissible, because the life of the poem can never be separated from that of its author. The reader's relation with Byron's *Don Juan* hence parallels that which we have to Tirso's Don Juan. In both cases, we anticipate an indefinite sequence of episodes kept in being by erotic life-force and intellectual trickery. In both cases, we anticipate Death's arbitrary intervention as necessary conclusion. But it is Byron's bravura rather than his Don Juan's which will be stifled at last. The poem's unintended final full stop after 'slept' (XVII, 14) is the only one of thousands of accidents in *Don Juan* which proves fatal. But, as with any death, the last moments of the poem become especially significant because they fix, preserve and lay bare for contemplative judgement the resources upon which it habitually depended. Until this point, *Don Juan* defies the essentialist's insistence upon form, but the last moments of its existence confer an essence upon it and provide the critic with a cross-section by which he may gain access to the 'process' of the poem.

It ought to be possible therefore to answer our questions — How does *Don Juan* proceed? and What kind of poem is it? — by reading the poem backwards.[11] This will be my enterprise in the bulk of this study and it must be acknowledged at once that Byron disapproves:

> Oh, reader! If that thou canst read, — and know,
> 'Tis not enough to spell, or even to read,
> To constitute a reader; there must go
> Virtues of which both you and I have need
> Firstly, begin with the beginning — (though
> That clause is hard); and secondly, proceed;
> Thirdly, commence not with the end — or, sinning
> In this sort, end at least with the beginning.

> (XIII, 73)

Byron's jokes, like Don Juan Tenorio's pranks, revolve round a single purpose. For what it is we 'begin with the beginning' and with which we 'secondly, proceed' is finally determined by the end which, here as everywhere, Byron evades but calls to mind. The poem is always in readiness for an end which its ever improved expertise is deployed to resist.

Save once. A real commandant (*commandante* rather than *commendatore*) is allowed to press the claims of real Death once in the poem. The assassination of the military commandant in Ravenna on 8th December 1820 is incorporated as narrative matter for reflection directly into Canto V. It is an example contributed by 'What Sages call Chance, Providence or Fate' (VII, 76) to the poet's own relentless imitation of inexplicable common occurrences. The rest of this chapter will be concerned with it and so I quote the section in full:

[33]

The other evening ('twas on Friday last) —
This is a fact and no poetic fable —
Just as my great coat was about me cast,
My hat and gloves still lying in the table,
I heard a shot — 'twas eight o'clock scarce past —
And running out as fast as I was able,
I found the military commandant
Stretched in the street, and able scarce to pant.

[34]

Poor fellow! for some reason, surely bad,
They had slain him with five slugs; and left him there
To perish on the pavement: so I had
Him borne into the house and up the stair,
And stripped, and looked to, — But why should I add
More circumstances? vain was every care;
The man was gone: in some Italian quarrel
Killed by five bullets from an old gun-barrel.

[35]

I gazed upon him, for I knew him well;
And though I have seen many corpses, never
Saw one, whom such an accident befell,
So calm; though pierced through stomach, heart, and
    liver,
He seemed to sleep, for you could scarcely tell
(As he bled inwardly, no hideous river
Of gore divulged the cause) that he was dead:
So as I gazed on him, I thought or said —

[36]

"Can this be death? then what is life or death?
Speak!" but he spoke not: "wake!" but still he slept: —
"But yesterday and who had mightier breath?
A thousand warriors by his word were kept
In awe: he said, as the centurion saith,
'Go,' and he goeth; 'come,' and forth he stepp'd.
The trump and bugle till he spake were dumb —
And now nought left him but the muffled drum."

[37]

And they who waited once and worshipped — they
With their rough faces thronged about the bed

To gaze once more on the commanding clay
Which for the last though not the first time bled:
And such an end! that he who many a day
Had faced Napoleon's foes until they fled, –
The foremost in the charge or in the sally,
Should now be butchered in a civic alley.

[38]
The scars of his old wounds were near his new,
Those honourable scars which brought him fame;
And horrid was the contrast to the view –
But let me quit the theme; as such things claim
Perhaps even more attention than is due
From me: I gazed (as oft I have gazed the same)
To try if I could wrench aught out of death
Which should confirm, or shake, or make a faith;

[39]
But it was all a mystery. Here we are,
And there we go: – but where? five bits of lead,
Or three, or two, or one, send very far!
And is this blood then, formed but to be shed?
Can every element our elements mar?
And air – earth – water – fire live – and we dead?
We, whose minds comprehend all things? No more;
But let us to the story as before.

(V, 33-9)

The incident described here is repeatedly described also in Byron's letters for December, 1820. He uses, for the most part, a similar vocabulary and refers to the same details. The commandant's death gains natural entry into these letters simply as news. Something has occurred and Byron has participated in the event. Secondly, the incident is used as an illustration of current political feeling and the corresponding dangers of living in Italy: 'You may judge better of things here by this detail than by anything which I could add on this subject.' (to John Murray, 9th December, 1820).[12] The reader receives more or less the same impression of this event as event in these letters and in *Don Juan* but it gains entry to the poem neither as news nor as political illustration.

Byron has been discussing whether satisfying appetites for food and sex has the immediate effect of cheering us up (see Voltaire's *Candide*) or depressing us (see Alexander the Great). Byron is of the latter opinion:

> I think with Alexander, that the act
> Of eating, with another act or two,
> Makes us feel our mortality in fact
> Redoubled; when a roast and a ragout,
> And fish, and soup, by some side dishes backed,
> Can give us either pain or pleasure, who
> Would pique himself on intellects, whose use
> Depends so much upon the gastric juice?

(V, 32)

Without further connection we are suddenly *in mediis rebus* of quite a different kind: 'The other evening ('twas on Friday last) —' (V, 33). The seven stanzas detailing the assassination are in fact a later interpolation added two days after the incident occurred but some six weeks after the canto had been completed in its first form. The ostensible link connecting this section with its context is the disparagement of intellect in the concluding epigram of stanza 32:

>   ... who
> Would pique themselves on intellects, whose use
> Depends so much upon the gastric juice?

and the more comprehensive but not dissimilar conclusion to the episode:

> Can every element our elements mar?
> And air — earth — water — fire live — and we dead?
> *We*, whose minds comprehend all things? No more;
> But let us to the story as before.

(V, 39)

This is presumably the reason why Byron selected this place in the canto for his interpolation. It would not of itself be sufficient to make the grafting 'take' for the connection, though real, appears superficial, the 'gastric juice' epigram is itself at a tangent from its preceding lines and the tone of the interpolation is sustained in quite a different register from its host stanzas. Compare, for example, the poised and self-conscious languour of stanza 30's conclusion:

> . . . When dinner has opprest one,
> I think it is perhaps the gloomiest hour
> Which turns up out of the sad twenty-four.
>
>   (V, 30)

which suggests that we ('one') have plenty of time in which to consider
wittily various civilised attitudes to digestion with the urgent directness
of 'I gazed upon him, for I knew him|well;' (V. 35). The opening
formula similarly, 'The other evening ('twas on Friday last) −' (V. 33),
seizes our attention with an Ancient Mariner's gauche insistence. We
might argue that such a narrative jolt often enlivens the doldrums of
conversational chatter which half expects interruption and gains
renewal by such formulas as 'You won't believe what happened yesterday.' Moreover, *Don Juan* depends upon unnerving shifts of tone.'

In fact there is no other example of an extended personal anecdote
of this kind in the poem.[13] And though the button-holing interjection,
'The other evening ('twas on Friday last) −' (V, 33), remains a conversational possibility, we receive it as an interjection by a different voice
of the speaker. In this way it is much closer to the normal mode of
Childe Harold's Pilgrimage than to that of *Don Juan*. For the earlier
poem, which had far more interpolations than *Don Juan*, comes to be
received by the reader as a dramatic ensemble of voices originating and
remaining in touch with real places and events (Cadiz, Epirus, Waterloo,
Venice, Rome, etc.) but expressing the history of a self (Harold/Byron).
Don Juan, ostensibly more realistic, is far more harmoniously distanced
from external interjection. It is set, like the *Divine Comedy,* some 30
years before the openly acknowledged time of writing. Hence, though
past action is continually interrupted by present comment, the action
remains securely within its own recalled time and place. The narrator
on the other hand, who does live within his present, by assuming the
role of commentator forfeits his ability to initiate any action other than
that of comment. So there *is* something odd in the sudden reminder
that the narrator is capable of his own kind of action.

Having established this and without gainsaying it, we must try to
account for the apparently contradictory fact − which I will simply
assert − that the reader does not perceive the oddity of this section
when he reads the canto even though, uniquely, it sets up a mini-action
of its own within the commentary. Three factors contribute to this. In
the first place, this action is fact not fiction and set in the writer's time
and place:

> The other evening ('twas on Friday last) —
> This is a fact and no poetic fable —
> Just as my great coat was about me cast,
>
> (V, 33)

Hence it does not threaten or rival the fictional past historic of Juan's antics. Secondly, though Byron does do something,

> . . . So I had
> Him borne into the house and up the stair,
>
> (V, 34)

the main actor, albeit passive, is the commandant. Byron's role as commentator is not undermined,

> I gazed upon him, for I knew him well;
>
> (V, 35)
>
> . . . I gazed (as oft I have gazed the same)
>
> (V, 38)

The third factor is, however, crucial and central to my contention. The poem receives this interjection so readily not as any old incident which can be recycled into Art[14] but as a peculiarly corroborating instance of the poem's abiding concerns. Byron welcomes the dead commandant into his house with the same alacrity that Don Juan Tenorio welcomes the dead commendatore into his. Byron's motives for this act, though not without Tenorio's bravado (no one else has the nerve to defy possible reprisals), are, needless to say, not Tenorio's but those of the Good Samaritan:

> . . . so I had
> Him borne into the house and up the stair,
> And stripped, and looked to, —
>
> (V, 34)

just | as Juan, in the main narrative parallel to the assassination, is impelled to the 'pious duty' of helping the London highwayman whom he has, in self-defence, shot:

> . . . I can't allow
> The fellow to lie groaning on the road.

So take him up; I'll help you with the load.

(XI, 15)

But if charity lifts the commandant into Byron's house, quite other factors bring him into Byron's poem and subject him to Byron's gaze in and out of the poem. Other incidental allusions to actual occurrences[15] are readily subordinated to the poem's conversational manoeuvres as mere instances or illustrations, but the dead commandant refuses to be simply an occasion for reflection or even a stable object of attention. La Rochefoucauld maintains: 'le soleil ni la mort ne se peuvent regarder fixement'[16] (Maxime 26). ('It is impossible to gaze steadily at either the sun or death.'). Byron, in a way, does attempt to hold such a 'fixed regard' upon the dead commandant but cannot maintain it:[17]

> . . . I gazed (as oft I have gazed the same)
> To try if I could wrench aught out of death
> Which should confirm, or shake, or make a faith;
>
> But it was all a mystery.

(V, 38, 39)

Like La Rochefoucauld's sun, the dead man is too evidently 'there' to be gazed at for long. Much as the incident is imposed upon the reader: 'The other evening ('twas on Friday last) —' (V, 33), so the commandant, initially the passive object of Byron's concerned attention, imposes his passivity upon the poet. He refuses to answer Byron's questions, refuses to reveal whether he has the answers to them or not and, for a moment, forces Byron into the submissive puzzlement of the soldiers who

> With their rough faces thronged about the bed
> To gaze once more on the commanding clay.

(V, 37)

The oxymoronic 'commanding clay' tells all. He who once commanded is now clay. If this is true, all those who command do so with ludicrously 'brief authority'. This customary Byronic *sententia* here receives a new twist:

> And they who waited once and worshipped — they
> With their rough faces thronged about the bed

> To gaze once more on the commanding clay
>
> (V, 37)

Clearly, the soldiers still wait and worship their officer. Clearly, their 'rough faces' still remain in a class set below the 'commanding clay'. It is Death, however, rather than military rank which is conferring the commandant's authority.

Customarily in *Don Juan*, awkward sticking points in the narrative are manoeuvred back into flow by the interpolation of the narrator's banter. Correspondingly, the narrator's necessary immobility needs to be countered by narrative novelty. In the commandant section, both narrative and comment terminate in the little stillness separating stanzas 38 and 39:

> . . . I gazed (as oft I have gazed the same)
> To try if I could wrench aught out of death
> Which should confirm, or shake, or make a faith;
>
> But it was all a mystery.
>
> (V, 38, 39)

It is not my intention though to claim that these stanzas represent some indispensable crux in *Don Juan*. Remove from the Siege of Ismail those stanzas concerned with Leila, the old Tartar Khan, or Daniel Boone, and the episode reads differently. Remove the death of Haidée or even the lines addressing Catharine the Great, and the whole poem alters character. Remove the dead commandant, and the poem remains as it was. What this section does is to fuse momentarily narrative and comment in a baffling image of real death. The next time this is to happen is when the poem fails to resume after 'slept' (XVII, 14), for Byron, in and out of the poem, is dead. We know this without separate recourse to literary biography. Only Byron's death could halt the renewal out of death which is the poem's stock in trade.

These stanzas then are not a normal instance of Byron's accretive tendencies, nor are they one amongst many examples of one poem's intrinsic openness to the adventitious. They are accepted by the reader without fuss because he has understood that the poem's openness to continuation by the adventitious is also openness to the intervention of actual Death. This is a formidable equivalent to the commendatore's intervention into the doings of Don Juan Tenorio. Death is invited mockingly into the action of both fictions for he is the only opponent of equal rank to Don Juan Tenorio or to Byron the poet. Only he can over-master their ability to escape from the traps which they live to create for themselves. In the end, Death, without irony, takes up the initiation.

The commandant's death in Canto V is a foretaste of this reversal. It is particularly appropriate because, as an officer, he represents the powers of the human mind under the aspect of Will. This ready identification went deep with Byron. Years earlier he had written of Conrad:

> What is that spell, that thus his lawless train
> Confess and Envy — yet oppose in vain?
> What should it be, that thus their faith can bind?
> The power of Thought — the magic of the Mind!
> Linked with success, assumed and kept with skill,
> That moulds another's weakness to its will.
>
> (*The Corsair*, I, 179-84)

Hence the importance in *Don Juan* of the commandant's authority over others:

> A thousand warriors by his word were kept
> In awe:
>
> (V, 36)

Italian politics, which caused the assassination and intrigued Byron, play no part in the poem's version of events. We have instead a concern with the human mind and its thwarted powers of will (in the dead commandant) and thwarted understanding (in the baffled narrator):

> And air — earth — water — fire live — and we dead?
> *We*, whose minds comprehend all things? No more
> But let us to the story as before.
>
> (V, 39)

The blank resumption of narrative here leaves the reader of the next few stanzas deprived of that gusto he has come to think of as always available in the poem. But we would be wrong in thinking that the interpolation has unsettled us simply by some customary cynicism or predictable lack of faith.

T.G. Steffan, for example, concludes his fine account of these stanzas with just such an assertion:

The last exclamatory stanza of the insertion poses the mystery of the astounding and discouraging frailty of flesh and mind. "Here we are,/And there we go:- but *where*? five bits of lead,/Or three, or two, or one, send very far!" Can we "whose minds comprehend all things" die, blank out, with such absurd ease, while all matter survives? [It was a question that Shelley posed in the middle of *Adonais* and answered before the end of the poem. But the skeptical, negative mind of Byron will shake rather than confirm or make a faith, will bitterly swing the contemplation back to the previous question in stanza 32: "who/Would pique himself on intellects, whose use/ Depends so much upon the gastric juice?"[18]

This basically 'Whig' view of Byron undoubtedly has truth but it is not, here or elsewhere, the whole truth. Byron is always as close to Pascal as he is to Voltaire. The most striking element in the lines quoted by Professor Steffan is not the intellect's inherently sceptical inability to choose between differing interpretations of death, but Death itself. It is not the intellect, in dead commandant or living commentator, which is sovereign. That, it is true, *could* unmake a faith. Byron was often drawn to that familiar amalgam of neo-Platonic and Stoical notions about the immortality of Reason which attaches small importance to gastric juice. Such notions single out the mind's capacities to grasp or at least reason towards an ideal order of changeless reality. Plainly the commandant's murdered corpse suggests a less transparently ideal version of reality than that advertised by the death of Socrates, or Cato, or (via David's painting) Marat. Moreover, the last stanza of the episode generalises the argument, juxtaposing vulnerable corpse and unlimited mind. This is Byron's normal way of distancing himself and his reader from the particularity of his comment or narration before changing tack. It also enables him to rejoin the narrative at an apparently similar point to that which preceded his interpolation.

We betray the whole force of the episode, however, if we assume that the story of the commandant has merely illustrated the dismissive couplet which now serves to introduce it:

> Who would pique himself on intellects whose use
> Depends so much upon the gastric juice?

> (V, 32)

Such an epigram, though dismissing intellects, promotes the intellect-based poise of the speaker. It is incorrect also to assume that Platonic/

Stoic faith is the only one in question or that the poem automatically sides with 'the skeptical, negative mind of Byron' which 'will shake rather than confirm or make a faith'.

I have already demonstrated that neither these stanzas nor the event to which they bear witness represents a normal instance of illustrative allusion. They intrude themselves upon narrative and commentary alike. But even in the last stanza, where the narrator is reasserting control, the reader's response to his question,

> Can every element our elements mar?
> And air — earth — water — fire live — and we dead?
> *We*, whose minds comprehend all things?
>
> (V, 39)

must be that it seems impossible to believe either that the mind survives death or that it does not. If our conclusion was simply negative then there would be no force in the incredulous repetition of 'we'. There are more substantial reasons still for taking seriously 'But it was all a mystery.' (V, 39). These will require a small diversion and necessitate some account of Byron's *Cain*.

It is a normal assumption of Byron's poetry that the intellect is inherently negative. Certainly 'Reason' is a good word for him and is often associated with Promethean powers of concentrated defiance as in Canto IV of *Childe Harold's Pilgrimage*:

> Our right of thought — our last and only place
> Of refuge; this, at least, shall still be mine:
> Though from our birth the Faculty divine
> Is chain'd and tortured — cabin'd, cribb'd, confined,
> And bred in darkness.
>
> (*Childe Harold's Pilgrimage*, IV, 127)

At best, however,

> Sorrow is Knowledge: they who know the most
> Must mourn the deepest o'er the fatal truth,
> The Tree of Knowledge is not that of Life.
>
> (*Manfred*, I.i, 10-12)

Byron's poetry recurs to this paradox and seeks to surmount it. *Cain*, in particular, written shortly after this stanza from *Don Juan*,

allows the negative intellect (Cain, Lucifer) full play. Thus the cate-
chism answers of Adam to Cain's questions about the origins of evil and
death seem ridiculously thin. Hence the outraged reaction of the
English church-going public[19] when the poem first appeared; an outrage
which prefigures that accorded to Darwin's *Origin of Species* and which,
it now seems probable,[20] was, like that, fed by a specifically English
anxiety to preserve the relation between Christianity and optimistic
reasoning cultivated in the eighteenth century.

Byron wrote a play not a tract, however, and appeared to be genuinely puzzled by English reaction to it. It is plain that whilst *Cain*
does not articulate forceful intellectual positions to counter Cain's
acceptance of Lucifer's negative reasoning, the action of the play certainly prevents us from acquiescing in those negatives, for there is a
direct route from Cain's negative thought to Cain's murderous action.[21]
His intellectual sophistication (gained through encountering abstract
Death in Act II) highlights his naïvete in the presence of a real death in
Act III. The play concludes with a sense of the baffling quietness of
Abel's corpse and the corresponding bafflement in Cain's normally
confident mind. The action of *Cain* crosses the gap between the
narrator of *Don Juan*'s casual familiarity with sceptical conclusion and
Byron's painful blankness in the presence of an actual dead commandant. The response of the reader to *Cain* is a similar inability to accept
that Cain's reasoning is at fault or that his action is good. Yet both of
these cannot be simultaneously true.

We could call this a conundrum or a problem. Byron, however, called
Cain 'a mystery'[22] and he did not do so merely 'in conformity with the
ancient title annexed to dramas upon similar subjects which were
styled "Mysteries or Moralities"'[23] but for the same reason that in *Don
Juan* he decides 'But it was all a mystery'. (V, 39).

Shelley, if Trelawney's record is to be believed, after discussing *Cain*
with Byron, was forced into reluctantly complaining to Mary Shelley
later: 'I do believe, Mary, that he is little better than a Christian!'[24]
Certainly the play is more consonant with orthodox Christian conceptions of the origin of evil and death than is, say, Coleridge's 'Christabel'
or 'The Ancient Mariner', or Blake's 'The Poison-Tree'.

If Shelley, like Byron, was held by the Prometheus story, he knew
that he could not communicate his admiration for some aspects of that
story without altering its conclusion. In the same way Blake, deriving
his ideas from biblical and Miltonic narratives, dare not simply allude to
his sources without carrying over their version of the concepts which
he takes from them. Thus he has to rewrite the Bible and *Paradise Lost*

in *Jerusalem* and *Milton*. Outraged by Byron's *Cain*, he rewrites the biblical story in *The Ghost of Abel* (1822). Blake alters the story of Cain in order to dramatise his own current preoccupations with forgiveness, blood-scacrifice and visionary phantasms. Byron has his own preoccupations too, but, unlike Blake, he subordinates them to the original Biblical narrative which he is careful to preserve. Thus if we encounter a negative voice in *Cain* which is recognisably Byronic, this voice remains situated within a narrative whose meaning Byron chooses but does not seek to control. Hostile reaction to Byron's play was undoubtedly in part outrage at the puzzling nature of the original|biblical story, for audiences were used to Gessner's popular *Death of Abel* (1758) which retells the story but carefully glosses or bowdlerises those elements in it which 'Reason' might dislike.

If this is true of *Cain*, we should be especially sensitive to the possibility, in those stanzas on another murder in *Don Juan*, that here too Byron is simultaneously upholding Lucifer's contemptuous clarity in the face of death, establishing Death's mysterious priority over any intellectual statement whatsoever and, finally, suggesting some still uncontradicted force in something 'little better' than Christianity.

It is the third of these elements which remains to be substantiated. It is Byron's reference to the centurion by which it will stand or fall.

"Can this be death? Then what is life or death?
Speak!" but he spoke not: "Wake!" but still he slept: —
"But yesterday and who had mightier breath?
A thousand warriors by his word were kept
In awe: he said, as the centurion saith,
'Go,' and he goeth; 'come,' and forth he stepp'd.
The trump and bugle till he spake were dumb —
And now nought left him but the muffled drum."

(V, 36)

The inclusion of the centurion is warranted as a familiar exemplum of authority analogous to the commandant's. In addition, the allusion picks up and authorises the oddly solemn tone and diction of the stanza which firmly distances us from the banter of intellectualised doubt. This may seem sufficient reason perhaps but the curiously archaic tone and the centurion's sudden appropriateness at this point will repay further enquiry.

Unlike Blake, Byron's literary and biblical allusions work straightforwardly. He uses them either as amplifying illustrations or with evident irony. In both cases, the original meaning of the allusion within its own context is a necessary part of the amplification or the wit.[25]

The centurion, it will be recalled from Matthew, 8, 5-13, is not primarily there as an example of authority but of faith found in an unlikely person (a Gentile officer in an occupying army).

> And when Jesus was entered into Capernicum,
> there came unto him a centurion, beseeching him,
> And saying, Lord, my servant lieth at home
> sick of the palsy, grievously tormented.
> And Jesus saith unto him, I will come
> and heal him.
> The centurion answered and said, Lord, I
> am not worthy that thou shouldest
> come under my roof: but speak the word
> only, and my servant shall be healed.
> For I am a man under authority,
> having soldiers under me: and I say
> to this *man*, Go, and he goeth: and to
> another, come, and he cometh; and to
> my servant, Do this, and he doeth it.
> When Jesus heard *it*, he marvelled,
> and said to them that followed, Verily
> I say unto you, I have not found so
> great faith, no, not in Israel . . .
> And Jesus saith unto the Centurion,
> Go thy way; and as thou hast believed,
> *so* be it done unto thee. And his servant
> was healed in the selfsame hour.[26]

The faith of the centurion, which is the effective transference of his own authority to that authority recognised in Christ, is the occasion for a miracle of healing. Christ uses the authority acknowledged in Him by the centurion to cure the centurion's paralysed servant. The miracle is not one of raising from the dead but it is not too far-fetched to find hints of such miracles as that described in the next chapter of St Matthew in Byron's insistence on the sleeping appearance of the commandant:

> And when Jesus came into the ruler's
> house and saw the minstrels and the

people making a noise,
He said unto them, Give place: for
the maid is not dead, but sleepeth. And
they laughed him to scorn.
But when the people were put forth, he
went in, and took her by the hand, and
the maid arose.

(Matthew, 9, 23-5)

This is perhaps to put the cart before the horse since Byron had emphasised that the dead commandant seemed asleep in letters written prior to this stanza: 'His face not at all disfigured — he seems asleep.'[27] It cannot be the centurion who suggests sleep then, indeed, as we have seen, the miracle in question has to do with paralysis, but it is more than likely that a death which looks like sleep suggested the New Testament, that the commandant's status suggested the centurion, and that this explains the exalted idiom of the whole stanza.

Byron rules out in the poem many contexts for the assassination established in his letters. Three things matter to him: first, the unexpected and 'given' nature of the commandant's death; second, the disparity between his undoubted murder ('butchered in a civic alley', V, 37) and the calm, undead appearance of the corpse ('He seems to sleep', V, 35); finally, the sudden passivity and quiet of a man accustomed to activity and dominion.

The centurion's covert significance and force lies in the possibility — awakened by allusion to him — that faith such as his would make sense of all three facts, i.e. accident, death-like sleep, true authority. It is this covert possibility that fully authorises the sudden exaltation of stanza 36 and it is only by marking such expectations, or at least their possibility, that we can understand why the habitually cool gaze of the narrator is enlisted:

> To try if I could wrench aught out of death
> Which could confirm, or shake, or make a faith;

(V, 38)

There is an excess of attention here which appears to embarrass the speaker:

> But let me quit the theme; as such things claim
> Perhaps *even more attention* than is due

From me: I gazed (*as oft I have gazed the same*)

[my italics] (V, 38)

No sooner does Byron claim to be leaving the topic than he reverts instinctively to 'I gazed'. This is no customary play with artfully placed digressions. When Byron declares suddenly that he is going to change the theme (cf. IV, 74) that is normally what he does.

I am not here arguing for some settled Christian purpose. Byron is clearly not in possession of a Christian faith sufficiently explicit to be 'confirmed' or 'shaken', nor can a dead man, as opposed to a risen one, 'make a faith'. It is another thing altogether to attribute a settled negativity to him as though Cain's end and the centurion's presence pass unnoticed by their author. The attempted cool gaze at death follows but does not confute Byron's earlier impulsive warmth of action in bringing the commandant into his house nor the possibility of faith which the juxtaposition of sleeping corpse and the centurion's acceptance of Christ's authority necessarily activates.

If then, we are to characterise this peculiar section of the poem, we cannot do so in a way that guarantees dominance to the intellectual voice of the narrator. Faith is neither made nor confirmed but its possibility is specifically activated, nor is that possibility shaken. The intellect is not quite displaced but it yields in the first place to charitable action and, in the last place, to 'a mystery' which it cannot articulate or fathom. At the centre of these diverging forms of attention is a particular death which obtrudes upon our reflections and our instinctive trust of life just as it demands entry into the poem as an event permanently relevant to its dual processes. This relevance is exhibited in this section but it cannot be separately stated for then it would merely be an item within the narrator's intelligent discourse.

The whole section is stitched cleverly into Canto V but the reason for its appearance in this canto lies in the time and place of the death itself which lies outside the poem. This is not because Byron automatically writes his own current doings into the narrator's stanzas of *Don Juan* for, on the contrary, he excludes them. It is simply because of the appropriateness of Death's intervention at any point in the poem. This episode is not crucial to the poem's meaning, but it reveals decisively that latency for Death's intervention into its process which is comparable to the commendatore's intervention in *El burlador de Sevilla*. The poem's incessant risk-taking charges it with a vitality doomed to an end that will appear both arbitrary and necessary. The art of *Don Juan* is to bring together Juan's rush forwards via a sea of particulars (mimicked in the poem's haphazard process) and the proximity, mysterious and absurd, of that onrush to Death's intervention (mimicked by the narrator's interjections but also by the disclosure of his own vulnerability to actual death). The poem's outrageous openness to continuation is also openness to an ending as surprising in its sudden reversal as that of the commandant. Any termination proffered within the narrative, even such a decisive full stop as the death of Haidée, can, we learn, be laughed into another future as a prisoner on the open sea (IV, 74-5). But Byron's gaze at the dead commandant which claims 'perhaps even more attention than is due' (V, 38) is a permanently relevant reminder of a mysterious inertia beyond his powers of resurrection. To that full stop he, and therefore the poem, will come at last.

The narrator, unlike the reader, cannot counter the force of melancholy reflection by the comic renewals of the narrative because he stands outside it. The most the narrator can expect is that, in so far as he is a work of fiction, he will persist in the poem as the voice of a perennial melancholy wisdom. The most the narrator can expect, in so far as he is Lord Byron, is death and a fame whose value will be undermined by his own reflections. An alternative to this is faith which offers its own rival version of comic renewal. If openly embraced, such a faith would subvert, or excessively clarify, many of the assumptions upon which the poem depends. But the presence of this possibility is virtually inescapable in a European poem when the clash between sex-based comic confidence and intellectualised negation yields no resolution. For if the naturally exaggerated language or Eros once falters it can only be revivified as metaphor for the life of the spirit. Conversely scepticism, though hostile to faith, must also undermine the absoluteness of doubt ('I doubt if doubt itself be doubting', IX, 17; 'He who doubts all things, nothing can deny' XV, 88).

I am thinking, needless to say, of Haidée's transformation into Aurora Raby in Canto XV but that is to anticipate a conclusion as yet unearned. An example that might be more casually granted is the ending of *As You Like It* where Jacques, voice of anti-comic commentary, avoids the comic conclusion by slipping out to meet Duke Frederick — principal agent of anti-comic action — who we learn

> (*Jacques*) . . . hath put on a religious life.
> . . .
> To him will I. Out of these convertites
> There is much matter to be heard and learn'd.
>
> (V, iv, 180, 182-3)

This is lightly handled by Shakespeare and, though not without resonance in the play, is clearly not central to it. But then, though all kinds
of villainies are planned and perpetrated in *As You Like It*, the play
carefully avoids actual deaths. When Shakespeare does accommodate
death in a comic play, as for instance in the deaths of Mamillius and
Antigonus in *The Winter's Tale*, he is forced to rely on Time (16 years),
Byronic farce (Autolycus, 'exit pursued by a bear') and, centrally, on
religious intensification (the oracle, Leontes' penitence, Hermione's
'resurrection').[28]

Don Juan has to incorporate far worse than the deaths of Mamillius
or Antigonus. Not only the explicit death of its major heroine and a
slaughter bloodier than *Macbeth*'s but, by implication, the death of the
poet himself have to be faced, passed, and made occasion for a fresh
commitment to comic verve.

The demands this makes as the poem both leisurely prattles on and
hurtles forward are so considerable that what we come to discern as its
three habitual resources — intellectual ingenuity, erotic confidence and
the not foreclosed possibility of religious faith — are forced to become
almost grotesquely explicit and what we could label 'the centurion's
presence', discernible only as undertow in Canto V, moves, in the final
canto, to the centre of the stage. The next three chapters will examine
each of these resources in turn.

Notes

1. 'Preface to Anabasis' in Frank Kermode (ed.), *Selected Prose of T.S. Eliot*
(London, 1975), pp. 79-80.
2. Much critical ink has been spilt in the last 50 years about 'authors',
'narrators', 'speakers', etc. in general and in Byron's *Don Juan*. Whatever may be
true elsewhere, Byron makes it impossible for us to regard the narrator of *Don
Juan* consistently as himself or as wholly other than himself, and, in any case, the
Byron of the Letters, Journals and Conversations is partly a dramatic construct.
I will be similarly inconsistent, though never arbitrary, in subsequent references
to 'Byron' and 'the narrator'.
3. Extensive parallels between *Don Juan* and Homer's *Odssey* are suggested
in Hermione de Almeida, *Byron and Joyce through Homer* (London, 1981).
4. Byron devotes a stanza to this point (III, 23).
5. 'You ask me for the plan of Donny Johnny — I *have* no plan — I *had* no plan
— But I had or have materials.' *Byron's Letters and Journals*, Leslie Marchand
(ed.) (12 vols., London, 1973-81), vol. 6, p. 207 (to Murray, 12th August, 1819).
6. In Tirso's play he is 'Comendador' but Mozart's opera *Don Giovanni* has
stabilised reference to him as the 'Commendatore'.
7. The similarity between Sardanapalus and Don Juan Tenorio is an obvious
one, e.g. Don Juan's valet in Molière's *Don Juan* calls him 'un vrai Sardanapale'
(*Don Juan*, I, i, 74). *The Plays of Molière*, A.R. Waller (ed.) (Edinburgh, 1907).

8. It seems simplest to distinguish Tirso's hero from Byron's by always giving him his full name.

9. J.J. McGann, *Don Juan in Context* (London, 1976), p. 129.

10. 'It is a poem that must, appropriately, end with the death of the narrator not of the hero.' M.K. Joseph, *Byron the Poet* (London, 1964), p. 304.

11. Mark Storey in *Poetry and Humour from Cowper to Clough* (London, 1979) commends a similar procedure for *Childe Harold's Pilgrimage*: 'It might seem perverse to be reading the poem in this way. But in practice this is what happens — we need to keep checking our bearings in a continuing process that is unnerving.' (p. 87)

12. *Letters and Journals*, vol. 7, pp. 247-8.

13. A glance at such parallels as present themselves will confirm the difference, see I, 210; II, 209; IV, 103, 104; IX, 50. 51.

14. T.G. Steffan in *Byron's Don Juan: A Variorum Edition*, T.G. Steffan and W.W. Pratt (eds.) 4 vols. Austin, Texas, 1957), vol. I, pp. 80-5 discusses the commandant stanzas extensively but treats them as a typical instance of Byron's accretive art. Philip W. Martin in *Byron, a poet before his public* (Cambridge, 1982) pp. 196-9 also discusses the stanzas, sees the link with *Childe Harold*, but is unconcerned with the thematic implications.

15. See I, 210; II, 209; IV, 103, 104; IX, 50, 51.

16. La Rochefoucauld, *Maximes* (Bordas, Paris, 1966), p. 55.

17. Ronald Gray's general comment is pertinent. The reader can judge whether it fixes or misses the point of these particular stanzas: 'One of the distinguishing features of Romanticism, and thus of intellectual life in the nineteenth century, was the determination to face the worst that might be experienced, without recourse to any saviour from a transcendental world. It was part of the determination to face experience as a whole and unflinchingly . . . '. Ronald Gray, *Goethe* (Cambridge, 1967), p. 6. Byron himself wrote on the death of his mother: 'There is to me something so incomprehensible in death; that I can neither speak nor think on the subject. — Indeed, when I looked on the Mass of Corruption which was the being from whence I sprung, I doubted within myself whether I *was*, or whether she *was not*.' (*Letters and Journals*, vol. 2, p. 69, to Hobhouse, 10th August, 1811). We may compare this with Byron's sustained gaze at a public execution in Rome: 'The first turned me quite hot and thirsty — and made me shake so that I could hardly hold the opera-glass (I was close — but determined to see every thing, once — with attention)' (*Letters and Journals*, vol. 5, pp. 229-30, to Murray, 30th May, 1817), and also with his reaction to the discovery and cremation of the bodies of Shelley and Williams (see Edward John Trelawney, *Records of Shelley, Byron and the Author* (Harmondsworth, 1973), pp. 170-3, 314 n. 43)).

18. *Variorum*, vol. I, pp. 84-5.

19. See T.G. Steffan, *Lord Byron's Cain* (Austin, Texas, 1968), pp. 309-426.

20. See James R. Moore, *The Post-Darwinian Controversies* (Cambridge, 1979). Moore argues that orthodox Christians were accustomed to invoke Providence as a theories than liberal Christians who wwere accustomed to invoke Providence as a means of suppressing grim or merely contingent realities much as Adam does in *Cain*. Orthodox Christians were not, however, thick on the ground then or earlier. Vincent Newey, for instance, argues convincingly that even Cowper defended orthodox teaching 'full of a sense of dissolution' in his contemporaries of doctrinal conviction. (Vincent Newey, *Cowper's Poetry* (Liverpool, 1982), p. 145). See also Stephen Prickett, 'The Religious Context' in his *The Romantics* (London, 1981), pp. 115-63.

21. There is an excellent account of *Cain* in McGann, *Don Juan*, pp. 31-3. See also Wolf Z. Hirst, 'Byron's Lapse into Orthodoxy: An Unorthodox Reading of

Cain' in *Keats-Shelley Journal*, vol. XXIX, 1980, pp. 151-73.

22. There is undoubtedly a certain jokiness in this, as in most of Byron's prefaces, but here as elsewhere he gains access to a vocabulary which is intended to affect his readers in more ways than a joke.

23. Steffan, *Cain*, p. 155.

24. Trelawney, *Records*, p. 99.

25. See, for instance, the reference to Alexander the Great (V, 32) where the phrase 'with another act or two' depends for its full effect upon knowing the much plainer statement of this familiar story in Plutarch.

26. The quotation is from the Authorised Version which Byron presumably used (see Travis Looper, *Byron and the Bible* (London, 1978) p. 12). 'I am sure that no man reads the Bible with more pleasure than I do; I read a chapter every day, and in a short time shall be able to beat the Canters with their own weapons.' Ernest J. Lovell, Jr., *His Very Self and Voice: Collected Conversations of Lord Byron* (New York, 1954), p. 596.

27. *Letters and Journals*, vol. 7, p. 247, to Murray, 9th December, 1820.

28. *Cymbeline* uses similar devices to contain the death of Cloten. In the final battle, we see submission but no deaths or woundings. 'There are no "events" in comedy; there are only "happenings". Events are irreversible and comedy is not concerned with the irreversible, which is why it must always shun the presentation of death.' (Helen Gardner, *'As You Like It'* in John Garnett (ed.), *More Talking of Shakespeare* (London, 1959), p. 21.)

2 THE NARRATOR'S CANTOS

The most direct way to tackle the procedure question in *Don Juan* is to look first at the construction and linking of narrative episodes in the poem. Here the exposed ending of the poem, characteristically felt to be appropriate and significant, even if unintended, is particularly instructive.

The poem ends with the Duchess of Fitz-Fulke's attempted seduction of Don Juan which concludes Canto XVI. Canto XVII, which begins 'The world is full of orphans', is clearly to be about the orphan Aurora but we discover that it does not break narrative continuity for the last three stanzas of the 14-stanza canto reveal Juan and Fitz-Fulke at breakfast in a 'morning-after-the-night-before' situation unique in the poem. In between orphans and breakfast, stanzas 5 to 12 of Canto XVII re-establish a confident, bantering tone defending, in the narrator's usual manner, individual freedom and subversive sages (Pythagoras, Locke, Socrates). Although narrative continuity is not formally disrupted, the abrupt reminder of orphans, hence Aurora, sobers and distances the reader from his uncritical acceptance of the magically warm and vibrant Fitz-Fulke in the closing stanzas of the previous canto. Moreover, the reassumption of Whiggish superiority in the narrator distances us still further from the more primitive fear of Death and sudden arousal by Sex which pinioned narrator and reader in the account of Juan's encounter with the Black Friar and Fitz-Fulke.

Certain features of this ending are precedented, others are new. Both repetition and novelty help us to determine procedure. The deliberated nonchalance of the narrator is a familiar distancing device in the poem after any events that have made laughter difficult for his readers. Thus,

> Our Hero was in Canto the Sixteenth,
> Left in a tender moonlight situation,
> Such as enables Man to show his strength
> Moral or physical:
>
> (XVII, 12)

appears to be much the same in force as those celebrated distancing stanzas after the death of Haidée:

> We'll put about, and try another tack
> With Juan, left half-kill'd some stanzas back.
>
> (IV, 74)

The assumption of superiority is the same but in Canto IV the narrator does manhandle us away from unpalatable event towards the comic future. Here in Canto XVII, the narrator lingers. In the final words of the poem, he is speculating uneasily:

> Which best is to encounter — Ghost, or none,
> 'Twere difficult to say — but Juan looked
> As if he had combated with more than one,
> Being wan and worn, with eyes that hardly brooked
> The light, that through the Gothic windows shone:
> Her Grace, too, had a sort of air rebuked —
> Seemed pale and shivered, as if she had kept
> A vigil, or dreamt rather more than slept.
>
> (XVII, 14)

As we read this stanza, we lost the sneery smile with which we had reacted to the implied inverted commas of 'tender moonlight situation' and the play upon 'man' as species and gender in

> Such as enables man to show his strength
> Moral or physical.
>
> (XVII, 12)

It is not simply that we now read with something of Juan and Fitz-Fulke's discomfiture but that the scene itself, which in stanza 13 promised the triumph of common sense:

> The morning came — and breakfast, tea and toast,
> Of which most men partake, but no one sings.
>
> (XVII, 13)

is, we discover, bathed in

> The light that through the Gothic windows shone:
>
> (XVII, 14)

The word 'Gothic' unobtrusively reminds us of ghost experience rather than sexual flirtation as does 'seemed pale and shivered' and 'A vigil or dreamt'.

The reader, we should recall, has been deliberately frightened by Byron in Canto XVI. The Black Friar is a credible and chilling ghost despite circumambient irony and evident Terror-fiction technique. We share Juan's amazement and relief therefore when, on the second visit of the ghost, he turns into the 'full, voluptuous, but not o'ergrown bulk' (XVI, 123) of the nymphomaniac Duchess. In the next canto the whole force of his experience is apparently dissipated by the confident innuendo of the narrator. In the very last lines of the poem, however, it is clear that this is not so. Fitz-Fulke herself is, in the morning, no longer confident or attractive;

> Her Grace, too, had a sort of air rebuked —
> Seemed pale and shivered, . . .
>
> (XVII, 14)

and that light filtered via 'Gothic windows' imposes itself even upon the narrator's posed insouciance. We are delivered from the narrator's vulgar alternatives (did they or didn't they?) to a more diffused bewilderment, for the suppressed Gothic side of Norman Abbey, which we thought we had faced and overcome in the night's escapades, remains as a force to disturb daylight experience.

Even without this delicate adjustment, any reference back to the previous night's experience is odd in *Don Juan* and undermines, what seems to be the most striking characteristic of its final section, the restoration of seduction as the habitual focus of narrative action.

In the early part of the poem, Juan's virtual seduction by Donna Julia and his love affair with Haidée (which she initiates) set up a pattern where the narrative proceeds ineluctably, despite digressions and shifts of tone, to sexual consummation. As soon as consummation occurs, there is a break in narrative continuity. For example, immediately after Julia and Juan's love-making, the narrator tells the reader that he must take a liberty with him:

> This licence is to hope the reader will
> Suppose from June the sixth (the fatal day
> Without whose epoch my poetic skill
> For want of facts would all be thrown away),
> But keeping Julia and Don Juan still
> In sight, that several months have pass'd.
>
> I, 121)

After coupling, Juan and Julia become a couple for the 'several months' mentioned but the next event in the poem is the disruption of the couple by Don Alfonso. Similarly, as soon as Byron can write of Juan and Haidée 'And now 'twas done − ' (II, 204), he can, after a flurry of digressions and some suggestion of their 'several months', move forwards to the return of Lambro who will disrupt couple and coupling.

The narrative then resumes its normal momentum from sea voyage to the harem where seduction and coupling are almost emblematically disconnected. Here it is important that the customary Don Juan progress to an illicit bed is maintained but Byron cannot afford to let his hero forget Haidée as readily as he did Julia; otherwise, indeed he would have recreated Don Juan Tenorio. Hence when the most explicit seduction yet seen in the poem is urged by Gulbeyaz, he resists. On the other hand, when put to bed with Dudù, whose 'talents were of the more silent class' (VI, 49), we can scarcely blame him for being the bee who 'flew out and stung her to the heart' (VI, 77). Indeed, if he had not done so, he would have participated in the epicene unnaturalness of the Seraglio not merely in his appearance 'in drag' but also in fact. Nevertheless the major momentum of the section cannot rest in this but swings back to the Sultana's failure to couple with Juan which Dudù's success highlights. Accordingly she turns into an Alfonso or Lambro figure intent upon Juan's destruction. As soon as this occurs, there is the usual break of narrative continuity and we, with Juan, find ourselves in the Siege of Ismail and a new canto.

It is clear then that the reader has come to expect, and is expected to expect, seduction to be the culmination of each section in the poem which, once clearly attained or unattained, involves a break in time. In this way, as well as in the movement from city ladies via shipwreck to island fisher-princess and back again to city seduction, the poem is a typically *Don Juan* story except that Byron's Juan is seduced rather than seducing. However, when the pattern is repeated yet again with Catharine the Great, it appears in a form so profoundly modified as to suggest its abandonment or overthrowal.

Essentially, it is true, the movement from battle horror to Catharine's bed is the same as that from shipwreck horror to Haidée's cave. In the battle, as in the shipwreck, Juan, though caught up in the horror, retains certain positive features. At sea, he did not eat his tutor; in the Siege, we do not see him kill anyone and we do see him rescue Leila. Nevertheless Juan participates in the battle in a sense which he does not participate in the mariners' cannibalism:

So Juan, following honour and his nose,
Rushed where the thickest fire announced most foes.

He knew not where he was, nor greatly cared,
For he was dizzy, busy, and his veins
Filled as with lightning — for his Spirit shared
The hour, as is the case with lively brains.

(VIII, 32, 33)

For this participation, the narrator later gazettes him with undisguised hostility: 'Don Juan, who had shone in the late slaughter,' (IX, 29).

It is not only Juan's behaviour, the dark side of his unthinking commitment to present intensity, that worries us. The scale and horror of the Siege, which lies within the poem but implicates the world outside it, disturbs our sense that, despite bizarre divergencies of tone and all manner of digressive interruption, we have a tolerable working sense of what to expect in the narrative sector. The Siege takes up two whole cantos, the shipwreck is only 73 stanzas. The siege is sufficiently lengthy to accommodate a specific digression of its own (the Daniel Boone stanzas), a variety of subordinate incident (the death of the old Khan, the saving of Leila), as well as a well-developed portrait of Suvarrow. It straddles the poem. Certainly Juan is carried through it as a triumphant survivor just as, after the shipwreck, he survives the waves that drown his companions and is borne to the rich safety of Haidée's isle. Yet we can forget Juan's companions more readily than we can obliterate the memory of the soldiers who, despite the narrator's mock-Homeric catalogue (VII, 15-22), remain an anonymous

Forty thousand who had manned the wall,
Some hundreds breathed — the rest were silent| all!

(VIII, 27)

Juan, invariably well intentioned, did not will this slaughter but is undeniably accomplice in it. We lose our comic sense that our hero survives because of fictional strategy, inherent virtue and kindly providence which, for example, accomplish Juan's arrival on Haidée's isle:

Not yet had he arrived but for the oar,
Which, providentially for him was wash'd,
Just as his feeble arms could strike no more.

(II, 107)

Rather, as he is rushed to Catharine's approving eyes and arms, he seems to be merely an instance of natural selection who earns his chance of mating with the Queen by accident and his own murderous vigour. When he does couple with Catharine, without any formal show of reluctance, we are not at all surprised nor do we expect or wish them to form a couple. 'Couple' and 'coupling' have been sundered. Here there is no privileged, first-time consummation which, lyrically saluted will inaugurate their status as a couple. Juan merely has his social and bio-logical duty to perform:

> The favour of the Empress was agreeable;
> And though his duty waxed a little hard,
> Young people at his time of life should be able
> To come off handsomely in that regard.

(X, 22)

The sexual puns in these lines are typical of this section of the poem alone. They are associated with an explicitness which is also unusual. For the most part, *Don Juan*, though easy to read and dependent upon disconcertingly apparent manoeuvres, is hard to describe accurately and interpret correctly. We have to work hard if we are to understand and then point to Byron's delicate maintenance of balance in it and the questing seriousness which enables the poem to be in touch with, participate in, and render a present mystery beyond the narrator's en-compassing. Many recent studies have helped us to see this but old habits of interpretation die hard, fostered in part by Byron's modest disclaimers and the narrator's own claims to interpret the poem for us. Here, how-ever, we do not have to work hard to render the opaque transparent. Byron, via his narrator, does the work for us. Take these stanzas for instance:

> O, thou 'teterrima Causa' of all 'belli' –
> Thou gate of Life and Death – thou nondescript!
> Whence is our exit and our entrance – well I
> May pause in pondering how all Souls are dipt
> In thy perennial fountain:– how men *fell*, I
> Know not, since knowledge saw her branches stript
> Of her first fruit; but how he falls and rises
> *Since, Thou* hast settled beyond all surmises.

Some call thee 'the worst Cause of war', but I
Maintain thou art the *best:* for after all
From thee we come, to thee we go, and why
To get at thee not batter down a wall
Or waste a world? Since no one can deny
Thou dost replenish worlds both great and small?
With, or without thee, all things at a stand
Are, or would be, thou Sea of Life's dry Land!

Catharine, also was the grand Epitome
Of that great Cause of war, or peace, or what
You please (it causes all the things which be,
So you may take your choice of this or that) —
Catharine, I say, was very glad to see
The handsome herald, on whose plumage sat
Victory.

(IX, 55, 56, 57)

The reader has very little room for manoeuvre in stanzas like these.
The representative, helpless movements of Juan, comically falling
and rising, in bed and out of it, are here displayed, understood and
arraigned. Where Haidée helped to assuage Juan and the reader's
memories of horrors at sea, Catharine, it is clear, will offer no such
solace for she is the presiding procreative deity over the horrors of
battle. The configuration of her sex incites men to

> . . . batter down a wall
Or waste a world . . .

(IX, 56)

just as they did to 'get at' Helen of Troy. As in Shakespeare's *Troilus
and Cressida*, killing and love-making are no longer decorously distinguished for the noises made during them are indistinguishable:

Oh Catharine! (for of all interjections
To thee both *oh!* and *ah!* belong of right
In love and war)

(IX, 65)

This is so inclusively and unambiguously anti-comic a point of view that
it is hard to see how the narrator or Juan can win their way back to free

comment and free action. It is not surprising that Juan's life-force suddenly stops nor that the narrator is short of explanation:

> I don't know how it was, but he grew sick:
> The Empress was alarmed, and her physician
> (The same who physicked Peter) found the tick
> Of his fierce pulse betoken a condition
> Which augured of the dead.
>
> (X, 39)

This is a turning point in the poem. Sex, which restores Juan to whole
life on Haidée's isle after the shipwreck, now seems to be agent and
symptom of his Russian distemper. Of course he loved Haidée, whereas
with Catharine,

> He, on the other hand, if not in love,
> Fell into that no less imperious passion,
> Self-love.
>
> (IX, 68)

But it is not only Juan who has fallen. Narrator and reader alike have
travelled from battle to bedroom and acquiesced in the declared inde-
terminacies of sex and war, love and lust:

> . . . the Sovereign was smitten,
> Juan much flattered by her love, or lust;
> I cannot stop to alter words once written,
> And the two are so mixed with human dust
> That he who *names one*, both perchance may hit on.
>
> (IX, 77)

Juan's sickness is the only chance he has of recovery. The poem too
cannot be propelled forwards in the same way as in previous cantos.
There is a gap of seven cantos before the next attempt is made to
seduce Juan by the Duchess of Fitz-Fulke. But we know that although
Fitz-Fulke's escapade appears to reinstate seduction right at the end
of the poem, it does so in a strange mode or perhaps not at all. In particular, in the last stanzas of the poem as we have seen, instead of
cutting decisively to new time in the old way as the new canto (XVII)
appears to promise, we are left looking back uneasily on the events of
the night before. To understand this better we need now to look at the

movement of the poem in between Catharine the Great and the Duchess of Fitz-Fulke. What happens or, more precisely, how does the poem proceed when seduction can be no longer its 'staple narrative device?

I

While this high post of honour's in abeyance
For one or two days, reader, we request
You'll mount with our young hero the conveyance
Which wafted him from Petersburgh.

(X, 49)

These lines in Canto X inaugurate what we might call 'the narrator's cantos'. Throughout the rest of the canto, together with Cantos XI and XII, the narrator exercises an undisputed control over the poem. His ascendancy persists, though it is being eroded, until the end of Canto XV. When Juan, in the lines quoted above, packed into a barouche, begins a new journey, it is a journey thought out in advance by the narrator and not subject to contingent interruption. In this, it is quite unlike what we and the narrator are accustomed to. Earlier in the poem we would not have accepted a succession of stanzas set out like these:

They journeyed on through Poland and through Warsaw

(X, 58);

From Poland they came on through Prussia Proper,
And Königsberg the capital

(X, 60);

And thence through Berlin, Dresden and the like,
Until he reached the castellated Rhine

(X, 61);

But Juan posted on through Mannheim, Bonn,

(X, 62);

From thence to Holland's Hague and Helvoetsluys

(X, 63);

Here he embarked, and with a flowing sail
Went bounding for the island of the free

(X, 64);

> Don Juan now saw Albion's earliest beauties, —
> Thy cliffs, *dear* Dover! harbour and hotel
>
> (X, 69);
>
> On with the horses! Off to Canterbury!
>
> (X, 71).

Manifestly the narrator is taking Juan somewhere. If there is any interruption, such as that of the highwaymen on Shooter's Hill (XI, 8-20), it is but a calculated diversion which does not challenge the narrator's authority and clear purpose,

> But Tom's no more — and so no more of Tom.
> Heroes must die; and by God's blessing 'tis
> Not long before the most of them go home. —
> Hail! Thamis, hail! Upon thy verge it is
> That Juan's chariot, rolling like a drum
> In thunder, holds the way it can't well miss,
> Through Kennington and all the other 'tons',
> Which make us wish ourselves in town at once.
>
> (XI, 20)

Juan is trapped inside both Byron's orderly recollection of his own English experiences and the narrator's firm intention of taking him first to London and then to a country house. Since Byron often pretends to be narrator and the narrator often claims to be Byron, there is a particular appropriateness in that the narrator's fiction of Norman Abbey is, transparently, Byron's Newstead Abbey. Juan, that 'thing of impulse' (VIII, 24) is a picaresque puppet in their hands. Why do we readers put up with this?

Readers often resent[1] the thinness of Cantos X to XII but they have been caught up in the crisis of confidence which has produced this anorexic disorder. In effect, a poem which, like ancient epics, has two centres (gods and men, narrator and Juan) is now left with trust in only one of them. This process, though we only see its effects clearly now, began in the Siege of Ismail.

Juan participates in the siege; the narrator does not. But Juan's participation is simple in kind. It consists of alert excitement, constant activity, and moments of pity. The narrator's relationship with events is of far greater interest to the reader for he presents a much more complete picture of the battle than Juan can comprehend. Moreover the narrator's response to what occurs is, even by the customary standards of the poem, amazingly multi-faceted. Terms such as 'a controlling indignation' may offer themselves to characterise this account of modern warfare but they would not be accurate. Mad gaiety, elegiac tribute, pity, horror, bitterness and admiration mingle in the narrator's presentation and response involving constant adjustments of diction. In Canto VIII, for example, warfare of this kind is presented on two occasions as an historical curiosity before coming revolutionary changes wipe it out (VIII, 50-1; 133-7), yet, in between these occasions, warfare is also said to be typical of modern life (VIII, 68) and then said to be a perennial human activity (VIII, 104). The reader reacts with the narrator and looks to him rather than to Juan for directions here. The narrator dominated the shipwreck stanzas in a similar way but Haidée's isle promptly restored narrative solidity. The scale and duration of the Siege cantos make such restoration implausible.

In fact, at the end of Canto VIII, Juan is merely 'sent off with dispatch' to St Petersburg (VIII, 139) and we begin a new canto. This opens with 28 stanzas where the narrator holds forth. Each canto so far has begun with a flourish by the narrator but the longest have been seven stanzas (Cantos I, IV and VII). Thus 28 introductory stanzas both is and appears to be unusually extended. Clearly the narrator is acting as though he is in full control. The reader has not experienced this hitherto for he is as accustomed to having the narrator's commentary interrupted and exposed by events as much as he expects events to be checked and satirised by the narrator's interpolations. Rough and ready statistics here are helpful though it is not always clear whether a given stanza in *Don Juan* is a digression or not since it may, though digressive in manner, directly relate to events or characters.[2]

In the first eight cantos, digression takes up just under a quarter of the poem. In Cantos IX to XV, the digression averages a half of the whole. Canto XVI, the ghost canto, however, again has less than a quarter digression. The change from a quarter to a half is initiated by the 28 stanzas which open Canto IX. Such a scale of scale is undoubtedly noted by the reader. We could explain it in either of two ways. It could be that, just as in *Childe Harold's Pilgrimage* the fictional device of Harold, prominent in Cantos I and II, is discarded in the later and better Cantos III and IV where Byron is seen to intervene and direct the poem openly, so in *Don Juan* we could see the supremacy of the narrator in its second part as a clarification of the poem's true purpose and nature. Or we could see the foregrounding of the narrator as a prolonged but temporary response to the unpalatable collusion of the Siege and Catharine which severely damages the recuperative energies of the poem. *Don Juan* has sustained such attacks before, indeed it depends upon them for its outrageous feats of renewal. This attack, however, is nearly fatal. The narrator's subsequent exposure functions like an invalid's crutches. It is the over-use of an undamaged or less damaged part of an organism whilst damaged tissues elsewhere are allowed to revive. The sick person is still able to get about even though the strain on his or her arms and their consequent over-development is considerable. The narrator in *Don Juan*, though forced into analogous over-activity, is not to be instated as sole permanent mode of locomotion in the poem. This second explanation of the narrator's prominence is vindicated by the return to the same proportion of digression in the last full canto (XVI) as we find in the first two cantos. But the reader cannot be sure that this is so until he reaches Canto XVI. It may be, however, that some answer to our question – Why do we readers put up with the narrator's apparently complete manipulation of the poem from Cantos X to XV? – is that the reader, though unclear as to the outcome, does not surrender the possibility that the lost other centre of the poem may be recovered. The reader, after all, is invited not only to intimate participation in the narrator's prodigious feats of improvisation from the outset but also, from Canto II, to some judgement of the poem's consolidating procedures and values in the face of the nihilism and mobility of its surface. We learn to laugh at but also to wait with events.

The Siege then prepares us for the narrator's assumption of centrality. In the next (Russian) canto, though we have a seduction episode as before, it is now kept entirely within the narrator's habitual point of view of which it offers bitter confirmation. From this point the narrator is on his own without even an episode such as this to threaten his hegemony. Hence, even though digressive stanzas in these cantos take up half of the poem and, in Canto XII, nearly three-quarters of it, even these figures do not reveal how pervasive is the narrator's presence. For when the narrator is perfunctorily taking Juan through several countries, it is the narrator's commentary that is decisive rather than Juan's experience. When Juan arrives in England, the narrator's knowledge of the nation and his ambivalent attitude to its inhabitants and customs is matter both for digression and for such narration as exists. Obviously it is far more difficult in these circumstances to know where digression begins and ends. This state of affairs persists until the narrator has taken everybody off to Norman Abbey but the house has surprises for the narrator as well as for its inhabitants.

As Norman Abbey is based on Byron's Newstead, the house is

acutely and nostalgically detailed (XIII, 55-67). Invention and memory fuse just as Byron and narrator appear to do. At the beginning of *Childe Harold's Pilgrimage*, the over-experienced Harold flees from another fictional version of Newstead to set out on his 'pilgrimage'. Here, at the end of *Don Juan*, Byron's Spanish hero finishes up where Harold began in what appears to be a triumph for the uncontrolled narrator. He has locked up Byron's fictions in Byron's house about which he can discourse indefinitely. Instead of this, both house and characters assume a real fictional independence and, by-passing the narrator, engage the reader's interest as directly as he does. For the present, however, we are concerned with that section of the poem in which the narrator rushes on without restraint. What does he do with his freedom?

Thought is a major activity of the narrator. In his cantos it becomes a major and controlling activity within the poem. The narrator thinks in so far as he abstracts, generalises, argues and moves rapidly from one concept to another. Thought is exhilarating for these reasons but it is also an unwelcome visitant not easily removed especially without the continual interruption of Juan's adventures.

> I won't describe — that is, if I can help
> Description; and I won't reflect — that is,
> If I can stave off thought, which, as a whelp
> Clings to its teat, sticks to me through the abyss
> Of this odd labyrinth.
>
> (X, 28)

'Abyss' and 'labyrinth' are guiding words here. 'Abyss' suggests profundity but also falling and the Fall. 'Labyrinth' suggests circularity, darkness and confinement though also a 'clue' which might lead us outside it. In any event, it is not easy to 'stave off thought'. On the other hand, it is impossible to persist with thought either:

> For ever and anon comes Indigestion,
> (Not the most 'dainty Ariel') and perplexes
> Our soarings with another sort of question:
> And that which after all my spirit vexes,
> Is, that I find no spot where man can rest eye on,
> Without confusion of the sorts and sexes,
> Of being, stars, and this unriddled wonder,
> The World, which at the worst's a glorious blunder.

If it be Chance, or if it be according
To the Old Text, still better

(XI, 3, 4)

The narrator's impulse to think cannot be staved off but it will lead him no way out of 'this odd labyrinth'. Such a diagnosis is well suited to the interpolating narrator of the early Juan stories but how can labyrinthine circularity give forward momentum to the poem from Canto X onwards?

It is for this reason, we must presume, that the narrator so evidently plans Juan's linear progression through Poland, Germany, Holland, to London and on to Norman Abbey. There is no intrinsic momentum within the journey itself for we witness it always from the narrator's point of view and the end-point is predetermined from the outset. On the other hand, such a clearly disclosed narrative sequence does formally counter the sticking points of 'thought' which the narrator can neither stave off nor move through. Again, such a travel narrative authorises a continually shifting topography inviting detached intellectual comment in the manner of Montesquieu's *Les Lettres Persanes* or Goldsmith's *Citizen of the World*. Travel invites commentary and thought, there is no need to 'stave' it off. In addition, travel disposes of the problem of 'the abyss' and 'the labyrinth' by providing always something different for the mind to annotate and discuss. In this way the poem may be kept going but we pay a price.

Clearly, continuous travel and intellectual comment will become monotonous. Indeed the attempt to divert the vacant or preoccupied mind by travel is a familiar ploy to Byron (hooked on travel accounts from an early age) and his audience. As the journey of the poem proceeds along familiar routes to London and to Byron's country house, the author's *divertissement* is one that he is sharing with the society that is the object of his criticism. Like Byron, the Amundevilles divert themselves by changing from London to Newstead Abbey. Like the author, the Amundevilles' guests seek relief from a single form of life by wandering round the lake, hunting, chatting, dreaming of dinner or looking for adultery. Thus 'ennui' becomes a much more prominent theme of the digressions but it forms a bond between the narrator and the characters which undermines the presumed superiority of the former. We note for instance the inclusive 'we' of such comments as

And hence high life is oft a dreary void,
A rack of pleasures,where we must invent

A something wherewithal to be annoyed.

(XIV, 79)

There is more evidence of this. Byron's editors comment that:

> There are only about four French words in Cantos IX and X, and
> the frequency is even lower in preceding cantos, but in the last six
> Byron uses French words at least eighty times, including several that
> are repeated. Many are rhymes. French is most abundant in Cantos
> XIV and XV (the banquet), then declines to about seven words in
> Canto XVI.[3]

There are evident satirical purposes at work here and Byron's dislike
of French is well attested; nevertheless these facts indicate the extent
to which the narrator in these cantos shares the same vocabulary and
conversational manners as the society which he is observing. It is
possible that Byron's recollection of such idioms was heightened by his
conversations with Lady Blessington in Genoa from March to May 1822
which released a flow of reminiscence in him but also sharpened his
naturally acute sense of the already historical character of his earlier experience of English social life. Certainly the narrator's immersion in the
lingo of Blank Blank Square (XIII, 25) is part and parcel of his delineation of a society which the narrator too reflects in his poise but also by
his doomed and temporary flaunting of that poise. Byron in 1822 is
describing English society after an exile of six years, moreover his hero
is supposed to be in the England of the 1790s. Hence the coincidence
of the narrator's vocabulary with that of this historically fixed world
makes him, for all his bitter superiority to it, something of a Mr Turvey-
drop embalmed in his Dandy deportment. Both Lady Blessington's
reactions to Byron and English reaction to his poem suggest that *Don
Juan* preserved the idioms of a social world already discredited when
Byron is writing but still capable of disconcerting its present audience.

Why does Byron immerse himself in remembered talk? Three factors
undoubtedly play their part here. We should not ignore the most
obvious of them. Byron had an acute ear for tricks of speech of all
kinds. He himself participated in English fashionable society from 1812
to 1816 and, through his acquaintance with older women such as Lady
Melbourne and Lady Oxford, would have had access to the gossip and
idiom of a previous generation. Just as he used the slang which he
picked up from Gentleman Jackson and others in the footpad episode
in Canto X or his memoirs of his visit to Aston Hall in 1813 for some

banter in Canto XIV (XIV, 100-102), so he must have raided his memoirs of Southwell, Cambridge, Holland House, Seaham, etc. for the vocabulary which is deployed almost as an aesthetic object in its own right in the English cantos. The absence of such a vocabulary in his depiction of the Russian army and court, or for that matter in the Tahiti of *The Island*, undoubtedly weakens their effect. *Don Juan*, unlike *Childe Harold's Pilgrimage*, depends upon the accurate delineation of the present societies through which Juan moves. Hence it must have been of evident advantage for Byron to have placed Juan in the society which he knew most intimately.

The second factor is that *Don Juan* is written, in the first instance, for an English audience. It is designed to counter contemporary English morals, politics and taste. Here Byron brings together a new kind of close social observation evidenced for example in the first part of Madame de Stael's *De L'Allemagne* (1810) and, later, in Balzac's novels, with his considered loyalty to neo-classical theory. The mocking imitation of current styles of talk has always been a staple ingredient of neo-classical writing as we see in Ben Jonson's plays, Restoration Theatre and Augustan satire. But there is a special poignancy and force in Byron's practice. For Jonson's Lady Politicick Would-Be, Etherege's Sir Fopling Flutter or Pope's Sir Plume depend upon Jonson, Etherege, and Pope's participation in the world which they describe. The English cantos in *Don Juan*, on the other hand, are a *tour de force* or sleight of hand. An entire social world is created and sustained by one man's virtuosity. It is true that Byron participated once in the world which he now describes, but that participation must always have had an outsider quality for it now to be recalled so completely. Regency society is here presented with something of the satiric and public immediacy of Pope or Swift yet it is shaped by memory and vivid with nostalgically glossed detail almost in the manner of Proust. Still discernible, though not fatally so, in Byron's exhibition of himself as a Regency talker, is a hint of snobbery deriving from uncertainty. Byron's shyness in society was both personal and linked with anxieties about the contrast between his rank and his drab, impecunious upbringing. He was never quite accepted by English Society. Cantos XI to XVII are a final bid by the exiled Byron for recognition as a then insider of that society.

The third factor is more elusive but of great importance. If thought is one characterising activity of the narrator, so is talk. By thinking in his poem, he aligns himself with a whole series of great thinkers and writers,

I say no more than has been said in Dante's
Verse and by Solomon and by Cervantes;

By Swift, by Machiaevel, by Rochefoucault,
By Fenelon, by Luther, and by Plato;
By Tillotson, and Wesley, and Rousseau

(VII, 3, 4)

By talk, however, the narrator aligns himself with present fashionable
society and with prattlers:

I rattle on exactly as I'd talk
With any body in a ride or walk

(XV, 19)

Thought and talk are not necessarily disjunctive. Shelley paid a
marvellous tribute to Byron's conjunction of thought and talk in the
opening section of 'Julian and Maddalo':

So as we rode, we talked; and the swift thought,
Winging itself with laughter, lingered not,
But flew from brain to brain

('Julian and Maddalo', 28-30).

This seems to corroborate Byron's own lines (XXV, 19) quoted above
but Byron's conversation with Shelley is more typical of Shelley's conversations than it is of Byron's. Shelley, in exile, talked to other like-
minded exiles. He gained access in this way to a sustained high-level
conversation on subjects that interested him. He forfeited his relationship both with the actual society of his current domicile and with his
matrix society in England to which his poetry, despite his Miltonic disclaimers, was addressed. In so far as he did consciously address his
English audience, Shelley will either write private verse letters to like-
minded Maria Gisbornes or, as in *The Mask of Anarchy*, assume the
role of a visionary prophet denouncing the society that does not listen
to him or to Truth. There is something of the latter, needless to say, in
the Byron who wrote *The Lament of Tasso* and *The Prophecy of Dante*
in praise of spurned prophet-poets. Nevertheless Byron never yields
common ground with his English readers, refused to be an outsider in
Venice, which still boasts of him as an inhabitant, or Ravenna, where he
formed part of local political and marital intrigue, or Greece, of whose

history he is a permanent part. To turn conversation and poetry into private and exclusive affairs was for him the heresy of 'the Lakers'. But with whom does Byron converse in Don Juan? We may well find the 'swift thought/Winging itself with laughter' but the only other brain to which it may fly is the reader's. There is no one of Shelley's status within *Don Juan*. There is no one anywhere in the poem who can provide any kind of intellectual rivalry to the narrator. He lays claim to be a Mephistopheles:

> For my part, I am but a mere spectator,
> And gaze where'er the palace or the hovel is,
> Much in the mode of Goethe's Mephistopheles.

(XIII, 7)

This sounds plausible enough until we recall that there is no Faust with whom this Mephistopheles can talk. Don Juan Tenorio is indeed a Faust figure but Byron's Don Juan is so only in limited ways. A better candidate would be Byron himself as narrator whose death, as we have seen, is built into the poem's structure and forms part of the reader's expectation. There are privileged characters in *Don Juan* (Johnson, Haidée, Leila, the old Khan, Aurora Raby) and figures of great practical intelligence (Lambro, Baba, Suvarrow) but no one speculates intellectually in the poem apart form Juan himself for a brief and ridiculed pubertal spasm (I, 87-96). Clearly this is to maintain the evident disjunction between thought and action which holds throughout the poem. Juan does; the narrator thinks. Even in sections of the poem where this seems threatened, as in the death of the Ravenna Commandant in Canto V, we have seen that the narrator does not really initiate actions of his own. If the narrator cannot act, none of the characters in the poem can be allowed to think as he does. Hence the narrator has no one to talk to except himself or the reader.

This is more of a problem than it may appear to be. It is true that good story-tellers often interrupt their narration by digressive comment which may take the form of apostrophe, reflection, jokes or apparent conversation with the audience. Moreover it is often the case that, through these and other means, the narrator is built up as a character in his own right. Fielding, much admired by Byron and invoked in Canto XIII (XIII, 110), is an obvious example. Narration in the first half of *Don Juan* follows this pattern though it extends it almost to breaking point. Talk is a natural feature of such narration for it arises out of a presumed reaction on the reader's part to the events of the story. Much ordinary conversation consists of anecdotes interrupted by comment initiated freely by the anecdotalist or others in the conversational group. The anecdote itself will tend to have an apparently independent existence. It is brought into light so that the participants in the conversation may be in the same relation to it as the anecdotalist and comment upon it for themselves. If anecdotes do not have this character but retain a primary link with the anecdotalist then he is either a confessionalist like Wordsworth in *The Prelude* or a performer such as a comedian.

In the first half of *Don Juan*, episodes do have a real independence from the narrator but this is not the case at all, as we have seen, in Cantos X to XII and not altogether the case from the Siege up to Canto XV. If the narrator continues to talk, this cannot now arise out of the credible fiction of shared response to independent events and therefore the narrator appears simply as a performer. What began as *Tom Jones* could topple into *Tristram Shandy*. It would not be difficult to adduce lines from the poem to illustrate this but they would precipitate a wrong inference. Something quite different from Fielding or Sterne occurs in the later cantos of *Don Juan*.

II

Conversation is a curious thing.[4] It is the first form in which any poet learns to handle words. Some poets, like Horace or Burns, seek to develop links between their poems and their conversation; others, like Keats or Rilke, try to sever them. Those who do the latter do so because conversation seems to them a secondary discourse too heavily implicated in the immediate rather than the perennial, or in social worlds rather than the inner world. Conversation, they claim, has 'Nothing that speaks to all men and at all times.' (XIV, 16). *Don Juan* is itself both contestant and exemplar in this debate and has often been presented as not a 'serious' poem for its apparently indiscriminate use of non-poetic registers. Something similar underlay Matthew Arnold's notorious contention that Chaucer lacked 'the high and excellent seriousness, which Aristotle assigns as one of the grand virtues of poetry'.[5] Part of the deficiency of this view is that conversation is not wholly a social or a temporal phenomenon or, to put it more precisely, conversation, like play, dance or friendship, though inescapably social and temporal, is an end in itself. It is not wholly immersed in the social and temporal contexts which shape it. The weight of Utilitarian assumption is of course against such a contention and I do not want to challenge such widespread assumptions here by protracted argument. Other assumptions remain intelligible and retain residual force; for the moment it is better to rely on them and the briefly invoked counter-example of Dante's *Divine Comedy*.

Dante's poem undoubtedly tethers its myriad subsidiary conversa-tions with the dead to the time, place and society which fixed them in their present location in *Inferno* or *Purgatorio*. On the other hand, Dante's conversation with the long dead Vergil and with his future reader suggests conversation's multiple entry points so that Dante, Vergil and his many different readers are not locked away in separate conversa-tional worlds wholly belonging to their originating circumstances. To this conversation, the inhabitants of *Inferno* and *Purgatorio* are sum-moned. In *Paradiso*, conversation of a kind is maintained with Beatrice and, finally, with St Bernard right up to the final vision of the triune godhead. These are fictions but intelligible fictions. They are intelligible because we would be less likely to accept the solidity of Dante's vision if it was not given conversational immediacy. The reverse and less popular proposition must hold too. Dante's supernatural conversation is credible because all conversation, even of the most ordinary kind, enjoys the free space which it occupies and, in this way, is open to and mimics a kind of timelessness. This is indicated in the ubiquitous time formulas with which we mark the transitition to ordinary sequence when we close a conversation('Is that the time?', 'How time has flown!', 'I must dash', etc., etc.).

Conversation in *Don Juan* has exactly this double character and this is the most considerable reason for the narrator's immersing himself in talk in the English cantos. It anchors the poem's time to historical time, society and place. On the other hand, it dissolves historical time, society and place into conversational flow and endless chat. Nowhere is this more marked than in the narrator's own cantos. What we see here is the narrator apparently most at his ease. He has got rid of independent incident. The poem is now set in a country which he can describe with an inexhaustible flow of witty corroborating detail. Instead of merely intruding into independent narrative, his chatter now superintends the narrative. However, the narrator's security is not abso-lute. Earlier in the poem, he had a narrative task as well as oppor-tunity for solo performances. His identity was not wholly given away, he was not the constant object of our attention, nor did he expect us to share all his reactions to events within the poem. Moreover, the early cantos in a way hide the narrator from us. Manifestly he is Byron, yet he is often a device and, even, in I, 14, VI, 70 and XVI, 82 claims to know some of the characters. None of this bothers us. We do not seek an explanation or a wholeness beyond this. Thus the narrator has, like Fielding in *Tom Jones*, a working independence. He is for much of the time a witty acquaintance whom we know quite well but we do not seek to know everything about him. We do not try to discover for instance where he learnt his skills as a narrator, for we are more interested in Juan's history than his.

When Juan arrives in England, however, the situation is different. The narrator's flow of detail and delight in revealing his extensive familiarity with the diction, tone and allusions of his high-society characters reveals him far more clearly to us. The reader knows very well that Lord Byron, author of narration and narrator, lived in a sociey and, later, in a house almost identical with this. It was through being a member of this particular society that the narrator acquired the poise which he used in earlier digressions and now uses to direct the poem and castigate that society. The narrator is one of those writers who 'Are grown of the *Beau-Monde* a part potential.' (XIV, 20). Two things follow. First this explains why the poem, ceasing to be Fielding, does not become Sterne at this point. Language, despite the solidity of Uncle Toby *et al.*, is largely a self-conscious medium for Sterne's solipsistic psychologising. In the later cantos of *Don Juan*, the narrator's language is more solidly instated in a disclosed social world than ever. Secondly, the narrator's superiority is once again shown to be of a vulnerable kind. He had previously some inscrutability as a narrator wholly other than his narration. Now he is merely superior to a particular social world of which he was once a part. Such superiority, like that of a dandy, can only be retained by constant vigilance. This explains the relevance of my earlier discussion of Byron's snobbery. The narrator is at ease in these cantos but that ease has to be exactly calculated and ceaselessly maintained. It advertises participation but may encounter rejection. In 1816 Byron was, or thought he was, rejected by just such a society as that which he here depicts. Now he courts an analogous rejection by his arrogant insider's portrait of the same society.

For the present rather than contemporary reader of *Don Juan*, the conduct of the poem as such is likely to be more crucial. It is a new experience for the reader to find a narrator so unfettered by narrative exigencies but it is a new experience for him also to see the narrator so fully discernible within the world which he describes. In particular this modifies the accustomed relation between thought and talk and reduces the paradoxical status of conversation which we have just established.

Speculative thought cannot be conversation's habitual concern but it is naturally linked with it for both conversation and speculation evade or transcend practical activities and specific communications. Socratic, and even Scholastic, methods rely upon the conversational model, for both dramatise a shared uncertainty in order to gain assent to an eventual truth. Of course, Socrates and the medieval disputant knew what point they wished to arrive at whereas free conversation cannot know this nor can be said to 'arrive' at all. Nevertheless Socrates, for instance, clearly takes advantage of that latency in conversation for unexpected intellectual discovery which still flickers intermittently, bereft of justification, in modern university tutorials. Conversation reveals our dependence upon our contemporary society for all our thoughts and feelings but it also allows and fosters in us some sense, intermittent but undeniable, of a direct, whole, and questioning relation with a reality, and there can only be one such reality, which transcends our particularity though it cannot be expressed except in limited and particular forms. *Don Juan* is, in its own quite different way, as brimful of this sense as is Wordsworth's *The Prelude*. However, the narrator's revealed proximity to and dependence on a social world which he shares with his audience makes it more difficult to suggest these possibilities. Instead of, like Dante, summoning the inhabitants of his comedy to his atemporal conversation, he is more likey to reflect their gossip or to stand apart from them only as the satirist of particular abuses. Even if his satire is more general, it is likely to confirm the generalities of his audience. A bored narrator may tellingly satirise a bored society but will hardly ruffle its surface. If, to relieve his boredom, he can produce endless comedian's patter, he will, whatever its satirical content, simply entertain his audience by relieving their boredom too and confirm their own deepest diagnosis of life.

I am not separating the reactions of Byron's contemporaries from that of later readers as clearly as perhaps I should. There are differences to be taken into account. On the other hand, we tend at this point in the poem to co-operate with Byron's very clear sense of present readership and that much stronger sense we now have of proximity to dated event and circumstance since the Siege of Ismail with its named historical characters. More generally those readers who are European or heirs to European traditions will recognise themselves to be in not dissimilar spiritual circumstance to the denizens of Blank Blank Square and Norman Abbey. Byron's profoundest criticism of these spiritual circumstances is not in the incidental satire of the narrator, which is tied to these circumstances, but in the revived narrative of Cantos XV to XVII as we shall see.

It seems clear then that, in these later cantos of *Don Juan* which can no longer trustfully commit itself to the unplanned turn of events after the Siege, the narrator, who can but think and talk, is loath to do so in a vacuum. We are given instead therefore a clear narrative line ('Juan was in x, is in y, and will be going to z') and the narrator's free flow of talk is held close to the world of English upper-class society from which it originated and to which it is addressed. In these cantos, which may be called 'his', the narrator talks and thinks as always but in quite altered circumstances. One of the oddest effects produced by these changed circumstances is the gap between the narrator and reader from the Siege outwards. This gap was an incidental feature of earlier cantos. It occurred when the narrator's response or sensitivity to narrative incident was other than the reader's. Since the narrator now controls incident, this gap is closed. The new division is caused by the ebullience of the narrator in the English cantos, apparently indifferent to the effect the disappearance of independent narrative is likely to have on the reader and making no allowance for the reader's markedly less buoyant expectations after the Siege. Helen Gardner, for example, commented: ' . . . there is a fundamental good humour in *Don Juan* which becomes the dominant tone when Byron finally gets his hero to England'.[6] That is perfectly true. The narrator's good humour alone, or very nearly so, preserves a sense of comic potentiality in *Don Juan* from Canto X and 'dominant tone' is exactly right. But this 'good humour' is like a comedian's performance stretched out miraculously to cover some awkward hiatus in a stage production. It is not clear whether, behind the scenes, a recovery is being mounted which will relieve the comedian from his astonishing improvisation and there is anxiety as well as admiring pleasure in our response. In *Don Juan*, the 'hiatus' is the disaster of Ismail and Catharine. The narrator's good humour thus appears not only admirable but callous. Earlier that callousness, as in his enjoyment of Juan's sea-sick response to Julia's letter, assisted the renewed comic narrative. Now there is no narrative to assist and the narrator's 'good humour' persists as a separated entity enthralling but distancing his anxious readers.

Their anxiety may be put like this. Does the course of the poem pare away everything external to it on which we may ground a comic view of life? Juan's comic survival at first, though wrought by fictions, seemed to be corroborated by forces that hold outside the poem. Such forces, however, also underlie the slaughter of Ismail and Catharine's insatiable lust. Hence they refute the solely comic character of Juan's survival and renewal. 'Good humour', consequently, can no longer be linked with that survival and can find no other corroboration than the narrator's style in which it is maintained.

We could stand this on its head, abandon our anxiety, dismiss *Don Juan* as comic, and claim the narrator's triumph of style as a forerunner of modernist aesthetics. G.M. Ridenour, for example, cites the well-known opening image of Canto VII:

> And such they are, such my present tale is
> A non-descript and ever-varying rhyme,
> A versified Aurora Borealis,
> Which flashes o'er a waste and icy clime.
>
> (VII, 2)

He comments that *Don Juan* is indeed such 'an attempt to give color, form, and warmth to a world naturally colorless, indefinitive and chill. Poetry sheds light and reveals.'[7] That indeed may be the force of these lines but it is not, I think, the force of the poem. Byron is neither Walter Pater nor Wallace Stevens. I am reminded of the English painter Keith Vaughan's reaction to Kandinsky's claim that 'the impact of an acute triangle on a sphere generates as much emotional impact as the meeting of God and Adam in Michaelangelo's Creation'. Vaughan's reaction was 'Not to me boy!'[8] Professor Ridenour's point is less epigramatically contentious than Kandinsky's but it drives a sinister wedge between 'color, form, warmth' in fiction and in fact. However superior the former, it must presuppose the latter in order to be intelligible at all. Of course, the narrator and Byron, on occasion, see the world as Lucifer presents it in Act II of *Cain*, a place of lifeless shadows. Of course, Byron, sometimes, privileges poetry as a|fiery Promethean relict in a fallen world.[9] But these are not Byron's only views on the matter. *Don Juan*, in particular, though it contains many viewpoints and is, in its way, a triumph of fictionality and reflexive consciousness, resists mutation and remains a spectacularly beleaguered comedy. There are many traditional enemies of comic viewpoint — law, convention, parental tyranny, intellectualised negation and, pre-eminently, Death. Comedy depends upon their opposition and incorporates them into its triumphing dialectic. The narrator's isolated pre-eminence from the Siege onwards is just such a counter-agent to comic confidence whose pride precedes his fall. If Ismail, Catharine's court and Regency London are the whole of reality then such 'a waste and icy clime' does stand in need of 'A versified Aurora Borealis' to 'flash o'er' it and lend it fiction's 'color, fire, warmth'. This is a plausible temptation but one which reader and poem alike come to reject. The reader, for example, is eventually brought to clear impatience with the maddeningly foregrounded narrator. Even if we, too, can see nothing on which to rely other than the narrator's capacity to keep on talking, we, by reading on, suggest the possibility of an underlying or possibly renewed momentum which is implied by that impatience.

If we take, for instance, one of the most outrageous stanzas in *Don Juan:*

> But here is one prescription out of many:
> 'Sodae-Sulphat. 3vj, 3fs. Mannae optim.
> Aq. fervent. F. 3ifs. 3ij. tinct. Sennae
> Haustus.' (And here the surgeon came and cupped
>   him)
> 'R. Pulv. Com. gr. iij. Ipecacuanhae'
> (With more beside, if Juan had not stopped 'em).
> 'Bolus Potassae Sulphuret. sumendus,
> Et Haustus ter in die capiendus.'
>
> (X, 41)

We are quite prepared to accept the appropriation here of a bizarrely unpoetic but accredited mode of discourse as a triumph for the poem. It is the occasion for some routine anti-medical satire, it reminds us of the frightening distance between medical professionalism and human suffering but it is chiefly relished for its poetic daring. Pedantry and medicine are made to dance. We are likely to share the narrator's evident glee in this achievement without reservations. When, however, several cantos later, Canto XV begins like this, our reaction is likely to be different:

> Ah! — What should follow slips from my reflection:
> Whatever follows|ne'ertheless may be
> As à propos of hope or retrospection
> As though the lurking thought had follow'd free.
> All present life is but an Interjection,
> An 'Oh!' or 'Ah!' of joy or misery,
> Or a 'Ha! ha!' or 'Bah!' — a yawn, or 'Pooh!'
> Of which perhaps the latter is most true.
>
> (XV, 1)

We might admire here, of course, the balancing of rhyming poly-syllables ('reflection', 'retrospection', 'interjection') with inane mono-syllabic exclamations ('Oh!', 'ah!', 'ha!', 'bah!', 'pooh!'). We will notice the relevance of this realised boredom to the later discussion of ennui in general and in Norman Abbey. It is, however, our diminished reaction to this stanza as a *tour de force* which will differ from our delight in the poetic prescription of X, 41. The reader, though, accus-tomed to sceptical introductory stanzas in the cantos of *Don Juan*, is as likely to be as much appalled as thrilled by the risk-taking here. *Don Juan*, like conversation, understanding and erotic impulse, comes most tellingly when unbidden. It is a human characteristic to seek to catch and 'know' those moments of unbidden prompting and to enjoy those situations (e.g. argument or games) which rely upon their occurrence. *Don Juan* plays this game of consciously knowing its origins: 'I'll have another figure in a trice' (XIII, 37) and relying upon unconscious sources of renewal: 'Eureka! I have found it! What I mean/To say is . . . ' (XIV, 76) to excess. What worries the reader of the first stanza of Canto XV is the blasé and off-hand character of this renewal signalled by its ostentatious placing at the beginning of a canto: 'Ah!|– What should follow slips from my reflection:' (XV, 1). It is difficult to describe this correctly. If we are heavy-handed about it, we will over-look the sense in which this is, in a way, no different from the cele-brated shocker which opens Canto III: 'Hail, muse! *et cetera.* – We left Juan sleeping,' (III, 17). Moreover the narrator certainly takes into account the reader's discomfiture and is adjusting his flippant cock-sureness to our presumed outrage. Laughter should and does result but the reader's reservations and impatience are more loyal to the poem than the narrator's remorseless invention at this point. It is the narrator who will, in effect, climb down. For here we have a trivialisation of that co-operation between chance and significance which holds the poem together and which, whatever the narrator or Professor Ridenour may say, is not, the poem presumes, confined to it alone. After all, if the narrator is right and the creative art of the poem is no more than the meaninglessly alternating exclamations of joy and misery which 'interject all present life' then the poem has no standpoint or insight other than that of the denizens of Blank Blank Square or, for that matter, of the Sultan's palace in Canto V. No reader of *Don Juan* can think this for long. Nor would it be sufficient to locate that further standpoint or insight within 'art' itself when that art is no more than the ingenious spinning out of Canto XV, stanza 1. Debasement is essen-tial to the poem's comic and satiric procedures but its own larger pro-

cedures could also become debased and then we would lose the capacity to react to debasement upon which the poem depends.

Certainly by Canto XV the reader is unlikely to be simply amused
by all this. The presence of countering viewpoints would help but the
narrator has dominated the poem since the Siege. Little by little, it is
true, we have had a new social world built up in the poem, first in
London and then in Norman Abbey. But this world cannot, it seems,
overturn the narrator's predilections. Unlike the similarly barren
Sultan's palace, it does not appear to contain within it that openness
to unexpected comic event nor to erotic warmth (Dudù's 'soft landscape of mild earth', VI, 53), which have been essential counters to
the narrator's desecrating intelligence hitherto. The opening of Canto
XV seems to glory in this bareness of options which highlights the
narrator's brilliance but cannot alleviate his confinement.

In general, Don Juan says 'Yes' and the narrator says 'No'. Both are
found out by their persistence in these modes. Juan's 'Yes' eventually
lands him in the Siege, pinions him in Catharine's 'vast arms' (X, 137)
and is finally checked by his sickness which 'augured of the dead' (X,
39). The narrator is thus landed with the poem but can say 'Yes' to
nothing in it except his own performance before an audience whom he
seems to despise. It is true that the narrator can muster certain liberal
preferences in the light of which he can satirise English society, but his
scepticism, which in part supports his liberal views, is allowed such
free rein as to disallow a tolerable working certainty to these values. If
we again ask ourselves what the narrator does with the poem when he is
in control of it, we might say that he infects it with his 'No'. But that is
not the end of the matter.

Understanding of Byron has usually polarised into primary
sympathy with either his positive or his negative drives. Carlyle instructed us to 'Close thy Byron; open thy Goethe' because of the
former's 'everlasting No' and the latter's 'everlasting Yea'[10] but others
in the nineteenth century saw Byron as a positive revolutionary force.
More recently R.F. Gleckner has persuasively documented Byron's
pessimism, whilst E.D. Hirsch has emphasised the inherent affirmation
of Byron's poetry.[11] Need we be so anxious to sunder and choose
between Byron's 'Yes' and his 'No'? A couplet in Canto IV suggests
otherwise:

While life's strange principle will often lie
Deepest in those who long the most to die.

                                                                 (IV, 11)

Certainly the 'strange principle' of life in *Don Juan* is forced to emerge from within the shadow of the narrator's isolation and nihilism in the final cantos of the poem.

III

Byron could discriminate finely between different kinds of 'No'. Manfred, for example, reveals its eponymous hero in Act I about to jump off the Jungfrau. The scene is apparently an exalted one and appears as such in John Martin's well-known painting. Byron, however, undoubtedly wants to make Manfred look slightly ridiculous, for after his magnificent rodomontade he is 'in act to spring from the cliff' when 'the Chamois Hunter seizes and retains him with a sudden grasp'. Manfred replies with some meekness:

> I am most sick at heart — nay, grasp me not —
> I am all feebleness — the mountains whirl
> Spinning around me — I grow blind — What art thou?
>
> (II, 113-15)

He is then led down the mountain 'with difficulty' by the chamois hunter. Byron had a peculiar horror of suicide and manifestly disapproved of Manfred's willed 'No' at this point. The latter is humbled by the chamois hunter's ordinary good sense. At the very end of the play, however, when demons come to take him with them like Faust, he rises superior to them and dies in a most un-Faustian speech to the Abbot who has tried to convert him. Their interchange looks as though it is intended to recall Manfred's reply to the chamois hunter:

> *Man.* 'Tis over — my dull eyes can fix thee not;
>   But all things swim around me, and the earth
>   Heaves as it were beneath me. Fare thee well —
>   Give me thy hand.
> *Abbot* Cold — cold — even to the heart —
>   But yet one prayer — Alas! how fares it with thee?
> *Man.* Old man! 'tis not so difficult to die.
>
> (IV, 146-51)

Here, though Manfred is again 'all feebleness' in his physical being, he is at one with his condition. We could adapt a distinction very dear to Rilke and say that Manfred now finds his death rather than seeking it.

Instead of being a solitary seized by the chamois hunter, he asks for the Abbot's hand. His last words: 'Old man! 'tis not so difficult to die.' express a coincidence of his mastering will with a natural surrender of life. E.H. Coleridge comments:

> In the first edition (p. 73), this line was left out at Gifford's suggestion (*Memoirs, etc.*, 1891, i. 387). Byron was indignant, and wrote to Murray, August 12, 1817 (*Letters*, 1900, iv, 157), 'You have destroyed the whole effect and moral of the poem, by omitting the last line of Manfred's speaking'.[12]

This 'whole effect and moral' must lie in the proof which the last line offers of Manfred's growth since the false 'No' of his Jungfrau attempt. The problem with *Manfred*, as with Milton's *Samson Agonistes*, is how this change is effected in the course of the play. That need not concern us. We need only to mark the importance of this distinction to Byron.

In Canto XIV of *Don Juan*, the narrator discourses in an important passage about the Manfred experience and relates it to his own present trivialising consciousness:

> The very Suicide that pays his debt
> At once without instalments (an old way
> Of paying debts, which creditors regret)
> Lets out impatiently his rushing breath,
> Less from disgust of life than dread of death.

> 5

> 'Tis round him, near him, here, there, every where;
> And there's a courage which grows out of fear,
> Perhaps of all most desperate, which will dare
> The worst to *know* it: — when the mountains rear
> Their peaks beneath your human foot, and there
> You look down o'er the precipice, and drear
> The gulf of rock yawns, — you can't gaze a minute
> Without an awful wish to plunge within it.

> 6

> 'Tis true, you don't — but, pale and struck with terror,
> Retire: but look into your past impression!
> And you will find, though shuddering at the mirror
> Of your own thoughts, in all their self confession,
> The lurking bias, be it truth or error,

> To the *unknown*; a secret prepossession,
> To plunge with all your fears — but where? You know
>   not,
> And that's the reason why you do — or do not.
>
>   7
> But what's this to the purpose? you will say.
> Gent. Reader, nothing; a mere speculation,
> For which my sole excuse is — 'tis my way,
> Sometimes *with* and sometimes without occasion
> I write what's uppermost, without delay;
> This narrative is not meant for narration,
> But a mere airy and fantastic basis,
> To build up common things with common places.
>
>   8
> You know, or don't know, that great Bacon saith,
> "Fling up a straw, 'twill show the way the wind blows";
> And such a straw, borne on by human breath,
> Is Poesy, according as the mind glows;
> A paper kite, which flies 'twixt life and death,
> A shadow which the onward Soul behind throws:
> And mine's a bubble not blown up for praise,
> But just to play with, as an infant plays.
>
>   (XIV, 4-8)

Here too we can discern different orders of negation. The 'secret prepossession,/'To plunge' into the abyss of Death as, earlier, into the abyss of Thought (X, 28) is, in its exalted excitement, quite other than the extended negativity of writing *Don Juan* as here described:

> In youth I wrote, because my mind was full,
> And now because I feel it growing dull.
> . . .
> Why drink? Why read? — To make some hour less dreary.
>
>   (XIV, 10, 11)

There are nevertheless links between the two as the narrator seems to admit. The narrator owns the wish to 'plunge' into the abyss but does not do so. Energy of a kind comes from proximity to this abyss but it is the trivialised creativity of 'poesy'; 'A paper kite, which flies 'twixt life and death,' (XIV, 8), for Art, from the narrator's viewpoint, can do no more than circle round the abyss, sometimes peeping into it and, at other times, distracting attention away from it by spectacular inventiveness. *Don Juan* is like this but, *pace* Professor Ridenour, is not this. A striking feature of these stanzas from Canto XIV is the casual movement from looking forwards in dread: 'You look down o'er the precipice, and drear/The gulf of rock yawns' (XIV, 5) to the retrospective organisation of verse: 'A shadow which the onward Soul behind throws:' (XIV, 8). This retrospective character of poetry is emphasised in subsequent stanzas:

> It occupies me to turn back regards
> On what I've seen or ponder'd, sad or cheery;
> And what I will I cast upon the stream,
> To sink or swim — I have had at least my dream.
>
> (XIV, 11)

The abyss, as it were, drives us back to the despised safety of present invention constructed from past experience. We shall encounter all this again when Juan meets the ghost in Canto XVI in that strange house, Norman Abbey, which has an abyss of its own permanently attached to it. There we shall be forced to move beyond the narrator's present assumptions and see the relation between past, present and future in a new light.

Even these present assumptions, however, contain within them a discernible appetency for their own overthrow. This is hard to demonstrate but easily grasped. In *Manfred* which, flawed as it is, undoubtedly works, we cannot say exactly how Manfred grows or attains the quiet authority of 'Old man! 'tis not so difficult to die.' (III, IV, 131), yet we accept that he has found this authority and ripe occasion for it. In the same way, reader and narrator in *Don Juan* wait for something other than the vivid acrobatics of Cantos X to XII to keep the poem going. We can, however, say more about this in *Don Juan* than in *Manfred*.

Waiting is the normal attitude of the observer and of human consciousness in so far as it sees itself primarily in a knowing relationship with being and occurrence. At one point, the narrator cries:

> If I agree that what is, is; then this I call
> Being quite perspicuous and extremely fair.
>
> (XI, 5)

Normally he is not content with this even though he often wishes to oppose sceptical commonsense to received speculation:

> "To be or not to be?" — Ere I decide,
> I should be glad to know that which *is being?*
>
> (IX, 16)

The problem is that commonsense, though dependent upon scepticism for its rejection of the supernatural or the *a priori*, cannot be wholly based on scepticism for scepticism also destroys commonsense. Some classic forms of sceptical thought have managed to overcome, or, at any rate, to face this difficulty, but scepticism *per se* threatens the privileged position of doubt as much as it does idealism or the supernatural:

> It is a pleasant voyage perhaps to float,
> Like Pyrrho, on a sea of speculation;
> But what if carrying sail capsize the boat?
>
> (IX, 18)

If sceptical enquiry, instead of simply demolishing metaphysical superstructures, also makes commonsense impossible and turns doubt back on itself,

> Oh, Doubt! — if thou be'st Doubt, for which some take
>   thee,
> But which I doubt extremely — thou sole prism
> Of the Truth's rays,
>
> (IX, 2)

then, instead of protecting us from 'the abyss' of thought, such scepticism plunges us back into the abyss with a vengeance. 'Waiting' in such circumstances seems intolerable. Practical activity (denied to the pure observer although he can mimic it in the rhetoric of political action), memories and 'creative' experiment are the only distractions from this intolerable attitude. These are the stock-in-trade of the narrator and serve him and his readers very well in the first half of the poem for we there have a narrative which does not simply confirm what the narrator says about it. Once Juan has come under the narrator's control, the whole poem is, from Cantos X to XV, restricted to the waiting character of the narrator's intelligence. We saw in the previous chapter how Byron's death rather than Juan occupies the end-position allotted to

Don Juan Tenorio in the source-play. Similarly, *El burlador de Sevilla*
and *Faust* plays are narratives of waiting for an end. In *Don Juan*, it is
not Juan whose waiting we nervously share but that of Byron as narrator. He, like Dr Faustus, is cruelly and continually exposed in Cantos
X to XV and reacts, like his tragic counterparts, with a dazzling display
of his normal tricks carried out with defiant energy but evident strain.
His relationship with the reader is necessarily more intimate than ever
but, rather like Dryden's in his dramatic prologues, the intimate tone
has an aggressive edge.

All this is to be expected. But we are given clear suggestions of a
different direction altogether, hints of '*Yes*-saying' on so extravagant
a scale that the narrator presents it in an odd mixture of direct statement, ironically embarrassed disclaimers and burlesque. If, for example,
we continue our quotation from Canto XI, we find —

> If I agree that what is, is; then this I call
> Being quite perspicuous and extremely fair.
> The truth is, I've grown lately rather phthisical:
> I don't know what the reason is — the air
> Perhaps; but as I suffer from the shocks
> Of illness, I grow much more orthodox.

>   6
> The first attack at once proved the Divinity;
> (But *that* I never doubted, nor the Devil);
> The next, the Virgin's mystical virginity;
> The third, the usual Origin of Evil;
> The fourth at once established the whole Trinity
> On so uncontrovertible a level,
> That I devoutly wished the three were four,
> On purpose to believe so much the more.

>   (XI, 5, 6)

It is necessary to submit these lines to rather unsubtle analysis in
order to demonstrate that though Byron as narrator has his tongue in its
usual place — namely in his cheek — that his words mean exactly what
they say. Byron has been ill. He is growing much closer to orthodox
belief than hitherto. There is a connection between the two. This is
what the lines say and it is what they mean though this meaning is not
the sum-total of their content and effect. It would not be necessary to
assert this if, almost from the outset, Byron was assumed to be of

wholly different disposition. Shelley, as we saw, may have detected more Christianity in *Cain* than he would have liked, but no less than Goethe had a different confidence:

> As to Byron's *Cain*, Goethe then showed me a short critique he had written.
> 'We see,' he said, 'how the inadequate dogmas of the church work upon a free mind like Byron's, and how by such a piece he struggles to get rid of a doctrine which has been forced upon him.'[13]

There is some truth in this critique but what principally motivates it is Goethe's assumption that he knows the direction of Byron's thought and that that direction is the same as his own in, for example, *Faust*.

I am as prejudiced in the direction of my own thoughts as was Goethe but the direction of Byron's remains susceptible of an attention which may be seen to confirm, by-pass or overthrow the prejudices of the critic. Let us admit at the outset then that the apparent sympathy of the narrator to orthodox belief in these stanzas from *Don Juan* is rendered both suspect and comical by its trivial occasioning:

> I don't know what the reason is – the air
> Perhaps; but as I suffer from the shocks
> Of illness, I grow much more orthodox.

(XI, 5)

It is not only the triviality of 'air' and 'illness' but the tone of 'perhaps' that is at odds with a declaration of belief. The next stanza, in its implication that a sequence of 'attacks' by illness leads to the acceptance of a corresponding sequence of increasingly incredible beliefs, from the Divinity to the Trinity, similarly does not appear to flatter the operations of faith. Finally, the gleeful sneeriness in the epithets of stanza 6 – 'mystical virginity', 'usual origin of evil', 'so uncontrovertible' – together with the expressed desire to believe that the Trinity were four 'On purpose to believe so much the more' make the reader snigger too and thus relieve him of the burden of taking Byron's religion very seriously. But then could a conversational tone such as this ever incorporate references to 'the Virgin's mystical virginity' or to the Trinity and not appear to make them objects which are, so to speak, at the mercy of discourse? The poise of an observer, if relentlessly maintained, must render everything within his observation a matter of curiosity rather than of wonder. In the preface to *Don Juan* Byron makes fun of Wordsworth's note on the insensitive narrator in 'The Thorn'. He was not in sympathy with *Lyrical Ballads*. The intolerable juxtaposition of naïvete and sophistication is, however, as central to his purposes in *Don Juan* as to those of Wordsworth. There are moments in *Don Juan* when sophistication topples over into naïvete and the reader is quite unclear as to the triviality or depth of the resultant discourse. These lines are a case in point. Are they a racy and assured sneer at the absurdities of religious doctrine or do they hoist the expected scepticism of reader and narrator with their own petard? Certainly the reference to 'illness' belies the narrator's tone. For the 'I' which is thus poised in conscious control in stanza 6; 'I devoutly wished the three were four,' has in fact admitted that it may be attacked and displaced: '. . . but as I suffer from the shocks/Of illness, I grow much more orthodox.' Both 'as I suffer' and 'I grow' imply duration and change rather than observation and performance. If then we are gradually returned to an observer's performance in stanza 6, we know that these detached and witty observations depend upon a being who does more than observe and 'is' beyond the exercise of his will. The stanza's second line too cannot be read wholly in the devil's sense:

The first attack at once proved the Divinity;
(But *that* I never doubted, nor the Devil);

This must mean that, prior to 'the shocks of illness', he has always believed in God (which in Byron's case was so) and therefore the first 'attack' confirms something which is true. This must carry the implication that the further, much more specifically Christian, doctrines are, though once doubted, now possibly credible and true in the same way. The tone of 'But *that* I never doubted' is unequivocal and leaves the reader confused as to what is coming next. It is only with 'nor the Devil' that the route is clear. For though Byron as narrator means that he has never doubted the devil's existence, the reader, correctly, adjusts after a moment's hesitation, to the familiar metaphorical interpretation that the devil must exist because we have overwhelming evidence of evil in the world rather than to literal belief in Satan. It is this element of ruefulness which establishes our hold on commonsense and distances us at once from 'the Virgin's mystical virginity', etc.

What is important here, however, is not the recovery of poise in the narrator, which he is bound to regain, but the allowed glimpse into what threatens that poise. Religious belief, like the narrator's compulsive ratiocination, is drawn to the abyss but claims to know and receive sustenance from it. The narrator's scepticism reduces him to 'what is' without giving him any more promise of certainty in this minimalism than would be the case if he were to believe in a whole series of unbelievable extras such as the Trinity or Mary's virginity. These remain unbelievably extra to commonsense but the return to commonsense is not to anything more solid or credible. The poise of commonsense is based simply on the skilled performance of the speaker and the wide-spread disinclination in his audience to take orthodox belief seriously. In these lines Byron is not flouting the allegedly solid Christian beliefs of his readers, rather he is tantalising them by a flirtation with the possibility of a belief or a rejection far more considerable than theirs. In *Cain* what outraged his audience was that he reopened a difficulty and the possibility of a religious understanding of the story as opposed to a moralistic simplification of it.

Once again we need to draw back a little from Byron and his imme-diate audience, though we cannot obliterate them, and consider any reader's relation to the narrator at this point. Here the most important fact is that the narrator's confession of 'shocks/Of illness' occurs only 40 stanzas or so away from Don Juan's illness in St Petersburg. Both hero and narrator are subject to illness at the same stage in the poem. Juan's illness is the hinge upon which the poem turns. It would be foolish to say the same of the narrator's brief admission but it is of real significance none the less. This can be neatly indicated by an incident in Homer's *Iliad*.

In Book V of the *Iliad*, Diomedes wounds Venus and then Mars. This attack has repercussions on later events, and warfare between gods and men may have been taken in his stride by an Ancient Greek.[14] Readers of the poem, however, Greek listener or otherwise, are bound to be particularly interested in this wounding of the gods by a man, for the contrast between the painful world of mortals and the similar but immortal world of the gods is basic to the poem's structure and signifi-cant effects. Human vulnerability to shame, pain and death we must take for granted, yet the reader is unprepared for Venus and Mars to flee howling and shamefaced back to Olympus. There are limits to this vul-nerability but that they are vulnerable at all and in this particular way modifies our understanding of the relationship between gods and men. We are interested in anything which suggests the vulnerability of the narrator in *Don Juan* in exactly the same way. We know that Juan can be ill and that his illness affects the course of events. We learn that the narrator can be ill and that this affects his thoughts and assumptions. We know very well, of course, that 'gastric juice' affects our 'intellects'

(V, 32) but the narrator has seemed immune from his own sharp observation. Normally he can comment, intervene in or turn away from the adventures of Juan with as much freedom as Homer's gods, but if he too is time-bound and vulnerable, the relationship between Juan and narrator alters. Moreover, we are bound to notice that the narrator's new vulnerability coincides with and occasions his mocking, tentative, yet covertly respectful, shift towards the affirming formulas of religious faith.

At the beginning of the poem, the narrator tells us

> . . . I
> Have spent my life, both interest and principal,
> And deem not, what I deem'd, my soul invincible.
>
> (I, 213)

and there are similar admissions of weakness and limitation elsewhere which apparently repudiate the claims of earlier poems such as *Childe Harold's Pilgrimage:*

> But there is that within me which shall tire
> Torture and Time
>
> (IV, 137)

If we confine ourselves to explicit admission then the narrator is now a much humbler fellow than this:

> And the sad truth which hovers o'er my desk
> Turns what was once romantic to burlesque.
>
> (IV, 3)

The narrator's humility here is presented very much in his own terms. In both cases quoted above his present admission of limitation is linked directly to Byron's own ageing:

> And would not brook at all this sort of thing
> In my hot youth — when George the Third was King.
>
> (I, 212)

> As a boy, I thought myself a clever fellow
>
> (IV, 3)

It is much less clear that the narrator as such admits limitation. If we return a moment to those splendid Promethean lines in *Childe Harold's Pilgrimage*, we should not overlook the acknowledgement of limitation whch precedes the flyting:

> But I have lived, and have not lived in vain: |
> My mind may lose its force, my blood its fire,
> And my frame perish even in conquering pain,
> But there is that within me which shall tire
> Torture and Time, and breathe when I expire

(IV, 138)

The claim here to persistence beyond the admitted limitations of mind and body is linked to the art of the poem for it is the persistence of *Childe Harold's Pilgrimage* as art which will vindicate Byron's own version of his private history. Nothing in *Don Juan* articulates this unmitigated bravura so directly. Byron's couplet

> And the sad truth which hovers o'er my desk
> Turns what was once romantic to burlesque

(IV, 3)

appears specifically to disclaim it. Nevertheless Professor Ridenour's contention that the poem claims a superior vitality to anything outside it is based on something. Byron and the narrator are to some extent one person, we can document 'the shocks/Of illness' in Byron's real life, but the narrator is also not Byron. He is a voice within a poem, the stage manager of events and characters, the free flow of a human mind. He will 'breathe when I expire'. He is what Byron calls elsewhere in *Childe Harold's Pilgrimage:*

> What am I? Nothing; but not so art thou,
> Soul of my thought! with whom I traverse earth,
> Invisible but gazing, as I glow
> Mixed with thy spirit, blended with thy birth,
> And feeling still with thee in my crushed feeling's dearth'

(III, 6)

Knowing this, the narrator will indeed see *Don Juan* as 'his' poem:

A versified Aurora Borealis
Which flashes o'er a waste and icy clime

(VII, 2)

In this way, the narrator, in spite of and partly through his modern disclaimers, has not given up the claim to be invincible. Hence his 'shocks of illness' do really threaten something.

We could resolve this problem by sundering Byron and the narrator altogether. Byron is the mortal poet; the narrator is an immortal fiction who is a projection of the mortal poet. Byron is subject to illness and death; the narrator is invulnerable, immortal and invincible. Or, since, through the surviving fiction, we seem to encounter the name and force of Byron long after he is dead, we could say that the narrator represents the immortal part of Byron ('spirit') and Juan the moral ('flesh'). But a sustained sense of the separation would run counter to the poem's central insistence upon connections of all kinds and especially between spirit and flesh, intellect and gastric-juice, Haidée's love and Zoe's fried eggs. Mortal, vulnerable Byron is caught up in the free play of mind and fiction but mind and fiction are implicated in pain and limitation. An alternative way of resolving this problem of course is laughter which arises at just such impossible junctures. But there is laughter and laughter. The discrepancy between 'Aurora Borealis' and 'a waste and icy clime' is based on disdain, disgust or horror. These are also the ingredients of the laughter provoked by the indecent puns of the Russian canto. We see the connection between sex and death, between Catharine's sexual surrender to her giant suitors and her mastering of virile men to warlike ends. Laughter here is bitter because the intellect detests the conjunction which it observes.[15] When we laugh, however, at the useful index of Juan's expurgated missal, or Dudù's dream, the intellect is happy to accept the connections which provoke the laughter. Either kind of laughter, sometimes in *Don Juan* they are difficult to disentangle, will have the effect summarised in Byron's aphorism in *Beppo:*

> . . . Laughter
> Leaves us so doubly serious shortly after.

(LXXIX)

For when we laugh, exuberance and anxiety, the meaningful and the meaningless, meet in a momentarily illumined empty space which, like the narrator, we may fear as 'an abyss' or, like the 'orthodox' or festive comedy, trust as plenitude. This is the answering principle to *Don Juan*'s:

> While life's strange principle will often lie
> Deepest in those who long the most to die.

(IV, 11)

but confirms and is confirmed by it.

We are less prone in recent years to treat *Don Juan* with the real but faint praise of New Criticism as though it represents a limited but creditable 'growing up' on the part of the immature author of *Childe Harold's Pilgrimage* and *Manfred*. It is still pertinent to observe, however, that Manfred's culminating utterance in tragic style 'Old man! 'tis not so difficult to die.' could also be claimed as the originating utterance of comic comfort. We do not laugh at Manfred's death though, as we have seen, we are directed to something close to laughter during Manfred's bungled suicide on the Jungfrau, but there is the same puzzling co-presence of emptiness and plenitude in Manfred's death as there is in the speculation, mirth and verbal dances of *Don Juan*. In *Manfred*, this authenticates a tragic conclusion, in *Don Juan* it furnishes a comic mode with its customary sceptical resonance and, yet, religious potentiality.

Comic laughter, in *Don Juan* and elsewhere, reassures us of the strength of secret underlying connections of all kinds, but especially and ultimately those between Life and Death. Satiric laughter on the other hand exposes with bitter triumph shamefully hidden connections of all kinds but especially and ultimately those between Life and Death. Laughter, in this way, can strengthen or undermine a *Yes* or *No* in us. *Don Juan* at first is carried along by comic laughter punctuated by satiric laughter. From the Siege onwards, however, comic laughter is hard to find. Catharine is the object of satirical attack because she draws comic energies to herself and allies them to Power and Death. Satiric laugher is not itself in league with a living forward movement and cannot therefore lead the poem on. Later cantos portray a static social world, whose secret relation with Death they can expose. Hence the necessity for the narrator to rush Juan from Catharine's court to England, the society which he can most tellingly satirise. Hence too his need to take Juan to Norman Abbey where the secret shameful connection between social vitality and Death is most tellingly disclosed in the fashionable house and religious ruin which together constitute the house. Of course, as we have seen, there are many reasons why Byron would want to take Juan to England but it remains a legitimate critical task to determine why Juan should visit England at this particular point (we have had no earlier intimation of it), and why this should coincide with a change of mode in the poem.[16] We could avoid giving Byron the benefit of the doubt and say that England itself induces the mode of the English cantos. It seems better as usual to follow Byron's family motto of 'Crede Byron' and conclude that England's sudden entrance into this European poem in English suggests some historical corroboration of Byron's fiction. Both have reached a similar point. England shares in and instances the hollow confidence of the narrator. It persists without any underlying connection between its non-pareil surface glitter and quiet replenishing energies which both once had. Those energies are, in *Don Juan*, replaced by the narrator's own architectonics.

We find the narrator then more invincible than ever, satirical exposer of a historical world which he has brilliantly reconstructed himself. Superior to and apparently unimplicated in Juan's temporal process, he is nevertheless closer than ever before to the idioms, hence assumptions, of the world which he satirises. Is there any sense at all in which the poem remains comic?

It is here that the difficulty of separating '*Yes*-saying' and '*No*-saying' is greatest. The narrator's persistence in his own cantos means that we change our attitude to him. His persistence in his separated gaiety is, we are bound to think, admirable but desperate. Jacques may be allowed to hold or even dominate the audience's attention for a time in *As You Like It* but we would resent his attempt to run the play altogether. The narrator's persistence, however, though substantially cut off from comic insight, is not inconceivably the harbinger of the mode he denies. Claudio in *Much Ado about Nothing* and, more strikingly, Leontes in *A Winter's Tale*, after they learn of the deaths, as they suppose, of Hero and Hermione, persist in uncomic penitential time and are rewarded by the full and unexpected restoration of comic hope. The persistent narrator of *Don Juan* may be perceived as the audience of *A Winter's Tale* perceives Leontes. They do not know how Leontes can be brought to a comic ending for they cannot consciously anticipate Hermione's resurrection but they do not exclude Leontes from the revivifying possibilities of Art and Nature. *Much Ado about Nothing* is particularly helpful because its separation of Beatrice and Benedick's intellectual comedy from the romance comedy of Claudio and Hero is analogous to the separation of narrator and Juan and *Don Juan*. Comedy may often utilise or depend upon an intellectual idiom consciously superior to the world which it derides but, in the end, this idiom will have to accept subordination of some kind just as Beatrice and Benedick have to submit to one another, society, Nature and the comic art of the play.

Shakespearian comedy throws more light on our present problem and Byron's procedures in his greatest poem than any other analogue. We know that, despite his disparagements of Shakespeare, Byron was steeped in Shakespeare's verse. Most of Byron's plays were written whilst he was writing *Don Juan*. It would appear that his long poem absorbed the Shakespearian structures which he was so intent on keeping out of his neo-classical dramas. That this is not likely to have been altogether unconscious we may deduce from the implication that Aurora Raby, a restored and better Haidée, is something of a Shakespearian heroine:

> Aurora . . .
> Was more Shakespearian, if I do not err.
> The worlds beyond this world's perplexing waste
> Had more of her existence, for in her
> There was a depth of feeling to embrace
> Thoughts, boundless, deep, but silent too as Space.
>
> (XVI, 48)

These extraordinary lines will need to be considered fully in the final chapter. However, the relationship of *Don Juan* to Shakespeare's comic pattern, which they appear to authorise, cannot be a straightforward one. *Don Juan*, though dramatic, is a poem not a play and it is written in and for radically different social and historical circumstances from those of Shakespeare's comedies. One particular divergence will naturally concern us. Shakespeare's comedies are rendered fully comic by their endings which reconnect an initially discredited social stability with vital energies. Byron's endless poem can only be comic in its mode. Sexual consummation is the end of Shakespeare's comedies; it is the means of Byron's. On the other hand, the mode of the poem, as we have seen, is based upon its capacity to recover vital energies in the face of all manner of threat. The mode of the poem is, in this loose sense, a series of comic endings, but stability is avoided for Juan does not renew a discredited society but moves on to a new one. Norman Abbey, for the first time, does represent a society in which we linger and which, though as hostile to love and comic insight as the Sultan's palace or Romeo and Juliet's Verona, could in principle find comic transformation.

My discussion, needless to say, has always presupposed the actual ending of the poem which does recover comic poise and, in surprising both reader and narrator, manages to re-subordinate the narrator to the poem as a whole. What we have been concerned with here is the narrator's part in this recovery. Waiting forms a part of it but it is not sufficient to see his virtuoso performance in Cantos X to XII, and even XIII to XV, as simply biding time. It is not as though the comic recovery when, not without qualification, it comes, is merely a reinstation of what was lost in the Siege of Ismail. The poem changes. Its loss of comic confidence necessitates a much deeper hold on and yet more explicit naming of the sources of comic life than hitherto. The dangerous game which Byron plays in the Shipwreck, the death of Haidée, the Siege, and Catharine the Great, forces him to explore the comic mechanisms upon whose functioning he ironically yet wholly depends. Each time that he places another insuperably anti-comic obstacle to his poem's persistence and surmounts it, he is betrayed into candour as well as further irony. The narrator may well share a running joke with his readers about the spectacular replenishment of his all-pervasive consciousness by those spiritual energies of which he is as much the master as Manfred is. But what if those energies come back to claim him or if he is forced to seek them out and stare them in the face? The narrator's task and his dangerous isolation in Cantos X to XV, is that of Manfred or the poet in Canto III or IV of *Childe Harold's Pilgrimage*. He, like them, is held to vitality in the midst of a perceived aridity but the distant adumbration of religious belief, transfigured Eros and comic laughter in Norman Abbey, place the Byronic Superman in an altogether different perspective. Persistence in *Childe Harold's Pilgrimage* or *Manfred* is based on the defiance articulated in Byron's poem 'Prometheus',

> Which even in torture can descry
> Its own concenter'd recompense,
>
> ('Prometheus', 56-7)

'Recompense' of a kind the 'concenter'd' narrator may find in Cantos X to XV of *Don Juan* but, like Aeschylus's Prometheus, he is to find release and recovery from his grotesquely renewed and ostentatiously isolated vitality provided he waits long enough and awakens within himself the capacity to submit. It is to that finally which we must turn.

IV

Canto XVI, the ghost canto, reduces the inflated proportion of the narrator's own stanzas to the proportion in existence before the Siege. It reinstates the seduction of Juan as a major focus of life and meaning within the poem. The last 14 or so stanzas of the previous canto, in which the narrator retains hegemony, provide a bridge between the two modes.

We have to talk of 'two modes' for the role of the narrator does change, as does the relation of the reader to him, but it is not as though we could detect the difference at a glance. The narrator, despite his ingenuity, has, like Don Juan Tenorio, only one mode. It is the maintenance of this mode as the only available form of life in later cantos which distinguishes it from the fictional role of Byron as digressing narrator in the early cantos. The brilliant conclusion to Canto XV seems to sum up the narrator's impasse but also acknowledges and marks a change.

The narrator's ascendancy in the English cantos is based on their much greater generality. He has, as usual, an epigram for this:

The difficulty lies in colouring
(Keeping the due proportions still in sight)
With Nature manners which are artificial,
And rend'ring general that which is especial.

(XV, 25)

In Cantos X to XV, English 'artificial' manners are presented in detail but in a general and satirical way which both confirms the narrator's intimate knowledge of them and his innate superiority to them. The reader is not allowed to have any reactions of his own. The general effect is closer to Peacock than to Shakespeare.

Two qualifications should be made. The first description of Norman Abbey in Canto XIII is of a singular house which makes a direct and particular impression on the reader before it is absorbed into a general satirical description of English country houses and their customary inhabitants. Secondly, among the inhabitants of Byron's Norman Abbey, certain characters assume greater definition and vitality than would be possible for characters in Peacock's Nightmare Abbey. This is so deftly done that we hardly notice the developing fictional life in Canto XIV of Lady Adeline, the Duchess of Fitz-Fulke and Aurora, until the meal towards the end of Canto XV for the narrator is always on hand to render 'general that which is especial'. It is clear, however, that the long account of Aurora (XV, 43-58), though she is introduced in the company of

> Miss Reading,
> Miss Raw, Miss Flaw, Miss Showman, and Miss Knowman
> And the two fair co-heiresses Giltbedding.

> (XV, 40)

separates her from the narrator's now habitual authority and occasions a different vocabulary. He acknowledges this himself:

> Juan knew nought of such a character —
> High, yet resembling not his lost Haidée;
> Yet each was radiant in her proper sphere:
> The Island girl, bred up by the lone sea,
> More warm, as lovely, as not less sincere,
> Was Nature's all: Aurora could not be
> Nor would be thus; —the difference in them
> Was such as lies between a flower and gem.

> Having wound up with this sublime comparison,
> Methinks we may proceed upon our narrative.

> (XV, 58, 59)

This sounds familiar and was so once but the narrator has not been forced to use this tactic since the Siege where we find a sublime comparison of a different kind:

> The bayonet pierces and the sabre cleaves,
> And human lives are lavished every where,
> As the year closing whirls the scarlet leaves
> When the script forest bows to the bleak air.

> (VIII, 88)

The narrator punctures this immediately:

> It is an awful topic — but 'tis not
> My cue for any time to be terrific

> (VIII, 89)

Between that reference and the appearance of Aurora, there has been nothing 'terrific' enough in the narration or metaphors of sufficient independence to warrant the narrator's anxiety that he might be excluded from the reader's consciousness by the poem's idiom.

The meal that follows seems at first to belong wholly to the narrator. It is in fact largely concocted from *The French Cook* by Louis Eustache Ude,[17] just as the shipwreck in Canto II is based on Sir John Graham Dalyell's *Shipwrecks and Disasters at Sea:*[18]

> Then there was God knows what 'à l'Allemande,'
> 'A l'Espagnole,' 'timballe,' and 'Salpicon' —
> With things I can't withstand or understand,
>
> (XV, 66)

This appears to be a satirical set-piece pillorying the snobbery and cold-hearted greed of high society and in contrast with the banquet over which Juan and Haidée preside in Canto III. It is certainly this but it is not set so firmly within the narrator's rational discretion as this suggests. Any large-scale meal, advertising as it does human contentment and rootedness in the world as it is, rouses a prophetic voice as well as a satiric disposition in Byron. One of his best *Hebrew Melodies* is the 'Vision of Belhazzar'. That same sense of apocalyptic reversal and admonition persists in the thunder heard during Sardanapalus's banquet[19] and may be discerned even in Juan and Haidée's love-feast. Their meal is haunted, we know it but they do not, by Lambro ('one deemed dead returning', III, 49) who will overthrow their contentment, their rootedness and the comic society built round them and leave their isle 'all desolate and bare' (IV, 72). Juan and Haidée, at the banquet, are spared this knowledge but are forced to attend to writing on the wall of another kind in the song 'The isles of Greece' which admonishes them in effect to leave their bower of bliss and 'Dash down your cup of Samian wine!' (stanza 16). Nothing like this occurs during the meal itself in Norman Abbey where Juan does not preside but

> By some odd chance too he was placed between
> Aurora and the Lady Adeline —
>
> (XV, 75)

Nevertheless this meal seems less and less generally satirical, as it proceeds, and more and more a particular fiction through which certain characters are moving forward swiftly within their own narrative time to nightfall and some coming event. That night in fact will provide a ghost of sufficient force to admonish any human rootedness and he will be the immediate subject of the only song in the poem other than 'The isles of Greece'. Between the meal and the events of the night comes the digression which concludes the canto.

We can see from this that the digression is being folded within a developing action which now exists for the reader in its own right. The digression itself falls into two parts with a coda. In the first section (XV, 86-94), the narrator chats on as usual. His point of departure is Aurora's purity which, he manages to imply, could coincide with or presage erotic feeling just as Socrate's cult of Ideal Beauty may, he suggests, be related to erotic 'phantasies' (XV, 86). This paradox confirms the narrator's habitual presumption of the contradictory nature both of experience and statement. We are back to 'He who doubts all things, nothing can deny;' (XV, 88). But as the narrator continues, he does more than simply reiterate his sceptical patter:

> He who doubts all things, nothing can deny;
> Truth's fountains may be clear — her streams are muddy,
> And cut through such canals of contradiction,
> That she must often navigate o'er fiction.
>
> Apologue, fable, poesy, and parable,
> Are false, but may be render'd also true
> By those who sow them in a land that's arable.
> 'Tis wonderful what fable will not do!
> 'Tis said it makes reality more bearable:
> But what's reality? Who has its clue?
> Philosophy? No; she too much rejects.
> Religion? *Yes*; but which of all her sects?

Once again, Byron as narrator means exactly what he says yet his tongue is far less in his cheek. Of course, irony is discernible but the primary sense of the lines on fiction is not that we cannot arrive at Truth because it is so wholly encumbered by fiction but that, however difficult it is to disentangle them, nevertheless fiction itself can disclose Truth. This meaning is threatened by ''Tis wonderful what fable will not do!', which demands and receives an exclamation mark. When we read the following line, ''Tis said it makes reality more bearable', it seems certain that we are back to an 'Aurora Borealis' view of art in general and the fable of *Don Juan* in particular. Yet this ground is then taken from under our feet:

> But what's reality? Who has its clue?
> Philosophy? No; She too much rejects.
> Religion? *Yes*; but which of all her sects?

These lines undermine any sceptical assurance that we can take away an ideal or supernatural superstructure and label what's left 'reality'. 'Clue' here refers us back to 'labyrinth'. 'Religion' refers us back to 'parable' in the first line: 'Apologue, fable, poesy, and parable,' which we too readily took to be a simple synonym for fiction. What is most striking is the unexpectedly clear and unequivocal division of the abyss of thought into Religion's 'Yes' and Philosophy's 'No'. Scepticism can lead to either but all the advantages lie with the former. All kinds of ironic qualification remain and the next stanza makes Religion's 'Yes' seem unattractive and unattainable for 'Some millions must be wrong, that's pretty clear.' (XV, 90). Nevertheless if, like Proteus, we can never hold the narrator for long, because he changes into something else, we should not underestimate the force of that possible 'Yes' which has taken shape within the narrator's persistence in his 'No'. Our interpretation of Byron's unbelieving but not disbelieving earlier references to the 'Virgin's mystical virginity' and to the Trinity lend and receive support here. Nor should we take less seriously the apologia for the true fable that is *Don Juan*. Byron disliked the cult of Imagination in so far as it appeared to replace inherited insistence upon Truth and Goodness as the primary values of Art by subjective fantasies. His greatest poem is ostentatiously modest but it exists for the same reasons and to the same ends as Dante's *Divine Comedy*,[20] to unite fiction with Truth.

The second part of the digression begins abruptly in stanza 95:

> Grim reader! did you ever see a ghost?

The line originally read:

> Pray reader did you ever see a ghost?[21]

It is possible that 'Grim reader' puns on Grimm, i.e. the reader of Grimm's tales.[22] It would be hard to determine whether this is so but since the narrator has already declared

> And now, that we may furnish with some matter all

Tastes, we are going to try the supernatural.

(XV, 93)

it is clear that we are meant to see the ghost episode as a version of the Gothic stories then in vogue. The sudden address to the reader is unusually direct after the self-preoccupied questionings of the previous stanza. It is designed presumably to disconcert the reader into a different kind of attention. This is effected too by the apparent frankness of the metaphor:

> The night (I sing by night — sometimes an owl
> And now and then a nightingale)— is dim,
> And the loud shriek of sage Minerva's foul
> Rattles around me her discordant hymn:
> Old portraits from old walls upon me scowl —
> I wish to heaven they would not look so grim;
> The dying embers dwindle in the grate —
> I think too that I have set up too late

(XV, 97)

This exquisitely managed stanza takes us apparently much closer to Byron as narrator than ever before. We are here encouraged to picture him alone, a little cold, writing his poem (as was his custom) in the middle of the night and in the very act of concluding the canto. Such intimacy is analogous to that which we have with the letter-writing heroines of Richardson's novels. In another way, as this analogy also suggests, we have an ostentatiously fictional emblem. The author is in the same position as so many frightened prisoners in Gothic houses. Old portraits look down and scare him as they did the occupants of Walpole's *The Castle of Otranto* and as they are about to scare Juan in Norman Abbey. The directly addressed reader, Juan and Byron as the narrator are about to find their experience fused in the coming fiction of the Black Friar which will frighten us by its reality and will be set in a fictional version of Byron's real, ghost-haunted and ruined house.

Byron uses the owl and the nightingale, perennial ornithic antitheses, to dramatise alternative ways of dealing with 'night'. These correspond roughly again with 'Philosophy' and 'Religion'. It is with 'night' as with 'the abyss', we can either peer into it (and the owl peers furthest) or sing it (and the nightingale sings best). The nightingale makes the night lovely and draws us into the darkness which we fear. The owl is the agent of Minerva's rational wisdom which throws light on the darkness but, by only allowing us to stay within that small space of light, makes the surrounding darkness appear more frightening than ever. Hence the 'shriek of sage Minerva's fowl' here acts as a frightening Gothic intensifier, paradoxically but also appropriately, for Gothic effects normally depend upon the presumption of rational expectation and explanation. Byron's art, as he asserts, is both that of the owl and the nightingale and the last stanza of the canto, which stands apart from the rest of the digression like a coda, reveals a fusion of the two.

> Between the worlds life hovers like a star,
> 'Twixt night and morn, upon the horizon's verge:
> How little do we know that which we are!
> How less what we may be! The eternal surge
> Of time and tide rolls on, and bears afar
> Our bubbles; as the old burst, new emerge,
> Lash'd from the foam of ages; while the graves
> Of Empires heave but like some passing waves.

(XV, 99)

T.S. Eliot did not like this stanza. He thought it one of Byron's 'sonorous affirmations of the commonplace with no depth of significance'[23] and declared that the verses 'are not too good for the school magazine'.[24] If this stanza was taken as an independent lyric then Eliot's comments, though intemperately over-stated, have force. In context, the stanza is moving and intelligent.

The stanza itself consists of a star image, suggesting uncertainty but also hope, an aphorism, and concluding sea imagery, suggesting uncertainty but also despair. Though the management of voice and syntax is masterly, all the ingredients are commonplace and literary. The narrator's voice is excluded in this way and by the sudden proliferation of 'we's' as opposed to the all-pervading 'I' of preceding stanzas. As it is the final stanza in the canto, there is no space for the narrator to say

> Having wound up with this sublime comparison
> Methinks we may proceed upon our narrative

(XV, 59)

It is the first time that the closure of a canto has been used to suppress the narrator who is normally at his chirpiest in a last stanza.

In context, these 'school magazine verses' produce a wholly original effect within the poem and formally represent the private anxiety which Byron as narrator has just shared with his readers. It is important to see that the aphorism in the centre of the stanza can be interpreted either in terms of the melancholy sea imagery or the star which precariously presides above the sea. The aphorism itself,

> How little do we know that which we are!
> How less what we may be!

is a version of Ophelia's 'Lord! we know what we are, but know not what we may be' (*Hamlet*, IV, v, 43-4). Byron's editors comment on this: 'Byron's rephrasing is in the sceptical tradition of Socrates, Montaigne and Hume'[25] which sounds authentic and final but the confidence with which the aphorism is shifted to the end of the stanza for its interpretation is quite misplaced. When Byron writes 'Between two worlds', he wishes to stress a radical uncertainty within our doubt-pressed knowledge not to clarify it by choosing 'Philosophy' or 'Religion''s version of this uncertainty. Critics owe so much to the scholarship and acumen of Byron's recent editors that it seems churlish to bite as well as to bark but, if pressed, it would be relevant to adduce Pamela's more or less identical rephrasing of Ophelia's remark in Richardson's novel; 'But after all, poor wretches that we be! We scarce know what we *are*, much less what we *shall* be.'[26] Byron loathed Richardson, but could have recalled *Pamela*. No one is likely to suggest, however, that Pamela's rephrasing derives from her loyalty to 'Socrates, Montaigne and Hume' for she, we are told, is 'religious'. We need to read Byron's life and letters in the light of his poems as well as reading his poetry in the light of his life and letters, otherwise we risk always approximating his most complex insights to the brilliant but specific pose he would adopt in a letter to John Murray. Byron's narrator habitually, and Byron himself on occasion, may align themselves with 'the sceptical tradition of Socrates, Montaigne and Hume' but *Don Juan*, though dependent upon it, is not an instance of that tradition. *Don Juan* exhibits scepticism in operation but also at bay.

If the narrator quotes Montaigne's 'Que sais-je?' approvingly (IX, 17), we should recall that the tradition which the poem does claim to be an instance of is that of the thinkers already listed in Canto VII:

> I say no more than has been said in Dante's
> Verse, and by Solomon and by Cervantes;

By Swift, by Machiavel, by Rochefoucault,
By Fenelon, by Luther, and by Plato;
By Tillotson, and Wesley, and Rousseau,
Who knew this life was not worth a potato.

(VII, 3-4)

To these he adds Cato, Diogenes, Socrates, Newton and 'Ecclesiastes'. This list consists of only three sceptics (Machiavelli, Rochefoucault, Diogenes) with whom we might here align Socrates, six religious figures (Solomon, Fénélon, Luther, Tillotson, Wesley, Ecclesiastes) with whom we might align Dante, Swift and Newton, and three figures (Cato, Cervantes, Rousseau) more difficult to classify. The preponderance of religious thinkers is obvious but the purpose of this gleefully improvised list is not to suggest a specific tradition of any kind but rather to invoke a widespread acknowledgement of 'the nothingness of human life' (VII, 6) in many cultures and by many clearly disparate personalities. The last stanza of Canto XV is deliberately fashioned out of the inherited stock of formulae and images which this acknowledgement has produced. Here, at the end of this canto and at the end of the narrator's impossible independence, the stanza summarises and embodies the radical uncertainty which underlies Religion's 'Yes' and Philosophy's 'No'. The effect of closure is stronger than in any other canto and yet a narrative movement of considerable force has already been initiated before it. The closure that this new reach of voice implies does not apply to the narrative but to the narrator whose subordination has now been accomplished.

It is worthwhile, finally, considering the scepticism of Hume a little further because there is a celebrated passage in which he talks about exactly the same issues as the final stanzas of Canto XV. The divergence between Hume and Byron should clarify and corroborate my necessarily tortuous argument in this chapter.

Hume argues, in the conclusion to Book 1 of the *Treatise on Human Nature*, that the operations of human reason must be ultimately based upon imagination. But, he maintains, it is impossible to live or act with the knowledge of this truth which destroys 'all science and philosophy':

The intense view of these manifold contradictions and imperfections in human reason has so wrought upon me, and heated my brain, that I am ready to reject all belief and reasoning, and can look upon no opinion even as more probable or likely than another. Where am I, or what? From what causes do I derive my existence, and to what condition shall I return? Whose favour shall I count, and whose anger must I dread? What beings surround me? and on whom have I any influence, or who have any influence on me? I am confounded with all these questions, and begin to fancy myself in the most deplorable condition imaginable, environed with the deepest darkness, and utterly deprived of the use of every member and faculty.

Most fortunately it happens, that since reason is incapable of dispelling these clouds, Nature herself suffices to that purpose and cures me of this philosophical melancholy and delirium, either by relaxing this bent of mind, or by some avocation, and lively impression of my senses, which obliterate all these chimaeras. I dine, I play a game of backgammon, I converse, and am merry with my friends; and when after three or four hours' amusement, I would return to these speculations, they appear so cold and strained, and ridiculous, that I cannot find in my heart to enter into them any further.[27]

Notwithstanding the lack of an assured foundation for philosophising, Hume is still drawn to it and recommends it above its rival 'superstition' for the latter may 'disturb us in the conduct of our lives and actions' whereas philosophy will normally not modify our behaviour and so 'generally speaking, the errors in religion are dangerous; those in philosophy are ridiculous'.[28]

Hume's strategy for dealing with the fears that his scepticism scorns yet intensifies looks much the same as Byron's in the penultimate stanza of Canto XV immediately preceding 'Between two worlds':

> And therefore, though 'tis by no means my way
> To rhyme at noon — when I have other things
> To think of, if I ever think — I say
> I feel some chilly midnight shudderings,
> And prudently postpone, until mid-day,
> Treating a topic which alas but brings
> Shadows; — but you must be in my condition
> Before you learn to call this superstition.
>
> (XV, 98)

Byron knew as well as Hume that 'chilly midnight shudderings' will normally appear unreal if prudently postponed 'until midday'. But, just as this is known in the midst of fear, so in the midst of our daytime confidence, we may recall dispelled anxieties. Juan, for instance, tries

unsuccessfully to control his recent fear of the ghost by reminding himself, via the perusal of an old newspaper, of midday matters:

> He read an article the king attacking,
> And a long eulogy of "Patent Blacking".

> This savoured of this world: but his hand shook —
>
> (XVI, 26, 27)

His fear persists the following morning, brings Juan to the notice of
everyone in the Abbey, and occasions the ballad of the Black Friar.
Hume, like the narrator, is wonderfully frank but he does not wish to
look at the experience of dread, which he recounts, in itself as a
possible discloser of Truth. Hume is not Heidegger. Though he may be
forced to grant Imagination's underpinning of human reason, Hume
wishes to preserve, so far as he can, the privileged apartness of the
sceptical spectator. Indeed Hume seems to revel in the impossibility of
the sceptical philosopher's stance and seek it out all the more for that
reason. *Don Juan's* diagnosis is the same as Hume's and, from Canto
X almost to Canto XV, the poem is run by a narrator 'in the sceptical
tradition of Socrates, Montaigne and Hume'. It is no accident that
conscious, like Hume, of the absurdity which is the conclusion of
sustained scepticism, the narrator takes the poem straightaway to
England where we can observe a society diverting itself sensibly in
Hume's fashion, 'I dine, I play a game of backgammon, I converse, and
am merry with my friends.'

My argument is that the poem's persistence in this impossible mode,
opened and held to the contrariety which Hume shies away from, is
evidence not of 'sceptical tradition' but of an original, Romantic revalu-
ation of comic process. The independence of the narrator, which
emerges decisively in the English eighteenth-century novel, instances
and helps to bring about the promotion of sceptical individual
spectators over the society and cosmos upon which they freely comment. The counterpart to their rise is the emergence of fiction as a
separate and potentially superior world of its own.

Don Juan could not have been written without the experiments in
eighteenth-century fiction which preceded it nor without the
eighteenth-century alliance between British and French sceptical philosophising with liberal political sentiment. We cannot talk about *Don
Juan* without naming and explicating these traditions but the poem also
does things which these traditions do not allow. It is an improvised but

deeply planned mimesis of life's continual triumphing emergence from Nothingness and Death through the uncontrollable force of Eros. Older comic traditions, with varying degrees of explicitness, depend on this pattern. The first half of *Don Juan* is created by the balanced antipathy of these traditions but it is not set up to sustain this equilibrium. It is not only the narrator who thinks. The poem thinks or, at any rate, is a paradigm of thinking. It is an experiment not only in fiction but also, like gambling, it ceaselessly takes risks without enquiring whether there is evidence or resource to support or reward this risk-taking. The poem, in this way, is an *exemplum* in the dispute between sceptical and comic versions of reality. Eros, which always encourages its devotees to take risks, seems to be naturally in league with comedy but the slaughter of Ismail and the indifference of Catharine to the deaths of thousands of handsome risk-takers appear to support Jacques's scepticism rather than comedy's Golden World. The poem, however, robbed of this staple confidence, persists in another. The narrator's maintenance of his scepticism and perilous centrality is, too, like that of the persistent gambler. Despite all the odds against him, the gambler superstitiously pins his faith on invisible connections and a miraculous future. So, in effect, does the narrator whom Hume might label increasingly 'superstitious'. The fortuitous coming right of events, upon which comic endings depend, characterises fictions but is intended to illuminate Nature rather than Art. Thus the narrator's increasingly explicit concern in Canto XV with Religion or Philosophy's claim to have the 'clue' of Reality, a theoretical problem, is exactly the practical problem of the poem itself now. Is there a clue binding it together? And if that clue has been lost, can it be recovered?

The argument of this chapter, however clarified by the manifest distinction between the movement and assumptions of Hume's thinking from that of Byron in an identical area of concern, may remain obscure in the centre. It would be foolish to exaggerate the difficulties here. Nevertheless the narrator's compulsion to make human life and the life of *Don Juan* explicit at the point where they emerge into intelligibility is unnerving. It makes further explicitness seem unnecessary and impossible just as Pope makes further annotation of *The Dunciad* seem unnecessary and impossible. More tantalisingly difficult still is the task of uncovering and naming what the narrator's explicitness brings with it or makes available, which, as it were, escapes that explicitness. The whole character of *Don Juan* is given by an exacting interplay between murderous self-consciousness and overflowing resource which Manfred holds to be impossible:

Sorrow is knowledge: they who know the most
Must mourn the deepest o'er the fatal truth,
The Tree of Knowledge is not that of Life.

(*Manfred*, I, i, 10-12)

Don Juan begins with a different premiss but, in the narrator's cantos, the value and possibility of sustaining this interplay between 'Knowledge' and 'Life' has become a dilemma for the narrator and the reader. This dilemma cannot be resolved or even fully understood by concentrating upon the narrator alone. We need now to look more closely at Eros, the narrative's declared agency of over-flowing resource which, in the suitable shape of the Duchess of Fitz-Fulke, makes a determined bid for Juan and the comic renewal of the poem in Canto XVI.

Notes

1. E.g. 'Cantos IX through XII are narratively the weakest in Don Juan', Karl Kroeber, *Romantic Narrative Art* (London, 1966), p. 160.
2. M.K. Joseph tabulates the proportion of Narrative to 'Comment' and 'Digression' in Appendix C of *Byron the Poet* (London, 1964). My own estimation (printed below) is identical with his on three occasions only but the general picture is exactly the same, indeed Joseph claims an even lower percentage of digression (15.4 per cent) in Canto XVI. The major difficulty is with those stanzas which are digressive in character but have some relation to adjacent narrative concern. Joseph thus attempts to distinguish clearly 'comment' from 'digression' but I have not found this to be feasible. Similarly, I exclude, Joseph includes, the Dedication and the fragmentary Canto XVII from these statistics. Decimal points, included by Joseph, are in my table rounded up or down except for Canto XIII:

Canto	Proportion of Digression to Narrative (per cent)
I	26
II	16
III	38
IV	24
V	19
VI	23
VII	22
VIII	17
IX	54
X	41
XI	50
XII	68
XIII	32.5
XIV	53
XV	43
XVI	18

These statistics show that the first eight cantos establish a norm of 23 per cent digression whereas in the next seven cantos this more than doubles (49 per cent). The last complete canto unmistakably| returns to the earlier proportion. Digression forms 34 per cent of the poem as a whole (Joseph, 33 per cent).

3. *Lord Byron: Don Juan*, T.G. Steffan, E. Steffan and W.W. Pratt (eds.), (Harmondsworth, 1973), p. 695.

4. See Michael Oakeshott's remarkable and insufficiently attended essay 'The Voice of Poetry in the Conversation of Mankind' in *Rationalism and Politics* (London, 1962), pp. 197-247.

5. M. Arnold, *Essays in Criticism: Second Series* (London, 1905), p. 33.

6. Helen Gardner, 'Don Juan', *London Magazine*, vol. 7, 1958, p. 65.

7. G.M. Ridenour, *The Style of Don Juan* (New Haven, 1960), p. 33.

8. Keith Vaughan, 'Extracts from a Journal 1943-6' in *Catalogue of retrospective exhibition, March-April, 1962* (Whitechapel Gallery, London, 1962), p. 41.

9. See, for example, *Childe Harold*, III, 6; *The Lament of Tasso*, 20-25; *The Prophecy of Dante*, IV, 1-39.

10. T. Carlyle, *Sartor Resartus* (London, 1908), p. 145.

11. E.D. Hirsch, 'Byron and the Terrestrial Paradise' in F.W. Hilles and H. Bloom (eds.), *From Sensibility to Romanticism* (New York, 1965), pp. 467-8. R.F. Gleckner, *Byron and the Ruins of Paradise* (Baltimore, 1967). Anne K. Mellor in *English Romantic Irony*, Cambridge, Massachusetts, 1980), catalogues negative and positive readings of the poem (p. 201 n. 43). She herself rejects a negative interpretation (p| 64). Travis Looper, *Byron and the Bible*, says simply: 'He is seen by some as a pessimist confronting a desolate universe and by others as an optimist' (p. 6). G.M. Ridenour himself seems to draw back, in 'The mode of Byron's *Don Juan*', *Publications of the Modern Languages Association*, vol. 89, September, 1964, pp. 442-6, from the negative implications of much of his argument in *The Style of Don Juan* by declaring some forms of irony to be less negative than others.

12. *The Works of Lord Byron:* E.H. Coleridge (ed.) (7 vols., London, 1898-1904), vol. IV, p. 136 n. 1.

13. J.P. Eckermann, *Conversations of Goethe*, trans. J. Oxenford, (London, 1930), p. 41.

14. There may well of course be other implications for the Ancient Greeks. W.K.C. Guthrie reaffirms the suggestion of H.J. Rose for instance that Homer's lack of respect for Aphrodite here is similar to the humiliations endured elsewhere in the *Iliad* by Artemis whom Hera whips and sends, weeping, off the field. The reason in both cases may be that Hera was at that stage 'fully naturalised as an Olympian' but Artemis and Aphrodite were not, and still retained something of their alien, oriental character. W.K.C. Guthrie, *The Greeks and their Gods* (London, 1950, paperback edn, 1968), p. 101 n. 2.

15. Compare the use of negative laughter in *Heaven and Earth* (I, iii, 55-66).

16. Byron had in fact decided to take Juan from Constantinople to Russia and then to England's 'town and country life' before he had started to write Canto VI (see *Medwin's Conversations of Lord Byron*, Ernest J. Lovell, Jr. (ed.) (Princeton, 1966), pp. 164-5). There is a gap between Medwin's account and the narrative form and circumstance| of the poem as written which it is still the critic's task to probe and interpret. Chapter 3 quotes Medwin's account at length and dicusses this problem. Medwin's veracity is confirmed by Byron's letter to Murray (16th February, 1821, *Byron's Letters and Journals*, Leslie Marchand (ed.) (12 vols., London, 1973-81), vol. 8, p. 78).

17. *Works*, vol. VI, pp. 561-2 n.2.

18. Ibid., vol. VI, p. 87 n.2; pp. 88-9 n.1.

19. 'A storm without, and Thunder occasionally heard during the banquet', *Sardanapalus*, III, i.

20. Steve Ellis in *Dante and English Poetry* (Cambridge, 1983) is helpful about Byron's relationship with Dante (pp. 36-65) but does not give a detailed comparison nor have much to say about *Don Juan*.

21. *Byron's Don Juan: A Variorum Edition*, T.G. Steffan and W.W. Pratt (eds.) (4 vols., Austin, Tesas, 1957), vol. III, p. 499,

22. Grimm's *Kinder und Hausmärchen* (1812-13) were translated by George Cruikshank in 1823.

23. T.S. Eliot, 'Byron' in M.H. Abrams (ed.), *English Romantic Poets* (Oxford, 1960), pp. 198-9.

24. Ibid., p. 199.

25. *Lord Byron: Don Juan*, Steffan, Steffan and Pratt (eds.), p. 739.

26. S. Richardson, *Pamela* (London, 1914), vol. I, p. 230.

27. David Hume, *A Treatise of Human Nature* (London, 1911), Bk 1. pp. 253-4.

28. Ibid., p. 256.

3 THE AMOROUS SPHERE

I

One clear sign of the narrative's emancipation in the final cantos is the renewed importance of half-submerged details which encourage the reader to resume discarded habits of attention. It is not at first obvious, for instance, that either of the two ghost-visitants to Juan is the Duchess of Fitz-Fulke. When, on the second occasion, Black Friar is metamorphosed into blonde duchess, it will seem quite plausible that this explains the previous haunting as well. If, on a closer look, this neither fits the differing circumstances (for example, the door of Juan's room is not pushed open) nor matches our larger sense of what is likely in the poem, then we may decide to 'leave the thing a problem, like all things:-' (XVII, 13) and assume that Byron's poem authorises this invocation of the uncertainty principle. If, however,we look at the details of Fitz-Fulke's behaviour we will come to a different conclusion and gain renewed respect for Byron's narrative art, but we may be puzzled by the resulting insight into the workings of Eros. Eros in Don Juan is our concern in this chapter.

When Juan emerges after his first haunted night, he is the recipient of three gazes. The first is Adeline's:

> She looked, and saw him pale, and turned as pale
> Herself; then hastily looked down, and muttered
> Something, but what's not stated in my tale.
> Lord Henry said, his muffin was ill buttered;
> The Duchess of Fitz-Fulke played with her veil
> And looked at Juan hard, but nothing uttered.
> Aurora Raby, with her large dark eyes,
> Surveyed him with a kind of calm surprise.
>
> (XVI, 31)

Some twenty stanzas later, having heard the story of the Black Friar,one of the gazers has now some very specific questions:

> Her Grace too also seized the same occasion,
> With various similar remarks to tally,

But wished for a still more detailed narration
Of this same mystic Friar's curious doings,
About the present family's deaths and wooings.

(XVI, 53)

Between the two quotations given above, if we may be allowed to read with the unfashionable literalness of A.C. Bradley,[1] the Duchess has clearly seen that the legend could provide cover for a night-time visit to Juan.[2] She alone of the three women who gaze on Juan in stanza 31 sees this information exclusively in terms of attainable erotic gains. Juan's past night of terror is immediately transformed by her consciousness into a future night of love-making. Of whom does this marking of prey, quick-witted improvisation and confident claiming of night, remind us if not Don Juan Tenorio? Kierkegaard's comments on Mozart's *Don Giovanni* are helpful here:

> To be a seducer requires a certain amount of reflection and con-sciousness, and as soon as this is present, then it is proper to speak of cunning and intrigues and crafty plans. This consciousness is lacking in Don Juan. Therefore, he does not seduce. He desires, and this desire acts seductively. . . To be a seducer, he needs time in advance in which to lay his plans, and time afterward in which to become conscious of his act. A seducer, therefore, ought to be possessed of a power Don Juan does not have — the power of eloquence.[3]

At first glance this may not seem to fit the brilliant scheming of the Duchess but Kierkegaard's point does in fact take us to the heart of its improvisatory quality, its suddenness, daring and conviction of success. Neither Don Juan Tenorio nor the Duchess are like the arch-seducer Lovelace in Richardson's *Clarissa* or that eloquent rhetorician Milton's Comus, both of whom need to plan well in advance, seize their victims, and talk incessantly. Duchess and Don prefer trickery, speed and silence. On the other hand though the Duchess may improvise seductive opportunity, it remains for Juan to take advantage of it. The Duchess may be said to seduce Juan (if she does so) simply by her proximity to him in exactly the same way as Julia, Haidée and Dudù may be said to seduce Juan. Her plan of seduction extends no further than presenting herself in immediate and glowing proximity to Juan. This is so simple a point that it may not seem worth making. Distance may lend enchant-ment to the view but it places insuperable obstacles to intercourse. The character of Eros in *Don Juan*, however, and it is a very specific one, is indicated by this feature.

L.P. Hartley's novel *The Go-Between* (1953) concerns a boy who moves between two lovers bearing their messages and being instrumental in their assignations. Such is the stuff of love encounters in many a picaresque novel where, for example, duennas employed to guard their ladies are often the means of providing them with letters and lovers. Friar Laurence performs similar functions for Romeo and Juliet and, less nobly, Pandarus goes between Troilus and his Cressida or Criseyde. Love comes into existence and thrives in the space between these lovers, in valedictions, memories and anticipations. In their turn, sonnets, tales, plays and novels grow up in the same space. Of this, there is nothing in *Don Juan*. Donna Julia's letter to Juan at the beginning of the poem is the exception which proves and proclaims the rule for its duration. Her letter is not defeated in its purposes solely by the accident of Juan's sea-sickness. It is rather that Juan's uncontrollably sea-sick condition (II, 19-23) highlights the unbridgeable distance between Julia and himself for we have witnessed Julia writing the letter earlier in some real distress but not without poise. The contrast is heightened in the final appearance of the letter when it is taken 'by force' from Juan by the murderous hands of his cannibal companions who will use it to draw lots for death (II, 74). The grotesque disparity between Julia's 'small, white fingers' (I, 198) carefully sealing the letter and this coarse violation is marked but it only underlines the earlier triumph of sea-sickness over Juan's love-sickness. The letter says nothing to Juan's present sea-sick or shipwrecked situation and cannot be a substitute for Julia's actual proximity. It was, on the other hand, the glow of that proximity which originally seduced him:

> But there were she and Juan, face to face —
>
> (1, 105)
>
> How beautiful she look'd! her conscious heart
> Glow'd in her cheek, and yet she felt no wrong.
>
> (1, 106)
>
> And Julia sate with Juan, half embraced
> And half retiring from the glowing arm,
> Which trembled like the bosom where 'twas placed;
>
> (1, 115)

Juan is not seduced by any conscious plan on Julia's part, nor does the event correspond to any fully conscious anticipation of his own. Juan contributes his own post-pubertal propensities (1, 93), Julia draws him to her simply by her immediate presence and the consciousness implicit in that presence of her own desirability. It is this consciousness which causes her to glow and thus renders her doubly attractive for it proceeds from her innate vitality of flesh and blood and it is reinforced by her own will and self-understanding which also speak and beckon in that vitality. Her glow is transferred to Juan whose arm is 'glowing' in the penultimate line quoted above. Juan is caught up in Julia's vitality but also feels and recognises his own vitality and Julia's quickened consciousness. Union is a natural consequence of this consciousness-conferring proximity. The narrator's mock-modest joke presupposes his reader's shared forecast of events!

> And then – God knows what next – I can't go on;
> I'm almost sorry that I e'er begun.

(1, 115)

If we compare this scene immediately with that between Juan and Fitz-Fulke, the resemblance is striking. It is true that the Duchess is far more calculating and knowing than Julia and that her glow does not include Julia's denied but discernible tincture of guilt. The context too could not be more different but the operating facts are the same:

> But still the shade remained; the blue eyes glared,
> And rather variably for stony death;
> Yet one thing rather good the grave had spared,
> The ghost had a remarkably sweet breath.
> A straggling curl showed he had been fair-haired;
> A red lip, with two rows of pearl beneath,
> Gleamed forth, as through the casement's ivy shroud
> The moon peeped, just escaped from a grey cloud.
>
> And Juan, puzzled, but still curious, thrust
> His other arm forth – wonder upon wonder!
> It pressed upon a hard but glowing bust,
> Which beat as if there was a warm heart under.

(XVI, 121-2)

It is the fact of proximity which is insisted upon here and it is wonderfully promoted by our previous sense of the 'spectre's' intangibility. It is astonishing what Byron can now gain from his apparently deflating admission in the next stanza where the 'spectre'

> . . . stole
Forth into something much like flesh and blood;

which, in itself, suggests something ordinary, common and disappointing after our heightened sense of a supernatural occasion but here confirms the miraculous superiority ('wonder upon wonder!') of this present flesh and blood to 'the stable frock and dreary cowl' of any mere ghost.

One thing, however, is missing from this account. Is Juan glowing too? The end of the canto intervenes upon this question. Certainly Juan has every reason to be grateful to this glowing vision of breathing life which rescues him from 'stony death'. At the end of the canto he, like the equally surprised reader, is transfixed between two worlds but, though 'he was of a kindling nation' (XVII, 12), the automatic consequence of union is, in the absence of any indication of Juan's response, not insisted upon.[4]

Our uncertainty as to what happens between Juan and the Duchess is of a very simple kind. Eros and the Duchess can make things happen but only two possibilities exist, Juan will or will not be drawn into the Duchess's 'amorous sphere'. I want to use this phrase here and elsewhere for the magnetic circuit within which lovers are drawn together. The narrator uses the phrase rather differently:

> Her Grace too passed for being an Intrigante,
> And somewhat *méchante* in her amorous sphere;
> One of those pretty, precious plagues, which haunt
> A lover with caprices soft and dear,
> They like to *make* a quarrel, when they can't
> Find one, each day of the delightful year;
> Bewitching, torturing, as they freeze or glow,
> And — what is worst of all — won't let you go;

> (XIV, 63)

The Duchess here is fixed within a special ambit of her own. 'Amorous sphere' denotes the exclusive circle of her operations which, like those of the Marquise de Merteuil in Laclos' *Les liaisons dangereuses*[5] or, for that matter, Don Juan Tenorio's, are wholly devoted to erotic pursuit. Like these, Fitz-Fulke's amorous schemes are motivated as much by pleasure in outrageous trickery as by Eros itself, or perhaps the two motives are fused together. We are told that

The Duchess of Fitz-Fulke, who loved *"tracasserie"*,
Began to treat him with some small *"agaçerie"*

(XIV, 41)

The rhyming conjunction of 'tracasserie' [mischief-making] and 'agaçerie' [flirtatiousness] suggests the bewildering confusion of the two motives. Unlike Don Juan Tenorio and the Marquise de Merteuil, however, the Duchess's mischief seems to be compatible with comedy. The customary epithet for the mother of Eros, Aphrodite, in the Homeric hymns and elsewhere, is 'laughter-loving'. The Duchess, like the poem which is her actual sphere, improvises the natural comedy of love for the sake of laughter. In other respects, she is not at all typical of *Don Juan*. She is one of those 'pretty, precious plagues which', and the word is well chosen *'haunt*/A lover' (XIV, 63, my italics),

Bewitching, torturing, as they freeze or glow,
And − what is worst of all − won't let you go;

The narrator here deploys the customary paradoxes of love poetry from Petrarch to Baudelaire.[6] Juan, however, save in his unfocused pubertal imaginings (1, 87-96), is never presented as tormented by these paradoxes. He is not, as we have seen, drawn across the 'go-between' space between lovers nor does he have to be kept within the amorous sphere by intrigue or calculated variety. The Duchess may use her wits rather than the accident of shipwreck to present herself to Juan but it is the presentation itself which is crucial. Indeed, the more this presentation is planned and willed, as it is with the Sultana and Catharine, the more probable it is that Juan will resist or, finally, grow sick.

Our uncertainty as to whether Juan 'glows' in response to the Duchess's teasingly immediate presence is tied up with the uncertainty of its occasioning. At first, her vibrant manifestation in the very accoutrements of Death must seem, as Eros customarily seems, both accident and necessary miracle. If there is, nevertheless, space for reflection before the inevitable answering glow then Juan will discern 'an Intrigante' as well as see a woman. None of Don Juan Tenorio's victims know him simultaneously as lover and trickster ('el burlador') and would, at least in Tirso's version, reject him if they did so. It is the nature of trickery which is in question here and returns us, by a different route, to the concerns of the last chapter and the recurring enigma of the poem.

If we view the Duchess negatively we will align her with the Sultana and see her as tainting the sources of erotic impulse by her all-invading will. Juan will become like Lord Augustus Fitz-Plantagenet, another prey for Fitz-Fulke's 'dead set' (XIV, 42). If we view her positively then her mischievous erotic intrigues will seem to emerge from the inherent predisposition of Nature to contrive sexual encounters out of random occurences. The Duchess's improvisations originate, in this view, not in her will but in the erotic forces which, however knowingly she represents them, operate in everyone. Here, the distinction between Julia's not wholly successful suppression of guilt and the Duchess's unflinching enthusiasm dwindles into unimportance. What is central and active in both cases is their present availability and their confidence (diffident or brazen) in the power which moves them to draw others into their amorous sphere.

A third possibility exists which would align the Duchess with Catharine the Great and undermine any comic confidence. We could see the Duchess as embodying the character of erotic energies only too well. It is true that her will does not taint these impulses but only because they are inherently tainted. Here the Duchess's appearance as the Black Friar is neither disguise nor mask but the counterpart to Catharine's mastery of men in bed and battlefield. Aphrodite, though 'laughter-loving' is aso 'Androphonous' [killer of men] and 'Tymborychos' [the grave digger].[7]

There is no doubt that all these are possibilities to the reader and that they contribute to that confusion, destructive of all systematic thinking, which the poem often celebrates. To know this, however, cannot be sufficient. Contradictory attitudes to love can easily be held within the poem but the underlying connection of Eros with Death, all too clearly understood in Cantos VII to X, cannot coexist with the comic confidence which it, in effect, parodies and pillories. The sudden absence of Eros from Canto X onwards, accepted as inescapable by the reader, cannot but be seen as a crisis for the whole poem as its own forward movement has, hitherto, closely paralleled Juan's erotically charmed life. The forward thrust of the poem reveals, as it were, more and more of the sources from which Juan acts and it springs just as the narrator's intellect tries to snatch a glimpse into the abyss above which it sustains a hovering dance. The return of Eros therefore, 'In full, voluptuous, but *not o'ergrown bulk*,' (XVI, 123), placed against a wall immediately in front of Juan's senses and the reader's imagination, presents us with an enigma which we cannot easily resolve. Like Juan, we may be grateful for the end of a canto and the helpful intervention of a gap. Does Fitz-Fulke proffer simply the restoration of a forgotten mode? Sexual life is inherently repetitive and, though on occasion shocked into suppression, the old game will in time seem a new one. Or does the Duchess represent, in changed circumstances, some altogether new confidence which could transcend the parody of comic renewal offered by Catharine? If the former, why should·we now accept what we earlier rejected? If the latter, what is the basis of this new confidence?

These questions cannot be avoided since they pose once again the originating questions of this study: how does *Don Juan* proceed and what kind of poem is it? For the moment nevertheless they can be put aside and, as a necessary preliminary to answering them, we will continue our characterisation of Eros elsewhere in the poem.

Haidée, for instance, is first seen by Juan in the closest proximity to him:

> And she bent o'er him, and he lay beneath,
> Hush'd as the babe upon its mother's breast,
>
> (II, 148)
>
> He woke and gazed, and would have slept again,
> But the fair face which met his eyes forbade
> Those eyes to close,
>
> (II, 149)
>
> And thus upon his elbow he arose,
> And look'd upon the lady, in whose cheek
> The pale contended with the purple rose,
>
> (II, 150)
>
> And Juan, too, was help'd out from his dream,
> Or sleep, or whatso'er it was, by feeling
> A most prodigious appetite:
>
> (II, 153)

Haidée's immediate presence awakens him from his nightmare experience of shipwreck, his death-like sleep ('or whatso'er it was'), and restores to him his confidence and appetite for life:

> And every day by day-break . . .
> She came into the cave,
>
> (II, 168)
>
> And every morn his colour freshlier came,
>
> (II, 169)

This restoration to health dissolves proximity into union:

> And saw each other's dark eyes darting light
> Into each other – and, beholding this,
> Their lips drew near, and clung into a kiss;

(II, 185)

The narrator suggests their union with warmth and tact but then deflates the situation and, in doing so, poses and answers a relevant question:

> But Juan: had he quite forgotten Julia?
> And should he have forgotten her so soon?
> . . .
>   . . . fresh features
> Have such a charm for us poor human creatures?

(II, 208)

This last aphorism, taken as a piece of narrator's wisdom, could (and to that extent *does*) mean that we like fresh features because they are new and/or because they are young. Within the poem, however, Juan is charmed by Haidée's 'fresh features' simply because they are present. He does not tire of Julia nor willingly leave her. He never does:

> But Juan never left them, while they had charms,
>
> Unless compelled by fate, or wave, or wind,
> Or near relations, who are much the same.

(VIII, 53-4)

He remains with Haidée for two cantos. In Canto IV still

> Juan and Haidée gazed upon each other
> With swimming looks of speechless tenderness,

(IV, 26)

When this sustained proximity and union are finally sundered by a 'near relation' in the shape of Lambro, Byron faces the apparently impossible task of suggesting that Juan virtually forgets Haidée whilst maintaining our sympathy for him. He does so by at once placing Juan in ridiculously direct proximity with the fresh features of an Italian opera singer full of that consciousness of sexual attractiveness which heightens it:

> And through her clear brunette complexion shone a
> Great wish to please — a most attractive dower,
> Especially when added to the power.

(IV, 94)

Juan is literally chained to this new charmer and, it must be acknowledged, does not oblige with an immediate answering glow:

> But all that power was wasted upon him,
> For sorrow o'er each sense held stern command;
> Her eye might flash on his, but found it dim;
> And though thus chain'd, as natural her hand
> Touch'd his, not that — nor any handsome limb
> (And she had some not easy to withstand)
> Could stir his pulse, or make his faith feel brittle;
> Perhaps his recent wounds might help a little.

(IV, 95)

Juan's resistance, if such it is, might in theory prevent us from criticising him but it is the ludicrous spectacle of his enforced proximity to fresh features, the very thing we most fear in the continuing poem, which releases us, almost without our noticing it, from our own desire to be loyal to Haidée. Laughter, acknowledging the absurdity, overthrows the earnestness upon which fidelity relies. We do not, to our own surprise, dissent from the narrator's Rochefoucauldian joke that Juan's virtue owes more to his physical weakness than to his moral strength for, as we remember, Juan needed time to recover from his physical weakness before he could return Haidée's glow.

Juan chained to an attractive Italian is a pretty device for manoeuvring Juan on from Haidée whilst the ship, and the poem too, sail past 'The shores of Ilion' (IV, 75), with all their burden of tragic|heroism, into a comic future. The sea too ('he found himself at sea', IV, 75, 'gazing on the deep blue surge', IV, 79) we recognise as the renewing sea of Shakespeare's final comedies but the emblem is not wholly a comic one. The permanent freedom of this sea is poignantly contrasted with the captivity of the slaves:

> ... each threw
> A rueful glance upon the waves (which bright all
> From the blue skies derived a double blue,
> Dancing all free and happy in the sun),
> And then went down the hatchway one by one.
>
> (IV, 90)

Juan in chains, precariously and only temporarily resistant to 'fresh features', appears amongst these captives as a slave of passion. Even with Haidée, the accusation of 'The isles of Greece' lyric is that the love-feast over which Juan and Haidée preside is a symptom of their slavery and that it would be better to accept the tyranny of Miltiades: 'Such chains as his were sure to bind' ('The isles of Greece', 12).

Juan's chains are those of the 'amorous sphere' itself. All this is clarified, extended, but also wilfully obscured in the Seraglio section of the poem which disentangles the paradoxes of love more fully than any other section in the poem.

As so often, Byron attains moderation by immoderate means. If Juan is to ennoble or escape from his role as a slave of love, he will first have to submit to it with a vengeance. Chosen and bought by a Sultana, he will be dressed as a woman, narrowly miss castration and sleep in the heart of the amorous sphere — a harem.

Harems were well recognised, mildly erotic features of eighteenth-century narratives, letters and travel accounts. Montesquieu's *Les lettres Persanes*, Le Sage's *Le Diable boiteux* and *Gil Blas* all have harem episodes. Mozart, interestingly, composed both a tragic *Don Giovanni* and a comic *The Seraglio*. Byron handles his Seraglio much more in the manner of Spenser's moral allegorising in *The Faerie Queene* than these precedents would lead us to except. He is primarily concerned with distinguishing what is natural from what is unnatural, showing the destructive nature of passion, and emphasising the integrality of gender to sexual life. The emblem of Juan in chains is encased in and modified by a sequence of emblematic tableaus to which the narrative is subordinated. Indeed one of the most characteristic features of harem accounts in, for example, Le Sage, the escape from the Seraglio (cf. Mozart's *The Abduction from the Seraglio*), is simply omitted altogether for reasons which must later detain us.

The Seraglio section (Cantos V and VI) is Byron at his best.[8] Obvious juxtapositions and crude contrasts support, as they do in *A Midsummer Night's Dream*,[9] a delicately adjusted and continuously intelligent life which we murder to dissect. The critic cannot hope to hold the section separately together as though he is responsible for its discovered unity[10] and, in any case, Byron practises a certain necessary sleight of hand in it which, except for our very specific purposes, is better left unexposed.

Let us turn to this straightaway. Juan in chains amongst 'the shivering slaves' in Constantinople is not an impressive sight. That he remains a sexually attractive one (for the Sultana first sees and chooses him in this condition) may occasion his freedom but leaves him more decisively than ever in slavery. A harem is thus the proper place for him. In many respects the mode of life there will not be very different from that of Haidée's isle as 'The isles of Greece' implies. If Juan were to comply with this situation he would be as evidently reprehensible as Don Juan Tenorio. If he were wholly to repudiate it, he would cease to be Don Juan. The interposition of Juan's fellow slave, Johnson, is Byron's first way of easing this problem. Johnson steadies Juan, is liked by the reader and represents certain qualities that Juan lacks. He is clearly useful too as a stereotype of masculinity with which Juan's metamorphosis into Juanna can be contrasted just as the innocent Leila is a contrasting stereotype in the Siege of Ismail. Byron uses Salemenes in *Sardanapalus* in exactly the same way. Johnson's main function, however, is to enable the reader to reassess Juan's amorousness and regain some confidence in it just at the point where we will be moving in the opposite direction. Once this function is fulfilled Byron suppresses Johnson, until he is again briefly useful in the Siege, because what is begun through Johnson is completed more effectively by the Sultana.

Johnson's experience of the 'amorphous sphere' differs from Juan's. One of his wives has died and the other left him. In this, if we count Julia's entrance into a convent as leaving Juan, Johnson's experience parallels Juan's, but then the difference is inescapable:

> "Well, then, your third," said Juan; "What did she?
> She did not run away, too, did she, sir?"
> "No, faith." — "What then?" — "I ran away from her".
>
> "You take things coolly, sir," said Juan. "Why,"
> Replied the other, "What can a man do?
> There are still many rainbows in your sky,
> But mine have vanished . . .

> (V, 20, 21)

Juan's comment on this is pertinent enough:

> "All this is very fine, and may be true",
> Said Juan; "but I really don't see how
> It betters present times with me or you".
> "No?" quoth the other; "yet you will allow
> By setting things in their right point of view,
> Knowledge, at least, is gained;

(V, 23)

Johnson, though still active in the world, is a resigned spectator of it just like the narrator. In comparison with him, Juan's attempt to remember Haidée, however unsuccessful, seems a model of fidelity. Again, Johnson's passive acceptance of chequered reality in contrast with Juan's suggestion that they might escape from the tutelage of Baba (the eunuch confidant of the Sultana) and Juan's indignant refusal of circumcision, make the latter seem the more active of the two. Thirdly, Johnson argues that:

> "But, after all, what *is* our present state?
> 'Tis bad, and may be better — all men's lot:
> Most men are slaves, none more so than the great,
> To their own whims and passions, and what not;
> Society itself, which should create
> Kindness, destroys what little we had got:
> To feel for none is the true social art
> Of the world's stoics — men without a heart".

(V, 25)

Here, the extension of the metaphor of slavery-to-passion beyond the bounds of Eros removes the exclusive nature of Juan's emblematic chains. The narrator, in his turn, confirms this extension of the metaphor by promptly devoting a whole stanza to it (V, 27). But Johnson's declared feeling 'for none', with its deliberate echoing of the uncommended stoic in (that other) Johnson's *Rasselas*, make us again side with Juan's warm-hearted impulses.

The reader will thus be placated. Juan, it seems, refuses ǀto be what he appears. In the Seraglio, we will be given two contradictory sets of information about Juan dressed as a girl. One will stress his androgynous attractiveness ('a perfect transformation', V, 80), sufficient to fool the Sultan and make him a suitable minion for the poniard-wearing Sultana. The other will stress his irrepressible masculinity which so alarms Baba:

"If you could just contrive," he said, "to stint
That somewhat manly majesty of stride,

(V, 91)

This doubleness corresponds to a double way of seeing the Seraglio
and also to its division into the Sultana's apartments and the harem
itself. The Seraglio is in part a dangerous 'Bowre of Blisse', Baba calls
it an anticipation of 'paradise' (V, 81) which, though given over to
natural pleasures, insists upon unnatural distortions. The presence of
eunuchs and dwarfs guarding the huge, lifeless rooms and Juan's
enforced crossing of genders, establish this. Eros exists without any
other context. The 'amorous sphere' alone prevails. Juan resents this
and is right to do so. Yet transformations exist here as in *Midsummer
Night's Dream* in order that identities may be regained. Juan does not
become a harem girl but is welcomed as an obtrusive male presence
within the harem. On the other hand, there are suggestions of fun,
romance, adventure and of innocence in the unnatural transformations
of the Seraglio:

"Farewell!" they mutually exclaimed: "this soil
Seems fertile in adventures strange and new;
One's turned half mussulman, and one a maid,
By this old black enchanter's unsought aid.

(V, 83)

Juan resists his transformation but his joke accepts and relishes it:

"Nay," quoth the maid [Juan] "the Sultan's self shan't carry me,
Unless his highness promises to marry me".

(V, 84)

Here Juan, in masquerade as a woman, en route to an assignation,
corresponds exactly to the Duchess of Fitz-Fulke gleefully disguised as
a monk. Unlike Fitz-Fulke, it is not his own plan but he is enjoying
the mischief of it which is appropriate, natural or unnatural, to Eros.
The palace may be lifeless but an attractive life-giving smell of food
('genial savour', V, 47) floats through it. Moreover, though it is policed
by maimed bodies it also has in abundance 'fresh features' and 'lovely
limbs' (VI, 64) which contrast with the unmoving corpse of the
Ravenna commandant who intervenes at the very beginning of the section (V, 33-9).

The poem also draws a distinction between the Sultana's apartments and the harem. The harem, it is true, is full of 'caged birds' (VI, 26) but, inside their own apartment they are 'freed from bonds' (VI, 34). They are 'like birds, or boys' or 'Waves at spring-tide', they 'sing, dance, chatter, smile and play' (VI, 34). When asleep, though shaped like statues, they are soft as fruit and flowers (VI, 65). Dudù is singled out to epitomise these qualities:

> But she was a soft Landscape of mild Earth,
> Where all was harmony and calm and quiet,
> Luxuriant, budding; cheerful without mirth,
> Which if not happiness, is much more nigh it
> Than are your mighty passions and so forth,
>
> (VI, 53)

Dudù is 'of a beauty that would drive you crazy' (VI, 41) but she does not represent 'mighty passions' in herself nor, so far as Juan is concerned, does she arouse them. This is because, unlike the Sultana, 'she never thought about herself at all.' (VI, 54). It is for this reason that Byron adopts the brilliant stratagem of the dream. Dudù's consciousness of herself and Juan cannot directly beckon him. She awakes screaming from her sleep with 'Juanna' and recounts her dream. The dream, like this whole section, is both coarsely obvious and delicately suggestive. The bee that flies out of the golden apple which she is about to bite and stings her 'to the heart' (VI, 77) is irretrievably phallic Juan, Eros with his dart, and the serpent in Eden but the knowledge which this represents cannot be fully acknowledged. When Juanna asks that Dudù be allowed to resume her sleep with 'her', Dudù who now understands why she too has pressed for this, cannot quite proffer her new consciousness of her own attractiveness to him but does so all the same:

> As thus Juanna spoke, Dudù turned round
> And hid her face within Juanna's breast;
> Her neck alone was seen, but that was found
> The colour of a budding rose's crest.
> I can't tell why she blushed, nor can expound
> The mystery of this rupture of their rest;
>
> (VI, 85)

If Dudù hides her glow in this fashion which still beckons and succeeds, the Sultana has, in the previous canto, asserted hers as soon as Baba has left them alone together in a less winning blend of stridency and doubt:

> When he was gone, there was a sudden change:
> I know not what might be the lady's thought,
> But o'er her bright brow flashed a tumult strange,
> And into her clear cheek the blood was brought,
> Blood-red as sunset summer clouds which range
> The verge of Heaven; and in her large eyes wrought
> A mixture of sensations might be scanned,
> Of half-voluptuousness and half-command.

(V, 108)

The Sultana is a magnificent natural phenomenon here but we are clearly guided to three kinds of reservation about it. She represents 'mighty passions' which are inextricably bound up with egotism. She wills the gender-crossing that Juan rejects by wishing simultaneously to command and to be possessed. Thirdly she fuses her political power with her sexual role. Hence the metaphor which Johnson extended is again narrowed:

> Something imperial, or imperious, threw
> A chain o'er all she did; that is, a chain
> Was thrown as 'were about the neck you' –

(V, 110)

It is no surprise that in the Sultana's bedchamber,

>   . . . many a vase
> Of porcelain held in the fettered flowers

(VI, 97)

How does Juan respond? The Sultana is present, proximate, at 26 years retains 'fresh features' and, manifestly, glows. How can Juan fail to catch the incandescence even though to do so is to accept his fetters? Here the sleight of hand begins. Juan's glowing response is, for once, stifled:

> But Juan, who had still his mind o'erflowing
> With Haidée's isle and soft Ionian face,

> Felt the warm blood, which in his face was glowing,
> Rush back upon his heart, which filled apace,
> And left his cheeks as pale as snowdrops blowing:

(V, 117)

When the Sultana responds by throwing herself 'upon his breast' (V, 125), Juan survives the 'awkward test':

> And looking coldly in her face, he cried,
> "The prisoned eagle will no pair, nor I
> Serve a sultana's sensual phantasy.
>
> "Thou ask'st, if I can love? be this the proof
> How much I *have* loved that I do not love *thee*!
> In this vile garb, the distaff, web and woof
> Were fitter for me: Love is for the free!

(V, 126-7)

The Sultana's response to this Achillean rejection of feminine disguise is to burst first into a rage and then into tears. This undisguised femininity now excites an answering masculine tenderness in Juan which reauthorises the answering glow which he had repressed: 'So Juan's virtue ebbed, I know not how;' (V, 144). It is only the sudden entry of Baba announcing the Sultan's unexpected arrival that seems to prevent their union but it is the logic of the poem which causes the interruption. We are not following a story so much as deciphering a masque within which the Sultana's role is now clear. A night with Dudù will make the poem's meaning clearer than union with the Sultana, whom, once united to, Juan would not be able to leave.

What has happened? We have shifted the blame that we were beginning to attach to Juan as a slave of love in this section onto the Sultana. She is sufficiently responsible for the gender changes, reversals, tyrannical restraints, exaggerated passions and hostility to natural life within the Seraglio for us to see Juan as an emblem of freedom and legitimate masculinity inside its strange world. Byron controls his readers always by the qualifying contexts which he sets up. Consider, for example, Juan returning with the other harem girls unable to resist their multiple proximity,

> And though he certainly ran many risks,
> Yet he could not at times keep, by the way

. . .
From ogling all their charms from breasts to backs.

(VI, 29)

In order to sustain this 'ogling' Juan has to act a part: 'Still he forgot not his disguise' (VI, 30). If we were to take away the episode of the Sultana, which in fact determines our response here, we would be appalled by this. We have assented to Juan's inability to resist more than one Italian opera singer but not to mass ogling. If we think separately about the context, as opposed to being guided by it, we will find it hard to see how Juan's recent invocation of loyalty to Haidée can be so readily cast aside or how the disguise which he then condemned as a 'vile garb' can now be so carefully cultivated. We do not do any of these things, however. We welcome Juan's masculinity, threatened and restored to him by the Sultana, and we discern a straightforward playfulness rather than prurient deception in his 'ogling all their charms'. Juan cannot be prurient any more than he can seduce, for both involve a maintained and superior separateness in the midst of desire and union. The narrator's objection to frigidity or to excessive passion such as the Sultana's is that they prevent what lovers such as Juan want:

Who fain would have a mutual flame confest,
And see a sentimental passion glow,

(VI, 17)

for, he argues, in another version of the slave metaphor,

For no one, save in very early youth,
 Would like (I think) to trust all to desire,
Which is but a precarious bond, in sooth,
 And apt to be transferred to the first buyer
At a sad discount:

(VI, 16)

Juan's union with Dudù could appear to be 'desire' alone and, without the interposition of the dream, might even now seem so. The dream, however, and the indirect dialogue between Juan and Dudù which it occasions, allows within the smallest possible compass, 'a sentimental passion' to 'glow' between them. The Sultana's grand passion, with which this uncomplicated, inevitable but not automatic coupling is contrasted, represents 'desire' alone of a thinner kind whose intensity is willed, contained and wholly known by the Sultana herself.

Through all this Byron successfully maintains an impossible balance. The Sultana is condemned but her too-consciously-stimulated energies are natural in themselves and we understand the frustrations inherent in being even the 'favourite' wife (V, 146) of the uncharismatic Sultan. Eros is an over-mastering force of Nature which love's masquerade diversifies but cannot overthrow:

> They lie, we lie, all lie, but love no less:
> And no one virtue yet, except starvation,
> Could stop that worst of vices — Propagation.

(VI, 19)

Slavery to this force is, at times, inescapable. Such slavery can be seen as a degradation, or, since it is in accord with our nature, can be an exercise of freedom. A 'mutual flame' is the best kind of love. It depends upon reciprocated tenderness and a dialogue of consciousness rather than direct speech. In such a dialogue, the flow of sexuality is dependent upon, and itself arouses, the necessary stereotypes of gender but there is a balancing equality and some interplay of gender roles. Both men and women initiate, respond, control and yield to one another and to the discernible force of Eros. They are fully conscious of this but they do not fully *know* it. At best, however, Eros is ambiguous. The bee's sting may be again desired but it is also feared and it betokens Death. Love is allied to mischief-making, disguise, fun but also to deception, forgetfulness and harm. Haidée forgets her father. Julia and the Sultana lie and deceive their husbands. The latter's deception of the Sultan is specifically called 'a prank' (V, 54). Byron wants to complicate and qualify our sense of Eros as much as he can whilst at the same time insisting upon a simple, reiterated distinction between positive and negative kinds of love. Hence the necessity for sleight of hand. He uses Johnson and the Sultana to redirect us towards Juan even when his hero's behaviour is contradictory and belies his pledged fidelity to Haidée. Nothing as complex as this has occurred in the poem hitherto. It anticipates the intricate but unfinished counterpoint of Norman Abbey.

The world of Catharine the Great is a direct counterpart to the Turkish Seraglio. The narrator is quick to point out that if only Catharine and the Sultan followed his recommendation,

> She to dismiss her guards and he his harem,
> And for their other matters, meet and share 'em.
>
> (VI, 95)

then there would be general peace and even the possibility of a mutual
flame between them. However, this Sardanapalian simplification,
acceptable before the Siege of Ismail, is certainly not so after it.
Catharine's court too has none of the imagined density and moral
ambivalence of the Seraglio. Juan, Catharine and Eros itself are together
subject to the same indictment which exposes all that Byron's earlier
sleight of hand concealed. What is accepted lightly in the Seraglio:

> They lie, we lie, all lie, but love no less:
> And no one virtue yet, except Starvation,
> Could stop that worst of vices — Propagation.
>
> (VI, 19)

comes home to roost in St Petersburg. Proximity is inescapable:

> ... perhaps, despite his duty,
> In royalty's vast arms he sighed for beauty:
>
> (X, 37)

Byron's facility for epigrams may mislead us a little here. There is something *de trop* about the Empress but she is not ugly despite the vast-
ness, real or metaphorical, of her arms. Catharine is said to be 'handsome' (IX, 63), 'rosy, ripe and succulent' (IX, 62) and she 'had a
touch// Of Sentiment' (IX, 54). Juan cannot therefore sigh 'for beauty'
in any straightforward sense. The glow of beauty has not disappeared
but reciprocated sexual consciousness, which participates in and magni-
fies that glow, is now reduced to commercial calculation:

> She could repay each amatory look you lent
> With interest, and in turn was wont with rigour
> To exact of Cupid's bills the full amount
> At sight, nor would permit you to discount.
>
> (IX, 62).

Indecency is an inevitable consequence of this sure calculation,
signalled both by the constant gossip of courtiers and the narrator's
puns, for both rely on an inherently reductive knowledge.

The central question for the reader and for this chapter is whether
Catharine should be seen as a local and unacceptable image amongst
many acceptable figures of love in the poem or whether she is that Eros
which underlies, and to that extent undermines, all images of human
love. Catharine, we might argue, is manifestly a particular case. Juan has
had a range of female partners and the reader has learnt to discriminate
amongst them. Just as Dudù is related to natural landscape, Haidée to
an isle, Gulbeyaz to a lifeless palace, so Catharine is an Empress related
to war, snow and court-life with its

> . . . waste, and haste, and glare, and gloss, and glitter,
> In this gay clime of bear-skins black and furry —

> (X, 26)

There is no reason to see this setting as more universal than its predecessors. Catharine the Great is, we might add, the most specific of all
Juan's partners because she, alone, is a real historical character. Finally,
what Catharine announces is not the truth about Eros but a truth about
Juan who 'about this time' grew 'a little dissipated' (X, 23). The poem,
we could say, uses Catharine and Leila in order to indicate the alternatives, both of age and type, between which other and better kinds of
loving may mediate and thrive.

These arguments appear solid enough but they blur the difficulties
which they claim to dissolve. For example, let us return briefly to the
apparently settled question of Catharine's beauty and enquire her age.
In Canto IX, 72 she is in 'Her prime of life, just now in juicy vigour,';
in Canto X, 24 she is

> . . . a *not old* Queen
> But one who is not so youthful as she was
> In all the royalty of sweet seventeen.

However, in X, 29 she is, perhaps for the sake of another epigram, 'an
old woman'. In X, 47, Byron appears aware of these discrepancies and
tries to sort them out:

> . . though her years were waning,
> Her climacteric teased her like her teens;

In fact, Catharine the Great would have been some 60 years old at
the time in which the poem was set and this would have been public

knowledge to the poem's first readers. The solution to this conundrum is not the naturalistic one which at first offers itself (i.e. Catharine the Great is still attractive though in the autumn of her years). The Empress has the appetites and energies of a teenager, her 'juicy vigour' is attractive to 'the standing army' (IX, 78) which surround her but she remains 'an old woman'. For her true identity we should look to an important passage in Canto XVI where the narrator modulates between the love inspired by Aurora Raby and the appearance of Fitz-Fulke as the ghost:

> Anacreon only had the soul to tie an
> Unwithering myrtle round the unblunted dart
> Of Eros; but though thou hast played us many tricks,
> Still we respect thee, "Alma Venus Genetrix"!

> (XVI, 109)

Venus is attractive in herself and presides over the generative forces which she epitomises. In another, and naturally linked, guise ('Venus Genetrix') she is an emblem of motherhood and nurture which is the end of sexual pleasure. Juan's mother therefore may be far-seeing as well as blind when, in her letter to Juan, she 'praised the Empress's *maternal* love' (X, 32). There is nothing necessarily Oedipal in all this and I am not concerned with those who interpret Don Juan Tenorio's betrayal of women as evidence of fidelity to his mother. Juan finds no difficulty in falling in love and desiring to stay with women of his own age. However, erotic life throughout the poem is seen in relation to natural forces of procreation, however disdainful the narrator may be about this:

> . . . What a curious way
> The whole thing is of clothing souls in clay!

> (IX, 75)

Even Haidée is an emblem of motherhood as well as of young love and would not be 'Nature's bride' if she were not so:

> She died, but not alone; she held within
> A second principle of life, which might
> Have dawn'd a fair and sinless child of sin;

> (IV, 70)

Catharine is partial to Juan's boyishness (X, 72) but she also requires

'Gigantic Gentlemen' (IX, 54). Like a Queen bee she presides over a huge and fierce society but she is an emblem of its renewal through generation. Juan with Catharine is a boy with his mother, Eros/Cupid with Venus as well as Mars with Venus. When, fresh from the Siege, he first appears before the Empress 'sword by side' he is thus identified for us:

> . . . He
> Seems Love turned a Lieutenant of Artillery!
>
> His Bandage slipped down into a cravat;
> His Wings subdued to epaulettes; his Quiver
> Shrunk to a scabbard,with his Arrows at
> His side as a small sword, but sharp as ever;
>
> (IX, 44-5)

As we have seen in Chapter 2, the narrator's bitter address to the 'great whole' for which every man sexually 'falls and rises' (IX, 55) supports these identifications of the narrative. Catharine *is* Venus Genetrix, bride and mother, life-giver and destroyer. She is 'the grand Epitome' (IX, 52) of what a cancelled line calls 'Dark Riddle of all Life! Earth's lifeless end'.[11] Cathererine is *de trop* not because she is 'an old woman' or a tyrant in bed and out of it but because she makes the play element of Eros into work (IX, 85), freedom into contract (IX, 62) and life-giving procreation into mere replacement of used procreators (IX, 56). This may be specific to her but she undoubtedly represents more than herself. Every love-episode in the poem, for example, is interrupted by some narrative machinery which relies upon an intervening 'near-relation'. Alfonso, Lambro, the Sultan, all interrupt an amorous engagement. Their intervention indicates a permanent restraint on the women whom they father or husband. Catharine, on the contrary, is the unconstrained fountain head of Eros. The narrative cannot therefore provide an intervention of its own. Juan has to fall sick and Catharine herself, reluctantly, commissions him for further adventures.

Finally, we encounter Catharine after Seraglio and the Siege. The former, because of its tableau character and Juan's position in the harem, has made us see and consider love in a more generalised fashion than the idyll with Haidée. The Siege similarly, and Juan's active participation in it, has made us aware of Death's scale and the close cooperation of erotic and aggressive drives. Catharine the Great is the epitome of natural energies as well as of absolutist government. She makes love and war on the grandest scales. The amorous sphere, it seems, 'Causes all the things which be,' (IX, 57).

There can be little doubt then that Catharine's confident and unshakeable vitality (she finds a successor to Juan within 24 hours, X, 48) does indicate that Eros is inherently tainted and, thus, disallows the now familiar resurrections of its narrative.

The form in which we express this conclusion is important if the correct consequences are to be drawn and in particular if we are to determine whether the Duchess of Fitz-Fulke is another version of the Empress. It is not as though Catharine alone represents the unacceptable face of Eros. Byron's long poems move in spiral fashion. They are both cyclic and linear. Childe Harold's predicament remains insoluble at the end as at the beginning of his pilgrimage but the poem's forward movement is authentic and brings clarification. Similarly, in *Don Juan*, Catharine does not bring a wholly new insight into the poem but she forces us to attend to previously contained characteristics of love as now presenting major impediments to comic confidence.

It is often observed, for example, that Haidée is not without taint.[12] Her eyes are 'black as death' and their glance is like the 'late-coild' snake who 'hurls at once his venom and his strength' (II, 117). Her brow is overhung 'with coins of gold' (II, 116) which, presumably, derive from her pirate-father's tainted stock of 'ill-gotten million of piastres' (II, 125). Above all her dream (IV, 31-5), which retraces her own love experience with Juan, reveals the shadow-side of that experience. These elements are, of course, not foregrounded and even contribute to our acceptance of the Juan and Haidée idyll as such by incorporating reservations. They qualify but do not undermine the poem's association of Eros with Nature or the reiterated opposition of Nature and Civilisation in Cantos II to IV. In the Seraglio, as we have discovered, some sleight of hand is required and damaging distinctions drawn. If Dudù is to be preferred to the Sultana because the latter is used to power and cultivates 'mighty passions', what are we to make of Haidée in whose air

> There was a something which bespoke command,
> As one who was a lady in the land.

> (II, 116)

Haidée is not only 'Nature's bride' but also 'Passion's child' (II, 202); her passions are tender with Juan (II, 141, 173, 186) but 'in their full

growth' she has her father's 'fixed ferocity' (IV, 41) and is like 'a
lioness, though tame'. When father and daughter glare at one another in
hatred, they parody and parallel the glowing interchange of lovers:

> He gazed on her, and she on him; 'twas strange
> How like they looked! the expression was the same;
> Serenely savage, with a little change
> In the large dark eye's mutual-darted flame;

> (IV, 44)

It is hard to imagine Dudù behaving like this.

We should conclude that Haidée represents a complex image of love
which is both ideal and seriously flawed. We are not intended to set one
element against another. Haidée unifies, idealises or at least contains a
representative, though not a complete, set of love paradoxes.

The wedge driven between the Sultana's self-instigated passion and
Dudù's passive tenderness makes such a unification implausible but
Byron manages to gloss over this. The Russian cantos remove this gloss
and reveal connections between tenderness and indifference, ultimately
between Eros and Death, that make unification, idealisation or contain-
ment impossible. For the moment, love disappears from the poem.
When it returns, it does so still in the clearly separated figures of Lady
Adeline, the Duchess and Aurora Raby.

Thus far in considering the character of Eros in *Don Juan* we have
examined Juan's various love-affairs in sequence. 'Proximity', 'glow'[13]
and the splitting up or holding together of various positive and negative aspects of love, have formed the main part of our account. Our
major concern, however, is with the forward movement and character of
the poem itself. Is there any sense in which Eros exists as a force in
the poem apart from Juan's sequence of encounters? This question
makes us look at *Don Juan* quite differently and warrants a section of
its own.

II

Richard Strauss's well-known tone-poem *Don Juan* is unified and
moved forward by an unmistakable mixture of erotic yearning, ardour
and energy. Music lends itself naturally to this but literature does not.
If we read Gottfried's *Tristan*, for instance, there is nothing in the
narrative method itself which, irrespective of particular narrative

circumstances, would suggest Eros. This, I suspect, is generally true. Even a blatantly erotic concoction such as Restif de la Bretonne's *Monsieur Nicholas* is not in any discernible sense moved forward by Eros; rather, as with all such fictionalised memoirs, erotic intimacies flicker within the cold continuum of the narrator's consciousness. There may be, as in *Les liaisons dangereuses*, some identity between narrative action and a seducer's plotting but this again is not, in its mode, erotic for this would also be true of other kinds of plotting such as Iago's in *Othello*. Similarly Byron's *Mazeppa* may represent in Mazeppa's punishment, strapped naked to the back of a wild horse, an emblem of the passion for which he is punished and the verse account may participate in these energies, but the narrative method itself is quite other than this.

Is it then possible for there to be a more direct linking of Eros and literary production? Lucretius seems to have thought so. At the beginning of *De Rerum Natura* he addresses Venus Genetrix under that title (it is the source presumably of Byron's own phrase in XVI, 109) and asks her in the very words of Dryden:

> ... since nothing new can spring
> Without thy warmth, without thy influence bear,
> Or beautiful, or lovesome can appear;
> Be thou my ayd; my tuneful song inspire,
> And kindle with thy own productive fire.

> (I, 329-33)

This, though exactly to our purpose, is no more than a superb local conceit in Lucretius. It is something more than this in Byron.

Byron's views on poetry are complex and interesting. They have too often been simplified. A recurring emphasis, however, relates poetic conceptions to sexual acts. In the evidence which we will need briefly to adduce, it should be observed that Byron is writing letters from Italy to Moore, Kinnaird and to John Murray rather than advocating a thesis. His letters to these, especially the last two, are often deliberately raffish in tone. They are intended both to recall and sustain a Regency *machismo* and to slightly shock as well as delight their recipients. We are concerned here only with their content and not, however unfortunate the temporary exclusion, with their tone.

It is worth adding that *Don Juan*, in comparison with such letters and Byron's own proclamation of his outspokenness in the poem, is noticeably discreet. There are scattered indecencies, of course, but clusters only occur in the Dedication to Southey and in the account of Catharine the Great. There are clear reasons for both. Byron never attempts to describe love-making in *Don Juan* as Shelley does in *Alastor*. We have been told time and again[14] that the idiom of Byron's letters is a major clue to the idiom of *Don Juan*. It would be odd if there were no connection but is there anything in *Don Juan* which resembles the idiom of the verse-letter to John Murray (8th January, 1818), part of which I quote below? In the prose-letter to Kinnaird, and there are many of this kind, Byron's words arrange themselves in brief bursts connected by dashes and rarely attain a true periodic conclusion whereas in the style of *Don Juan* flow and true conclusion are of the essence. Frequently a stanza will coincide with a single marvellously regulated sentence. It seems far more accurate to say that the idiom of *Don Juan* imposes a different character on Byron's flow of consciousness and, in part, activates a different kind of flow. The relationship of Byron's letters to his verse, which must be susceptible of something other than jejune approximation, cannot be pursued here at any length but it is not without its relevance to our concerns. I list first the twelfth stanza of the verse-letter to John Murray:

Now, I'll out my taper
(I've finished my paper
For these stanzas you see on the brink stand)
There's a whore on my right
For I rhyme best at Night
When a C-t is tied close to *my Inkstand*.[15]

This is Byron in what T.J.B. Spencer aptly called his 'scholar-rake' guise[16] and, on its own, this conceit would be nothing more than a *jeu d'esprit* in the manner of Rochester. But in a well-known letter to Douglas Kinnaird, written a year later, Byron takes up the same point and relates it directly to the character and excellence of *Don Juan*:

As to "Don Juan" — confess — confess — you dog — and be candid — that it is the sublime of *that there* sort of writing — it may be bawdy — but is it not good enough English? — it may be profligate — but is it not *life*, is it not *the thing*? — Could any man have written it — who has not lived in the World? — and tooled in a post-chaise? in a hackney coach? in a Gondola? against a wall? in a court carriage? in a vis a vis? — on a table? — under it? — I have written about a hundred stanzas of a third Canto — but it is damned modest — the outcry has frightened me. — I had no such projects for the Don — but the *Cant* is so much stronger than *Cunt* — now a days, — that the benefit of experience in a man who had well weighed the worth of both monosyllables — must be lost to despairing posterity.[17]

Both these letters could be interpreted as simply associating poetry with sexual experience, though the verse-letter's quibble on '*my Ink-stand*' fuses the two. In a revealing letter to Thomas Moore, however, Byron, in much more ordered prose, insists on their similarity:

> I feel exactly as you do about our "art", but it comes over me in a kind of rage every now and then, like ****, and then, if I don't write to empty my mind, I go mad. As to that regular, uninter-rupted love of writing which you describe in your friend, I do not understand it. I feel it as a torture, which I must get rid of, but never as pleasure.
> On the contrary, I think composition a great pain.[18]

Here the fusion of the two activities is not a matter of bravado but an admission of pain which could be seen as creative and significant or mechanical and trivial. In a journal entry, Byron balances these alterna-tives very finely: 'To withdraw *myself* from *myself* (oh that cursed selfishness!) has ever been my sole, my entire, my sincere motive in scribbling at all:'.[19] Finally, in a later letter to Moore, Byron adds this caveat: 'I can never get people to understand that poetry is the ex-pression of *excited passion*, and that there is no such thing as a life of passion any more than a continuous earthquake, or an eternal fever.'[20]

This association then is not unpondered. It can form the basis for the criticism of other poets. Byron objects to Keat's poetry, for instance:

> . . . his is the *Onanism* of Poetry[21]

> Such writing is a sort of mental masturbation — he is always f--gg--g his *Imagination*. — I don't mean that he is *indecent* but viciously soliciting his own ideas into a state which is neither poetry nor any thing else but a Bedlam vision produced by raw pork and opium.[22]

The point of this attack is not that Keat's verse is damagingly linked to sexual life as such but that since it is, unlike sexual intercourse itself, not produced by glowing interchange and naturally tending to fruitfulness, it is perversely self-regarding, knowingly produced and, instead of existing in living interchange with the reader, invites the reader to reproduce the poet's own stifled, reflexive contemplation. John Jones called this 'end-stopped feel'.[23] Byron's criticism joins together the particulars of Keat's verse, its origin and procedure.

Clearly there are limits to this analogy. Byron himself reminds us that 'there is no such thing as a life of passion' and therefore it is difficult to see how the life of a long poem could be an indefinite extension of the sexual impulse. If, however, we remind ourselves of the importance of proximity in the specification of Eros in *Don Juan* then, surely, there is a clear likeness between poetic and erotic procedures?

On the smallest scale, this likeness exists in the arbitrary but significant conjunctions of rhyme upon which the poem's invention depends more than any other English poem of its length. Byron's comic rhymes make us laugh because of what Paul West called their 'freakish bond'[24] but they also make us think, because the coupling is, as often as not, authentic: '"Kiss rhymes to "bliss" in fact as well as verse −' (VI, 59).[25] Rhyme is nothing other than a joining proximity based on the accidents of sound but suggesting the glow of sense. Byron's inveterate dealing in rhyme relies upon the co-operation of accident and significance to make witty nonsense of settled and decorous categories but yet hazards an exhilirating confidence in what underlies and could renew these categories. In this way, though the venture is much riskier, *Don Juan* is clearly using the familiar strategies of comedy. This point about rhyme in *Don Juan* could be demonstrated at length and with a wealth of example. It might be objected, for example, that *Beppo* and *The Vision of Judgement* uses the same stanza form as *Don Juan*. Beppo's theme, tangential but operative, is also love whereas in *The Vision of Judgement*, which is not concerned with love, spectacular comic rhymes are, significantly, avoided. For example, there are no trisyllabic rhymes at all in *The Vision* with the nearly notional exception of 'Castilian' and 'civilian' (stanza XXXVI). The appropriateness of evident and risky rhymes in a poem motivated by Eros will, however, be readily conceded. Are there any large-scale analogies to this procedure?

We must first observe that even comedy, though characteristically dependent on Eros for its subject-matter, and providential concurrences of accident, design and Nature for its conclusion, is not itself carried forward by Eros as such.[26] The initiatives of comic plot, as in many forms of story-telling, are occasioned by the interposition of some barrier to present or future happiness. The removal of these barriers is certainly promoted by erotically motivated heroes and heroines, and, it may be, the audience wills the comic conclusion in some kind of tacit support for the union-seeking couples as well as for their renewed communities. Yet comedy, though it prizes warmth and generosity, is itself cool in mode and procedure,[27] however festive in its occasions. Puck, like Cupid, darts amongst the inhabitants of the forest but he is situated within the action and mode of *A Midsummer Night's Dream*, he is not its life.

Don Juan, on the contrary, does not depend upon obstacles or barriers to its narrative progression — Lambro does not, as Egeus does in *A Midsummer Night's Dream*, intervene at an early stage to prevent his daughter from mating as she pleases. The Sultan's arrival prevents the union of Juan and Sultana but promotes that of Juan and Dudù. How exactly is narrative conducted in *Don Juan?*

Byron learnt how to construct narrative in the sequence of oriental Tales which, together with the first two cantos of *Childe Harold's Pilgrimage*, first gained a huge readership for his verse. Certain features of the tales anticipate the methods of *Don Juan*. For example, in *The Corsair*, Conrad is placed between the wilting, passive Medora and the active, resourceful Gulnare who murders Seyd, her lord of the harem, much as Juan is claimed by a bifurcated image of woman in the Seraglio. Similarly, in *The Corsair* and *The Bride of Abydos* there are many parallels drawn between slavery and love just as there are in Cantos V and VI of *Don Juan*. The differences are more instructive. We see Conrad's escape from Seyd with the aid of his would-be lover from Seyd's harem whereas we do not see Juan's escape at all. *The Corsair* has a beginning (Conrad on Medora's isle), a middle (Conrad's attack, imprisonment and escape), and an end (Conrad's return to Medora's isle and the discovery of her death). None of the episodes in *Don Juan* comply with these basic Aristotelian narrative requirements. If Lambro never left his island, then there would be a story of thwarted love. If we knew what happened to Lambro after Haidée's death and he lies alongside her in the grave (IV, 72) then we would have a story of a different kind. Such stories exist:

> But many a Greek maid in a loving song
> Sighs o'er her name; and many an islander
> With her sire's story makes the night less long; (IV, 73)

Lambro and Haidée, it appears, form the substance of other people's stories but they do not themselves constitute a story within the poem. Byron imposes a noticeable self-restraint here which helps us to see his quite other purposes.

When Byron tells a story, he usually identifies his readers at some point with each of the major characters within the narrative. In some extreme cases, we see the same event twice in order to see it with different eyes. For instance, in *The Corsair* we stand with Medora and watch Conrad descending the cliff path to the waiting boat (I, 482-504) and then, apparently, we go back a fraction in time and rejoin Conrad on the same descent. In the last two scenes of *Marino Faliero* we are first of all close to the Doge as his ducal cap is removed, as he speaks his prophetic denunciation, and as the executioner raises his sword then, in Scene IV, we are with the crowd outside the palace some moments earlier and the previous scene is replayed from this distant perspective. In *Parisina*, perhaps the best of all Byron's tales, we identify in turn with Parisina, then with Hugo her lover, and finally, to our surprise, with her husband Azo who lives on alone after the deaths for which he is responsible. Byron was as interested as Wordsworth in the experience of those who live on when it is impossible to do so and he was clearly moved by the feeling of parents for dead children (II, 88-90; VIII, 116-17). Lambro's continued existence after the death of Haidée, for which he is indirectly responsible, would therefore appeal directly to Byron's imagination yet he refrains from doing anything with it. The self-restraint here is the more remarkable because Lambro has hitherto functioned in exactly the same way as the characters in Byron's tales. We see the feasting of Juan and Haidée dramatically from Lambro's perspective and feel with him just as we feel, finally, with Azo in *Parisina* and, briefly, with Giaffir in *The Bride of Abydos* but this perspective, and the narrative technique that goes with it, is quietly laid aside and never again used in the poem.

There is even a sense in which there is virtually no narrative in *Don Juan*. Stories are constantly proffered[28] but then they are curtailed and suppressed before they can take full shape as a story which could be repeated apart from the poem. In picaresque novels, a new character usually obliges the reader with the story of his or her life and if we renew acquaintance with an old character, he or she tells us, in story form, all that has happened since their last appearance. If we compare this with the perfunctory details which Johnson gives of his life we see the emblematic nature of his characterisation. Picaresque novels make stories out of survival. Juan survives shipwreck and siege but he is never

without resources and, even in the shipwreck, though hungry and prepared in the end to eat his spaniel, he is never shown as desperate.
Movement forwards, as we have seen, is not that of comedy nor do
ordinary actions within it have the aesthetic completeness of epic.[29]
Byron's own habitual technique of dramatic identification with a
number of characters is, with the brief and clearly discarded exception
of Lambro, unused.

Yet *Don Juan* undoubtedly is a narrative but of a dramatic and
emblematic kind. It presents a sequence of significant narrative pictures
which establish clear episodes like *The Faerie Queene*, but where
Spenser's poem holds these sections together by a manifest intellectual
and moral framework,[30] in Byron's poem they are, as it were,
separately generated from their self-disclosing centre and joined only by
the outrageous gaps between them. Gaps that might seem analogous in
function, such as those in Ariosto's *Orlando Furioso*, depend upon the
intricate husbanding of plot material and a stable cast of major characters. Suppression of narrative links, of the 'before and after' of normal
story-telling, is in *Don Juan*, however, a necessary feature of the narrator's continuous squandering of his material. 'What happens next?' is
answered in *Don Juan* not by consequential narrative but by dazzling
improvisation which will make us forget our present loyalties rather
than keep track of them but will return us to identical concerns. Hence
when we are removed by force and laughter from one episode to
another, we at first resist the incongruity of the resulting juxtaposition
but then we see a connection between them. In this way, we react on a
large scale exactly as we do to the rhymes. Moreover it is the gap in
each case which joins. The shipwreck, for example, to take an apparent
instance of gap-filling, is clearly not a fictional transition from Seville to
Greek island but an episode in its own right which is the antithesis both
of civilised society and idealised Nature. It does not, as the Siege does,
wholly prevent that later idealisation but it is in troubling juxtaposition
with it. Haidée's dark dream makes her see this other destructive face of
Nature. She is Juan and Nature's bride but, via her father, she is also
bound to a cycle of destruction.

The shipwreck is not then merely a narrative device providing the
expected mode of entry into a Romance world, as in Heliodorus or
Sidney's *Arcadia*, nor into a satirised social world, as in *Gulliver's
Travels*, it exists in its own right within a sequence of bizarre but reconciled juxtapositions. The simplicity of this narrative construction corresponds to that simplicity which we marked in the poem's understanding
of Eros. 'Proximity' and 'glow' underlie the vitality and secret coher-

ence of *Don Juan*. They link its thematic concerns with its procedure and relate both to forces outside the poem.

Consider, for instance, the hypothetical effect of filling in the poem's most considerable gap by describing Juan and Johnson's escape from the Seraglio. Juan finds himself with Julia, shipwrecked, woken by Haidée, at sea chained to a woman, summoned to the Sultana's presence and put to bed with Dudù, we next find him, with Johnson, joining Suvarrow's army. We assume that Baba has helped their escape and that Dudù may be one of the two women who are with them (VIII, 60). It is inconceivable that the other woman is the Sultana, though the thought does flit through the reader's mind, but two women must signify something for Byron's narrative details are normally functional despite his own jests at their inert yet authenticating factuality.[31] Perhaps the other woman has been acquired by Johnson (this may be implied in VII, 76) but he has only shown an interest in food in the Seraglio and has a declared talent for losing women rather than for their acquisition. In default of other explanation, the deliberately mysterious 'two women' may subliminally continue Juan's association with two separated images of woman in the Seraglio, and one named woman (Dudù) would imply a sentimental attachment anchoring Juan to the immediate past. What we are trying to do here, as we have throughout, is to interpret a detail correctly in terms of the larger context almost as we would in *The Faerie Queene*. Narrative as such does not come into it. The excellent story of Baba's refusal to carry out the Sultana's order for Juan's execution, his scheme for their escape, Johnson's shrewd assistance and the tender compliance of Dudù and Johnson's girl friend is missing. We have no time to make it up ourselves nor does Byron enter his characters' fictional predicament, as I have just been doing.

As it happens we have direct evidence of Byron's refusal to bridge this particular gap. Medwin reports a conversation with Byron which appears to fill it in:

Someone has possessed the Guiccioli with a notion that my Don Juan and the Don Giovanni of the opera are the same person; and to please her I have discontinued his history and adventures; but if I should resume them, I will tell you how I mean him to go on. I left him in the Seraglio. There I shall make one of the favourites, a Sultana, (no less a personage) fall in love with him, and carry him off from Constantinople...

... Well, they make good their escape to Russia; where, if Juan's passion cools, and I don't know what to do with the lady, I shall make her die of the plague. . . . As our hero can't do without a mistress, he shall next become man-mistress to Catharine the Great. . . and shall send him, when he is *hors de combat*, to England as her ambassador. In his suite he shall have a girl whom he shall have rescued during one of his northern campaigns, who shall be in love with him, and he not with her.

You see I am true to Nature in making the advances come from the females. I shall next draw a town and country life at home, which will give me room for life, manners, scenery, &c. I will make him neither a dandy in town, nor a fox-hunter in the country. He shall get into all sorts of scrapes, and at length end his career in France. Poor Juan shall be guillotined in the French Revolution.[32]

It is clear from this conversation that the possibility of the Sultana's elopement with Juan, which the reader momentarily considers, was considered by Byron, and the mysterious other woman in Canto VII may be her ghost within the poem. We may be surprised too how detailed a sense Byron has of the future incidents, topography and general balance of the next cantos. These features, or many of them. survive in the poem as we have it but the manner of their narration has suffered a sea-change.

In the conversation with Medwin, Juan's adventures are picaresque, single-toned and at a regular fictional distance from the reader. In the poem, the unbridged gap between harem and siege destroys this distance and, in doing so, subordinates the Sultana's passion, imagined elopement and the convenient plague to the sterner contingencies of history and the poem. Byron may have learnt something of this intertwining of romance fiction with historical necessity from Scott's novels but the procedure here is original and profoundly in keeping with the evolving character of *Don Juan*. What we learn from Medwin's account, which gives us some of the facts but none of the feel of the poem, is to recognise Byron's sureness of judgement in allowing into the poem only those features of his projection for it which do not limit its peculiarly exposed vitality. We might say that however delightful the continuation of *Don Juan* projected in Medwin's account, Byron himself would learn nothing in writing it whereas *Don Juan* engages us because we do not only find out what Byron knows but also what he is learning. Gaps here are evidence of the deepest fictional strategy and of a relentless integrity which Byron's reported conversation is careful neither to name nor hint. We see too the disadvantages or relying on too clear-cut a sense of the identity or disjunction of the author and the narrator of

Don Juan. The 'real' Byron reported by Medwin is much like the 'fictional' narrator but is clearly not big enough to be, though he may temporarily represent, the author of *Don Juan*. The author of *Don Juan* is more present and disclosed to its attentive reader than he was to his would-be Boswell for whom he sketched an agreeable fiction. In the poem on the other hand,

> Besides, my Muse by no means deals in fiction:
> She gathers a repertory of facts,

(XIV, 13)

Byron points here, as so often, to the importance which he attaches to facts in themselves[33] and, more generally, he is claiming to be a moralist, not just a maker of fictions. But, as we have already seen, Byron's views on fiction are more complex than this:

> Apologue, fable, poesy and parable,
> Are false, but may be render'd also true

(XV, 89)

I want to argue that the gaps in *Don Juan*, such as the gap between Juan's fictional sojourn in the Seraglio and his participation in a real siege, are a device for rendering fiction 'true'. For if Juan's escape were to be written up in the customary picaresque fashion, as in Medwin's account, he would then be contained by a wholly fictional world. He might thereby acquire the solidity of Emma Bovary and move us by the lying verisimilitude of art but he would not engage us directly with the force, *hors* any possible *texte*, which moves the poem and the reader forwards in the very act of offering us art's instructive and pleasurable stillness.

It will be seen at once that if the poem is not simply a mimesis of life but is, so to say, as directly impelled by it as it is possible for a work of art, remaining a work of art, to be, then the termination of the poem by the real death of Byron, which we have established at the outset, is a necessary consequence of its procedure. The latency for such an interruption, which we examined in the Ravenna commandant section, is confirmation of this. We might say, accurately, if a little picturesquely, that Death could slip into and claim anyone of the gaps in the poem or establish one for himself. Each miraculous revival of *Don Juan* draws sustenance from an absence to which it will eventually succumb.

When we find Juan in the beseiging Russian army without any

detailed fictional link with the Seraglio we experience, directly, the disturbing identity of Juan's happy commingling with 'the lovely Odalisques' (VI, 29) and his joining

> In such good company as always throng
> To battles, sieges, and that kind of pleasure,
>
> (VIII, 24)

It is the context and associations, not the drive, which distinguishes 'ogling all their charms from breasts to backs' (VI, 28) and rushing 'where the thickest fire announced most foes' (VIII, 32). We could know this through a story and it is, in any case, pointed out to us in the most explicit way by the narrator (VIII, 111-15, IX, 55-7, 65) but the gap in the text puts us in touch not with a warning fable or a known truth but the thing itself. This is, in effect, Byron's claim in his letter to Kinnaird: 'is it not *life*, is it not *the thing*?' In a similar way, music may take advantage of a real and permanently available silence but so shape that silence by its own occasioning that we hear simultaneously a space now wholly consumed by musical use yet still existing in its pristine state. Art and sculpture provide similar parallels but I find it hard to find a close parallel in another literary text except in a hybrid such as the masque.[34]

It is here that the conversational flow of the narrator and the analogies between love-making and writing poetry, which Byron seems to take seriously, may be reconciled. The narrator's conversation is a very specialised affair and is available to later adjustment but it comes from wherever ordinary conversation comes from: 'I never know the word which will come next.' (IX, 41). It proceeds by leaps and gaps which can reclaim what they appear to abandon. Conversation does not know the truths which are discovered through its unregarded dialectic but it constantly proffers a present and available mystery which Philosophy 'too much rejects'. (XV, 89) It is in the gaps and jumps of the narrator's artfully mirrored consciousness that we come into closest contact with Lord George Gordon Byron himself for he does not know, yet makes available, the sources on which he relies. He gives himself away: 'To withdraw *myself* from *myself* (oh that cursed selfishness!) has ever been my sole, my entire, my sincere motive in scribbling at all:' (Journal, 27th November, 1813). The flow of sexual life, when it is not interrupted and self-regarding, involves a similar intensification yet yielding of consciousness and selfhood. There is no 'life of passion' and Byron's *Don Juan* is not written with the deliberated erotics of

Richard Strauss. Quite the reverse. Nor, despite the glancing allusions to Lady Byron, Sotheby, etc, is *Don Juan* a form of memoirs or confessions. If it were then, however sentimental the matter, the vantage-point could only be a knowing one and, like the letters, we would encounter Byron only in the bravura of his roles.

It should be admitted that not all gaps in *Don Juan* are as clear as that between the Seraglio and the Siege. The narrative here necessitates Juan's escape. This is a normal and often dramatised activity of Don Juan Tenorio which reveals both his heartlessness and his will for survival. Byron's Juan, on the other hand, can never escape of his own volition. Here, unthinkably for Tenorio, he is helped by the woman with whom he has slept and she escapes with him. Yet the freedom from the past which Don Juan Tenorio seeks ruthlessly but, finally, in vain is conferred unsought on Juan. We are not allowed to see this mechanism too closely, hence the size of the gap between the Seraglio and the Siege. Elsewhere in the poem, we do see Juan's escape from Julia's bedroom, knocking down a husband or two in the best *el burlador* fashion, but he is found out and sent away in a perfunctory four stanzas (I, 118-21) which are then buried and lost in 22 stanzas of digression which conclude Canto I.

When we see Juan in Canto II standing 'bewilder'd, on the deck' (II, 13) the effect is more like a new scene in a drama than a continuously unfolding fiction. Here, and the effect is even more marked in the sudden dispatch of Juan to sea after Lambro's return, Byron's strategy is best understood as a frail counterpointing of picaresque continuity superimposed upon the resilient and more discernible ground bass of dramatic technique cutting from one scene to another in the manner of the 'pantomime' Don Juan. The debt of Byron's poem to eighteenth-century novel is well established[35] but the history of picaresque novels themselves is closely tied up with the theatre.[36] Though the biographical genesis of *Don Juan* can be traced to confessional fragments,[37] it only gets under way when Byron abandons this linear model and re-employs the dramatic juxtapositions and sudden leaps which he had used in *Childe Harold's Pilgrimage* but which he now adapts to a different kind of emblematic narrative.

It cannot be repeated too often that Byron's greatest investment in dramatic writing coincides with *Don Juan*. In his supreme long poem, however, Byron uses the gaps that are a normal part of stage fiction for his own original purposes which attach the enigma and energy of his fictions to the real space which interrupts, founds and confounds them so that we encounter a free history. The gaps are more extreme in *Don*

Juan than in a stage performance, for a new scene in a play still forms part of a single whole but in Byron's poem a clearly developing fictional life is suddenly arrested and then replaced by another.

The centre of each new episode is either Eros or, in shipwreck and siege, Death. We do not see this clearly at first because the narrative is so often interrupted by digressions that it appears to be far more haphazard than it is and digressions are commonly used in stories in order to imply some duration in narrative episodes.[38] The major episodes of *Don Juan*, however, are not stitched to one another in this linear fashion but are, as it were, renewed immediately from the same starting point. This process cannot in itself reach any terminus.

When Shelley wrote of *Don Juan* that 'Nothing has ever been written like it in English'[39] he was, as usual in matters of verse, right but Byron understood literary tradition far more profoundly than Shelley. He has the capacity to awaken past precedents into new and living forms. He is not, by clear and conscious inclination, like 'The isles of Greece' poet who

> . . . praised the present, and abused the past
> Reversing the good custom of old days,

(III, 79)

We should not neglect the most obvious of *Don Juan's* many precedents. It is announced in the first stanza:

> I'll therefore take our ancient friend Don Juan,
> We all have seen him in the Pantomine
> Sent to the devil, somewhat ere his time

(I, 1)

Which version of the old play Byron had seen is not very important. It is the basic dramatic structure of opera, play or pantomime that matters. Teresa Guiccioli's sense that Byron's Don Juan and the Don Giovanni of the opera were 'the same person' is wrong but not misleading. I am indebted here to a study by H.G. Tan[40] which asks and painstakingly answers the question why the story of Don Juan Tenorio occurs in many forms and languages but infrequently as a successful novel. M. Tan argues that the gaps in Tirso's play, as Don Juan Tenorio flees from one seduction to another, constitute its character. No single act of seduction is constitutive or privileged. Repeated acts and flights give the sense, he argues, of Don Juan Tenorio's whole life and of its

essential character ('furor sexualis'). Hence the unqualified appropriateness of the final judgement upon that life in the arrival of the stone
guest. Tirso's play derives directly from medieval drama. In novels, on
the other hand, the emblematic stereotype of Don Juan, multiple
victims, and final avenger is replaced by an individuated sequence of
mere affairs with different women in each of whom we take a separate
interest. Consequently the avenger theme is minimised or omitted altogether:

> Le canevas des relations à remplir est devenu différent et la
> nature des relations amoureuses, devenues plus explicitement
> émotionelles ou affectives, n'admettent pas l'existence d'une statue
> vengeresse on châtiant.[41]

Hence, argues M. Tan, the essential 'matière' of the Don Juan story is
destroyed if he is pitched into the wholly (therefore merely) fictional
world of the novel. Byron's *Don Juan* seems to belong on both sides of
this divide. His Don Juan is not a seducer and does not flee, but the
structure of the poem does depend upon gaps which represent the
whole character of the drives in Juan and prevent their encirclement by
some all-containing fictional whole. Nevertheless Julia, Haidée,
Gulbeyaz, etc. are individuated and interesting figures. There is no stone
guest but the Black Friar and Byron's death impart an existential
frisson to characters and readers alike. Clearly Byron's poem draws on
both dramatic and novel traditions. In so far as Eros is a drive, a 'furor
sexualis', then dramatic structure is helpful; in so far as Eros is reciprocated in relationships 'émotionelles ou affectives' then the tender interi-
ority of the novel will prevail. We should not dissolve all our interpreta-
tive problems away, however, by such decent compromises. The
difficulty with *Don Juan* is that whereas we know what to do with
Tirso's *El burlador de Sevilla* or with Charlotte Bronte's *Villette*,
it is much less clear how we are to read *Don Juan*. In default of
such clarity, unhappy adjustments, condescension and widespread
throwing in the sponge displace affectionate analyses much as
follows.

The first two cantos of *Don Juan* present us with an amusing picaresque farce and a less amusing, less picaresque, shipwreck. Haidée and
Juan's love-affair then dominates the poem and, despite Byron's delicate qualifications, it is customary to react to the tenderness and
warmth of their coupling with an unambiguous tenacity as though the

poem's undoubted romanticism and marked satirical thrust simply coincide in the natural idyll of the island. If the poem does not then stay with Haidée, perhaps she represents some unattainable ideal which can linger in the subsequent debasements of Seraglio, Siege and St Petersburg in order to provide Romance corroboration of their satire. Or perhaps the poem is really satirical in essence and the narrative is merely a function of that bluff commonsense so often accorded the poet. The narrator must then be the centre of this almost twentieth-century masterpiece which is nevertheless almost attaining the form of the nineteenth-century novel in its interrupted final episode in Norman Abbey. The poem, in my experience, is often read more or less like this. It is enjoyed but ungrasped. Why should this be so?

Part of the answer is that the women in *Don Juan* increasingly represent a dramatic sequence but do not initially appear as such, Haidée, as it were, refuses to be simply number two between numbers one and three and the poem, as we shall see, in the end supports her. Secondly, as women rather than Juan initiate the affairs of love, it is harder to see the single force so unmistakably active in Don Juan Tenorio. Each woman too is particularised and inheres in a convincingly imagined setting. However, as the love-episodes multiply, the common force which binds them and the emblematic character of their differentiation, should appear. In both, Byron is the moralist which he always claims to be. Hence the extreme simplication of Catharine at the end of the first sequence of ladies as the unconstrained 'amorous sphere' itself, which cannot be missed by the reader, is a natural consequence of the poem's procedural clarification but is so on a scale and with such concomitants that we are freshly bewildered.

Here again M. Tan's thesis is helpful to the reader of Byron. He is concerned with Don Juan Tenorio's satanic destructiveness and inability to form lasting relationships:

Il est remarquable que les personnes qui vivent sous l'empire de Satan ne sont pas à même d'avoir des relations durables avec d'autres: il est toujours question de liens qu'on rompt, d'une relation rompue . . . [42]

l'homme-diable qui détruit tout ce qu'il rencontre, qui, bravant Dieu et les forces célestes, finit par sombrer dans le néant qu'il a créé.[43]

If Don Juan Tenorio constantly breaks relationships, destroys all whom he encounters and founders in the nothingness which he has created, Byron's Don Juan wills nothing of the kind. The pattern, however, discerned more and more clearly as both proceed, is the same. Relationships are broken, waste and destruction follow in the Dons' progress. In Byron's poem, women are at least as much the emblem of this process as Don Juan himself. Finally in that Catharine to whom Suvarrow offers up the fruits of the Siege ('"Glory to God and the Empress"', VIII, 135), wasting a world (IX, 56) and 'juicy| vigour' (IX, 72) coincide. We cannot therefore blame this on Juan nor even on Catharine. It is Eros itself which, drawing Juan and poem along by its wonderful energies, also builds up such piles of contaminated waste as the integral by-products of its lauded process that we come to doubt the value of these energies. When these same energies, drastically reduced in scope, persist in the ghastly chirpiness of the independent narrator who carries on talking across the largest gap in the poem in order to conceal, by a flimsy connecting narrative, the absence of renewed action in a purported change of scene, we may feel that Byron's claim for the vital truth of his fiction, 'is it not *life*, is it not the *thing*?', is tainted beyond redemption. Don Juan Tenorio's analogous chirpiness will heap whole coals of fire on his own head and thus confirms the genre which he instances, but by implicating Women, Life, Thought and the Art of the poem in this tainting, Byron appears to yield the comic foundations of *Don Juan*. The narrator's readiness to supply a network of transitions to take Juan from St Petersburg across the Continent and on to London replaces 'is it not *life*' by the realist fiction of an armchair satirist.

One must say therefore that Eros is not a drive which can be separately discerned in the poem as it might be in a work of music. If it were so, the note of yearning, incompleteness and suffering would inevitably characterise the poem and foreclose any relationship to Shakespearian or Dantesque comedy. The note which Byron's contemporaries so relentlessly isolated in the Paolo and Francesca episode of the *Divine Comedy*[44] is always side-stepped in *Don Juan*. Yet the gaps in its text make clear, and, in a way, present to the reader the Eros-based and repetitive character of Juan's adventures. Their symmetry is not occasioned by Juan's imposition of his simplifying will on diverse circumstances as with Don Juan Tenorio. Hence it is the circumstances themselves, in all their unforeseen contingency, which must carry some natural tendency to produce those kinds of proximity which provoke and promote the glow of conscious union. The forward movement of the poem itself is clearly analogous to this. Hence, precisely because we do not separately discern it, we attribute the character of Eros to the process of the poem rather than to Juan. This is contrary to what we do with Don Juan Tenorio but it is not unlike the given movement of love (Agape rather than Eros) which impels fiction, characters, readers and cosmos across the divisions of Dante's masterpiece. For the same reason, the Death which will interrupt Juan Tenorio's progress applies here not to Juan but to the author of the poem's process.

With this more detailed sense of the basic narrative devices of *Don Juan* and their demise in the narrator's cantos we can resume our customary vantage-point at the end of the poem.

III

The questions which now remain to confront us are these. How is narrative reconstituted in *Don Juan*? Does the separation of Aurora, Lady Adeline and the Duchess of Fitz-Fulke confirm the divisions which began with the Sultana and Dudù and make another Haidée impossible? Is the Duchess of Fitz-Fulke, that new Venus Genetrix, to be seen as the 'laughter-loving' muse of Comedy or as another Catharine 'killer of men'?

Byron's own death interrupts the poem and leaves a gap which the narrator will no more bridge than anyone will ever return and explain to the 'little town' in Keats's 'Ode on a Grecian Urn' why it is so 'desolate'. The Norman Abbey section is the fullest narrative episode in the poem and yet it remains, like the ruined Abbey, a fragment which we cannot fully interpret without timorous guess work as to the whole of which it forms a part. We should, however, be able to characterise its interrupted process sufficiently to answer our questions. Another difficulty is Aurora, who holds the key to some of the questions and will warrant a chapter of her own. With these provisos we can now try to conclude our present argument.

We can see at once that Eros does not lie at the centre of Norman Abbey. Unacknowledged in Juan's education, Eros yet dominates Seville ('Famous for oranges and women', I,8), Greek island, Seraglio, St Petersburg and, in distorted form, the Siege where

> For one rough, weather-beaten, veteran body,
> You'll find ten thousand handsome coxcombs bloody.
>
> (VIII, 112)

Norman Abbey, however, begins as an extension of the English society satirised in Cantos X to XII. Byron gives a representative sense of different classes, age groups and sexes:

> The gentlemen got up betimes to shoot,
> Or hunt: the young, because they liked the sport —
> The first thing boys like, after play and fruit:
> The middle-aged to make the day more short;
>
> (XIII, 101)
>
> The elderly walked through the library,
>
> (XIII, 103)
>
> The Ladies — some rouged, some a little pale —
> Met the morn as they might. If fine, they rode,
> Or walked; if foul they read or told a tale,
>
> (XIII, 104)

In this sequence, only the boys who, in Byron's witty and almost unobserved quibble,

> . . . liked the sport —
> The first thing boys like, after play and fruit:

appear to be motivated by Eros before settling into the serious boredom of maturity. It is not a central drive underlying a whole society. The ladies write voluminous letters, 'For some had absent lovers, all had friends.' (XIII, 105). Sisterhood appears to be more ubiquitous than Love. The house itself judges Eros unsympathetically. The unnamed, pregnant girl in a scarlet cloak who is brought before Lord Henry, a magistrate, is left waiting forlornly in the great hall whilst he bustles about on other business (XVI, 61-8). The inhabitants of the house represent a diffused image of power in the provinces which is related back to the smaller, but likewise diffused, group who dominate London. Byron, needless to say, was unsympathetic to absolute government but Sultanas, Empresses and fisher-princesses enable him to associate the Eros-drives of individuals with centres of power. In the oligarchy of Regency England, Eros is presented as a love-less diversion. The vigour of young nobles in London, 'in a thousand arms is dissi-

pated;' (XI, 75). Marriage, however, is of central importance for it preserves the oligarchy and is bound up with the transmission of property.

The narrative action of the last cantos emerges out of this satirical
perspective. It is initiated by Lady Adeline's desire to find a marriage
partner for Juan. She has two forces to contend with here. Eros, in the
evident shape of Fitz-Fulke, is making an independent bid for Juan
who, as Adeline discerns, 'was unlikely to resist' (XIV, 60). Marriage
therefore will divert Eros into acceptable social channels just as Lord
Henry and Lady Adeline have themselves displaced the erotic basis of
their relationship by a studied and socially admired correctness. The
other enemy whom Lady Adeline fears is Aurora Raby. More of her
later. But we can provisionally say that the Amundeville's Norman
Abbey is hostile to Nature and to Grace though the epigram is offered
in advance of the arguments to underpin it. Thus the idea of marriage
which it commends, unconnected with these two staple forms of value -
generating life, is the antithesis of that idea of marriage, nourished by
both, which is celebrated in Shakespearian and other comedy. It is
worthwhile distinguishing 'the Amundeville's Norman Abbey' from
Norman Abbey for, as Lady Adeline's ballad of the Black Friar tells us,

> But beware! beware! of the Black Friar,
> He still retains his sway,
> For he is yet the church's heir
> Who ever may be the lay.
> Amundeville is lord by day,
> But the monk is lord by night;

Lady Adeline's rational initiative, and its unconscious source in her
attraction to Juan, would constitute action of a kind that could be contained within the satirical framework set up by the narrator in the
cantos since the Siege. It is answered, however, by initiatives of quite
other kinds.

The Duchess of Fitz-Fulke is, of course, to wrest control of the plot
away from Lady Adeline's conscious strategy but does not do so by
any rationally pondered scheme of her own. As we saw at the beginning
of this chapter, if we attend to the narrative as closely as Byron again
requires us to, it is plain that the first appearance of the ghost is authentic and the Duchess's scheme is a quick-witted improvisation in response to this unforeseen occurrence. Where others react with dread to
the haunting, the Duchess foresees mischief and sex. Hence we must say
that it is the appearance of the Black Friar that first occasions and

authenticates the renewed possibility of adventitious incident on which, at the very end of the poem as earlier, the resurrections of erotic life depend.

By answering our first question in this way, we can now immediately see the answers to most of the others. For if Death, in the evident shape of the Black Friar, can, whilst retaining his terror, offer guise and opportunity to Eros, then the anti-comic connection between Eros and Death established with the Siege and Catharine is stood on its head. To stand this connection on its head is precisely the function of comedy and it is announced by the burst of laughter, comic not satiric, with which the reader greets the recognition of the disguised Fitz-Fulke. Such laughter is not heard in the day-time world of the Amundeville's Norman Abbey and it has not been heard in the poem for many cantos.

So precise and central is this dramatic emblem of renewed comic life, foregrounded by the abrupt ending of Canto XVI and the near termination of the poem, that we may be in some danger of celebrating the amorous sphere simply on the Duchess's terms.[45] Now that all standard editions of the poem conclude with the 14 stanzas of Canto XVII, however, we are unlikely to do this and the attentive reader should be at least as thoughtful as Juan himself here. Clearly the connection of the Duchess with Death, mischief and laughter, re-establish life-giving connections unavailable since St Petersburg but the very force which brings this about (the ghost) underlies and confirms the authenticity of Aurora's quite other life as we shall see. Hence, while there may be sufficient connections to refound comic narrative, the jarring questions posed by earlier cantos are not simply put aside but referred to an altogether new perspective. In this way, the poem again spirals forwards whilst retaining contact with what it supersedes.

Two other factors need to be included. The replacement of autocratic society by an oligarchic one certainly helps us to put aside the doubts occasioned by Catharine's unconstrained amorousness. By making Juan visit the free yet law-abiding society which is in clearest contradistinction to illiberal Ottoman or Russian regimes and then showing the coldness, selfishness and boredom of that society, Byron blurs the memory of that distinction upon which our condemnation of Seraglio and St Petersburg depended and re-awakens our sympathy for the known warmth of Eros.

Finally, though we have in this chapter and its predecessor separated the narrator's evolution from the fortunes of narrative, we cannot wholly do so. They are separated formally and the vocabulary of the one differs from that of the other but, as I have tried to show, both fictions and reflections in *Don Juan* leap across gaps which pre-exist the configurations imposed upon them and lend the actuality and energy latent in their enigmatic blankness to the fleeting colours of Byron's verse. Juan's Eros-enforced 'Yes' dwindles into the 'No' of his St Petersburg sickness. The narrator's own vitality ransacking 'le néant qu'il a créé' (to use again M. Tan's formula for 'l'homme-diable') encounters a present, immediate nothingness not of his fashioning. This nothingness nevertheless, without any intermediate stage or discernible transition, may be trusted as boundless replenishment, just as the ghost in a flash becomes flesh and blood. If this is so, and the argument of Chapter 2 depends on it, then even before the narrative's revival we are prepared for the confidence which it announces. That confidence may be put like this. Beyond the taintings, both of human experience and the immediate driving forces which move us, there are, simply available but not susceptible of separate articulation, untainted sources.

My argument is moving in a religious direction as openly as the poem is. The clear association of Aurora's untainted nature with her religious mode of being is surprising but, once understood, inevitable, as is Lady Adeline's distaste for her and the Duchess. Aurora exactly prescribes for us what our reaction to the Duchess should be. If there are untainted sources, then the old comic confidence can flow back into wonder before 'something much like flesh and blood'. Yet if these untainted sources are mediated in a world characterised by Catharine's destructiveness and London's boredom then Eros may both represent and, at the same time, sully the untainted. This insight will sufficiently authorise enthusiasm for the Duchess but warrant a necessary reservation.

We can say then that since Eros is clearly a force in *Don Juan* and yet it is not simply in Juan himself as it is in Tenorio, nor simply to be recognised in the 'go-between' yearning of most European love-literature, the question about the provenance, value, status and origin of its glowing life must be referred back to the adventitious yet repetitive circumstances upon which the poem and its similarly generated readers depend. It is a question whether the force inherent in these circumstances can be trusted to carry the poem forward beyond its tainted terminations with that kind of accompanying laughter which signifies untainted renewal. We may now add that it is some sort of comic law here that we cannot have a restoration of what we have lost without some manner of ascent. We lost a Mamillius and gain a Perdita. We would not so readily forget Julia and the horrors of shipwreck if we did not at once recognise both the superior force and the identical glow of Haidée's isle. Ascent is then apparently abandoned and Haidée's refusal to be one instance in a dramatic series seems to be unsupported by the continuing poem. Without ascent, we are left with an erotic sequence which inevitably deteriorates into Ismail and Catharine and cannot be immediately continued. When therefore we do again laugh not at the narrator's cerebral athletics but in delighted approval of the present flesh and blood of the blonde 'Intrigante', almost ridiculously free from that taint of Death which her monastic disguise would suggest, we must do so because some kind of ascent is authorising this restoration. This cannot be evidenced in the Duchess herself who, already in the next canto, is seen in a different and unco-operating light. We should find evidence of ascent and restoration simultaneously which will mean that the poem should regain contact with the lost Haidée, more thoroughly apprehend what was lost, and yet transcend the earlier values.

It is evident that we can no longer stay within the amorous sphere nor keep Aurora Raby out of the discussion of *Don Juan*. If the logic of Chapters 2 and 3 is right, she will herself unlock the logic of the poem for us.

Notes

1. See the famous notes to A.C. Bradley, *Shakespearian Tragedy* (London, 1904).

2. There would be no purpose in the Duchess's request for detail if she had already masqueraded successfully as the Friar. I cannot agree therefore with Professor McGann who argues that the story 'makes no judgement upon the existence of the ghost', though he acknowledges that 'the entire incident makes no negative pronouncement on spiritual phenomena. The legend of the abbey's ghost is real enough, in the story, and remains unexploded by Byron's comedy.' J.J. McGann, *Don Juan in Context* (London, 1976), pp. 135, 137.

3. S. Kirkegaard, *Either-Or*, trans. D.F. Swanson and Lillian Swanson (Princeton, 1949), vol. I, p. 80.

4. Earlier, when Juan is pursuing the 'ghost', his veins are said to be 'no longer cold, but heated' (XVI, 119).

5. Swinburne compares Adeline to the characters of Laclos. C.K. Hyder (ed.), *Swinburne as Critic* (London, 1972), p. 47. |

6. 'Freeze or glow', for example, is a Petrarchan conceit of considerable staying power. See Leonard Forster, *The Icy Fire: five studies in European Petrarchism* (London, 1969).

7. Carl Kerenyi, *The Gods of the Greeks* (Harmondsworth, 1958), pp. 70-1 ('Aphrodite's Surnames').

8. Not everyone agrees. Leslie Marchand, *Byron's Poetry* (London, 1965), p. 192 describes the narrative in these cantos as 'careless and pedestrian'. Andrew Rutherford, *Byron*, (Edinburgh, 1962), has only perfunctory references to Cantos

V and VI but has many pages on the Siege.

9. Bernard Blackstone compares *Don Juan* to *Midsummer Night's Dream* in *Byron: A Survey* (London, 1975), p. 290.

10. 'The merit of *Don Juan* does not lie in any part, but in the whole. There is in that great poem an especial and exquisite balance and sustenance of alternate tones which cannot be expressed or explained by the utmost ingenuity of selection.' Hyder (ed.), *Swinburne as Critic*, p. 39.

11. IX, 56, *Byron's Don Juan: A Variorum Edition*, T.G. Steffan and W.W. Pratt (eds.), (4 vols. Austin, Texas, 1957), vol. III, p. 210.

12. E.g. G.M. Ridenour, *The Style of Don Juan* (New Haven, 1960), p. 81.

13. We can trace Byron's insistence upon a glowing interaction between lovers to his early poems, e.g. 'To Caroline' ('You say you love, and yet your eye'). In stanzas 3 and 5, for instance, Byron complains:

3
Whene'er we meet, my blushes rise,
And mantle though my purpled cheek,
But yet no blush to mine replies,
Nor do those eyes your love bespeak.
. . .

5
For e'en your lip seems steep'd in snow,
And, though so oft it meets my kiss,
It burns with no responsive glow,
Nor Melts, like mine, in dewy bliss.

These verses of 1806, and others arising from Byron's flirtations at Southwell, have evident continuity with the concerns, and even the diction, of Eros in *Don Juan* but their awkward lyricism is countered and heightened by the surge and irony of Byron's narrative.

14. E.g. 'The style had from his earliest years been ready to his hand in *Letters and Journals*.' Ronald Boattrall, 'Byron and the Colloquial Tradition in English Poetry' in M.H. Abrams (ed.), *English Romantic Poets* (New York, 1960), p. 214.

15. *Byron's Letters and Journals*, Leslie Marchand (ed.) (12 vols. London, 1973-81), vol. 6, p. 5, to Murray, 8th January, 1818.

16. T.J.B. Spencer, *Byron and the Greek Tradition*, Byron Foundation Lecture (Nottingham, 1959), p. 6. See, for instance, Vivian da Sola Pinto, *The Restoration Court Poets* (London, 1965), pp. 21, 40. F.M. Doherty in *Byron* (London, 1968), pp. 155-6, describes the narrator as a 'gentleman-rake'.

17. *Letters and Journals*, vol. 6, p. 231, to Kinnaird, 26th October, 1818.

18. Ibid., vol. 18, p. 55, to Moore, 2nd January, 1821.

19. Ibid., vol. 3, p. 225, Journal, 27th November, 1813.

20. Ibid., vol. 8, p. 146, to Moore, 5th July, 1821.

21. Ibid., vol. 7, p. 217, to Murray, 4th November, 1820.

22. Ibid., vol. 7, p. 225, to Murray, 9th November, 1820.

23. John Jones, *John Keat's dream of truth* (London, 1969), *passim*. It is not perhaps surprising that the onanistic model for literary creativity associated with Rousseau's *Confessions* is, in the writings of Jacques Derrida and advanced circles generally, now considered normative. Byron's deployment of voice tone and the narrator's sustained conversation with the reader are at odds with Keats's production of a *texte* whose rifts are extensively loaded with ore.

24. Paul West, *Byron and the Spoiler's Art* (London, 1960), p. 62. See also M.G. Cooke's excellent comments on rhyme in *The Blind Man Traces the Circle*

(Princeton, 1969), pp. 150-2, and *Variorum*, vol. 1, pp. 170-6.

25. The quotation is given as in the first edition of the *Variorum*. Quotation marks should be closed after "Kiss.

26. This is self-evidently true of New Comedy and Shakespearian Comedy, less obviously true of Aristophanic Comedy and the sacred bawdy of archetypal comic festivities which Byron recalls and utilises in his account of Venetian carnival in *Beppo*. In these cases, narrative is obviously much less prominent.

27. See the reservations above in note 26.

28. A.V. Kernan in *The Plot of Satire* (New Haven and London, 1965), p. 176, calls this the '"but then" movement'.

29. A deliberate exception to this is the death of the Tartar Khan (VIII, 104-19) which is Byron's tribute to epic values and style in the midst of anti-epic narration. G.M. Ridenour, *Don Juan*, p. 111 argues that the last cantos of *Don Juan* are epic in character. Brian Wilkie in *Romantic Poets and Epic Tradition* (Madison and Milwaukee, 1965) mentions the Khan briefly (p. 207) and claims that the whole poem works within epic tradition but is 'The Epic of Negation' (pp. 188-226).

30. Spenser scholars must pardon this simplification of a very great poem.

31. E.g. 'June the sixth' (I, 121); 'Mr. Mann of London' (II, 129); 'fifteen hundred dollars' (IV, 114); 'Scherematoff and Chrematoff, Koklophti // Koclobski, Kourakin, and Mouskin Pouskin' (VII, 17), etc. There are fewer 'facts' of this kind in the narrator's cantos for the reasons suggested in Chapter 2.

32. *Medwin's Conversations of Lord Byron*, Ernest J. Lovell, Jr. (ed.) (Princeton, 1966) pp. 164-5.

33. See Anne Barton, *Byron and the Mythology of Fact*, Byron Foundation Lecture (Nottingham, 1968) and M.G. Cooke 'Byron and the World of Fact' in *The Blind Man*, pp. 91-127.

34. Dante's *The Divine Comedy*, Swift's *Gulliver's Travels*, Tennyson's *In Memoriam*, Lermontov's *A Hero of Our Times*, Pushkin's *Eugene Onegin* and T.S. Eliot's *Four Quartets* could be adduced as analogies to *Don Juan*'s use of gaps to suggest or instance actuality but their gaps function in more straightforward ways. W.P. Ker, never one to use words lightly, commented: 'Byron's poetry is alive; so full of life indeed that it threatens other more dignified sorts of poetry.' (W.P. Ker, *Collected Essays* (London, 1925), pp. 210-16).

35. See Andras Horn, *Byron's Don Juan and the Eighteenth Century Novel*, (Bern, 1962). Karl Kroeber argues that *Don Juan* is essentially a novel in *Romantic Narrative Art* (Madison, 1960). See also John Speirs, *Poetry towards Novel* (London, 1971), pp. 201-82.

36. Le Sage, for instance, wrote over 60 plays. Fielding's early experience as a dramatist is evident in his novels.

37. Elizabeth Boyd, *Byron's Don Juan* (New Brunswick, 1945), pp. 11-13.

38. The grandest example is Books V to VIII of Milton's *Paradise Lost* in which Raphael's answers to Adam's questions constitute a massive, if wholly relevant, digression which, paradoxically, gives the reader the sense that he has been in Paradise for some considerable time.

39. Letter to Byron, 21st October, 1821 in F.L. Jones (ed.), *The Letters of Percy Bysshe Shelley* (London, 1964), II. 323.

40. H.G. Tan, *La matière de Don Juan et les genres litteraires* (Leyde, 1976).

41. Ibid., p. 124.

42. Ibid., p. 34.

43. Ibid., p. 12.

44. See, for instance, Leigh Hunt, *The Story of Rimini* (1817). Byron himself translated the Paolo and Francesca episode in the *Inferno*. Dante's vignette is the most celebrated literary example of proximity and glow but it cannot be accorded

the central space allotted to it by nineteenth-century taste because of the serenely formal disposition of Dante's poem and its successful sublimation of Eros into Agape. In Byron's apparently haphazard comedy, where such sublimation is customarily seen as hypocrisy, Eros can, for much of the time, occupy this central space. In the end, however, the character and even the direction of *Don Juan* are closer to *The Divine Comedy* than they are to *The Story of Rimini*. Byron clearly admired Dante but, rather as in his attitude to Shakespeare, could also be caustic about him (see *Medwin's Conversations*, p. 161 n. 378).

45. Professor G. Wilson Knight, whose courageous and profound reading of Byron in darker days should always find an answering respect, may nevertheless be of the Duchess's party without knowing it. He writes of the Black Friar's transformation: ' . . . it is Byron's equivalent to Shakespeare's resurrection of Hermione in *The Winter's Tale*'. G. Wilson Knight, 'The Two Eternities' in *The Burning Oracle* (London, 1939), reprinted in *Poets of Action* (London, 1967) from which I quote (p. 254). Kernan, *Satire*, makes a similar simplification (p. 199) which will be examined in Chapter 4.

4 AURORA RABY

Aurora Raby surprises the reader of *Don Juan*. The vocabulary we employed in the last chapter will enable us to point to one element in this surprise with some precision. Aurora is a heroine who does not glow as her predecessors glow and is not a natural participant in glowing interchange:

> But what confused him more than smile or stare
> . . .
> Was, that he caught Aurora's eye on his,
> And something like a smile upon her cheek.
>
> . . .
> 'Twas a mere quiet smile of contemplation
> Indicative of some surprise and pity;
> And Juan grew carnation with vexation,
>
> . . .
> But what was bad, she did not blush in turn,
> Nor seem embarrassed — quite the contrary;
> Her aspect was as usual, still — *not* stern —
> And she withdrew, but cast not down her eye,
> Yet grew a little pale —with what? Concern?
> I know not; but her colour n'er was high —
> Though sometimes faintly flushed — and always clear,
> As deep seas in a Sunny Atmosphere.
>
> (XVI, 91, 92, 93, 94)

One possible interpretation of this lack of glow in Aurora is that of Lady Adeline whose judgement is often echoed by critics:

> She marvell'd "what he saw in such a baby
> As that prim, silent, cold Aurora Raby?"
>
> (XV, 49)

This judgement cannot possibly be right. No statement introduced by 'But what was bad' ('But what was bad, she did not blush in turn') can be straightforwardly bad in *Don Juan*. The tone will not allow it. The potentially worrying coldness of Aurora is, in any case, subtly associ-

137

ated here with depth, clarity and openness to cosmic warmth:

> . . . but her colour ne'er was high —
> Though sometimes faintly flushed — and always clear,
> As deep seas in a Sunny Atmosphere.

The flush here is not that of Aurora's natural life, to be readily awakened into the mutual flame of love, but is a direct reflection of the vast, distant sources of all natural life and warmth. Her stillness is the condition of this vital receptivity and stands in manifest contrast to the inert bustle of the house and its guests, the unacknowledged frustration of Lady Adeline, and the welcome but too mechanical glow of the Duchess of Fitz-Fulke.

Concepts of this kind should force us to enlarge our sense of what the poem is dealing with, instead of which critics and readers have too often preferred to follow Lady Adeline's lead and use a prematurely settled sense of the poem's values to situate Aurora, and thus ignore her. We should instead ascertain what the poem is by taking seriously what it becomes. Nineteenth-century readers of *Don Juan* were characteristically shocked by the poem's immorality and blasphemy. Twentieth-century readers, happy with sex, siege and shipwreck, are more likely to be shocked by the poem's morality and may be insensitive or hostile to its underlying orientation. A valuable anaesthetic aid here is Hazlitt's phrase 'a poem written about itself'[1] which suggests to the modern Western ear what it already wishes to hear, that a multi-policity of self-engrossed fictions will obligingly keep at bay intimations of immortality, moral concern and the strictures of commonsense.[2]

Hazlitt has a point. *Don Juan* is in a way about itself and its truth cannot readily be disentangled from fiction, but it excites also and goes some way to corroborate religious intimations. It takes morality seriously, and consistently distrusts the intellect's ready disengagement from the constraining paradoxes of good sense. Hazlitt's stance is a secular one. He stands alone in an unintelligible world without order and looks to the spell of words for his salvation:

Happy are they who live in the dream of their own existence, and see all things in the light of their own minds; who walk by faith and hope; to whom the guiding star of their youth still shines from afar, and into whom the spirit of the world has not entered! They have not been "hurt by the archers", nor has the iron entered their souls. They live in the midst of arrows and of death, unconscious of harm.

The evil thing comes not nigh them. The shafts of ridicule pass unheeded by, and malice loses its sting. The example of vice does not rankle in their breasts, like the poisoned shirt of Nessus. Evil impressions fall off from them like drops of water. The yoke of life is to them light and supportable. The world has no hold on them. They are in it, not of it; and a dream and a glory is ever around them.[3]

Hazlitt here takes the vocabulary of the Psalmist and the New Testament, familiar to him from his Unitarian upbringing, and reinterprets it with the rhetoric of unbelief in much the same spirit as Professor Ridenour understands the 'Aurora Borealis' passage in *Don Juan* which we discussed in Chapter 2 (see page 52). Hazlitt's stance is indeed proleptic of Western Art and Criticism in this century which seeks confirmation of liberal reverence for liberty and sexual feelings whilst at the same time contemning any wider ordering framework than that fitfully provided by the creative imagination so relentlessly 'frigged' (to use a Byronism) for this purpose.[4] *Don Juan*, on the other hand, a fable indeed of liberty and Eros, though claimed for this viewpoint and conscious of it, insists upon the disconcertingly given character of events, forces, and feelings. It does not seek out 'the dream of existence' or 'see all things' in the light of a mind such as Hazlitt's or even the narrator's.

It is not at all surprising that Hazlitt disliked *Don Juan* because the 'flashy passages' destroyed the effect of the 'serious writing'. For the 'flashy passages' are designed precisely to puncture the wholly unfounded vaunting of rhetoric such as Hazlitt's in the passage cited with its complacency of deep despair. The interaction of 'flashy' and 'serious' takes the curious character of the given more seriously than seriousness does. We cannot get at the world before we interpret it but we can, whilst interpreting, remain conscious of our stake in that which precipitates and outlasts our interpretation. The reader, like the narrator of *Don Juan* is, canto by canto, forced to try to acquire this contemplative knack in the midst of an array of galvanised phantasmogoria but Aurora Raby represents to us one who already has it in abundance. Hazlitt's words could be applied to her. Adeline's 'shafts of ridicule pass unheeded by', she is in the world 'not of it'. But Byron is not trying to cheer himself up in the creation of Aurora as Hazlitt so patently is in the beatitudes of 'Mind and Motive'. To our surprise, Aurora's stillness suddenly interests Juan far more than the dynamism of glow which it apparently displaces.

T.S. Eliot, in an overlooked passage praising the last cantos of *Don Juan*, recognises the force of Aurora and half-acknowledges that she does not fit his restricted conception of the poem and poet:

> His understanding may remain superficial, but it is precise. Quite possibly he undertook something that he would have been unable to carry to a successful conclusion; possibly there was needed, to complete the story of that monstrous house-party, some high spirits, some capacity for laughter, with which Byron was not endowed. He might have found it impossible to deal with that remarkable personage Aurora Raby, the most serious character of his invention, within the frame of his satire. Having invented a character too serious, in a way too real for the world he knew, he might have been compelled to reduce her to the size of one of his ordinary romantic heroines. But Lord Henry and Lady Adeline Amundeville are persons exactly on the level of Byron's capacity for understanding; . . . [5]

Eliot is right to call Aurora 'the most serious character' of Byron's invention and is right to recognise that continuing the poem with Aurora would be difficult. He does not grasp that continuing the poem without her would have been impossible. He thinks that Aurora's emergence is some fortunate but inexplicable aberration on Byron's part, which it would be if Byron had only the Amundevilles' 'capacity for understanding'. If it is true that Byron's understanding 'may remain superficial' because in comparison with Eliot himself or Baudelaire, Byron has no religious depth, then indeed Aurora may be saluted but left on one side. We may thus go on with Eliot to praise, 'Byron's satire upon English society' and his 'hatred of hypocrisy'[6] as though we stood at the centre of the final cantos.

Juan himself appears to acknowledge a different centre from this one. Aurora not ony captivates and stills the force of which he is the emblem but is herself an image of the wholeness denied to the other inhabitants of 'that monstrous house-party' and is thus exempt from the satire of which she is the ground. Eliot discerns the 'noticeable difference' between the first and second part of the poem[7] and he sees that Aurora belongs neither to the world of Byron's 'ordinary romantic heroines' nor to fashionable English society. If the poem is in two unconnected parts then Aurora appears as an aberration in both of them. If, however, there is some single evolution in *Don Juan* then Aurora could reconcile both the satiric and romance thrusts of the poem and suggest the containment of comedy. That is the thesis. To demonstrate it we must begin with a thorough scrutiny of Byron's presentation of Aurora in the last cantos.

I

Aurora is one of three women who are distinguished sharply from one another. Such character contrasts are familiar in novels. Thackeray's Becky Sharp and Emilia Sedley, Jane Austen's Fanny Price and Mary Crawford, D.H. Lawrence's ⎮Ursula and Gudrun Brangwen, are almost emblematically differentiated but remain within a single world. Byron's three women are not demarcated like these. Only one novelist provides a close parallel to Byron here. Byron was reading Scott's novels in preference to all other authors whilst he was writing these cantos as we have earlier emphasised.

In Walter Scott's novels, major differentiated characters, such as Flora Mac-Ivor and Rose Bradwardine in *Waverley*, belong to different worlds altogether. Scott is always concerned with the interpenetration and rival force of stilled images and fluid occurrence in human history. By and large, romance derives from the first and the novel from the latter though counter-claims are for a time set up. Byron and Scott respected and understood each other's work profoundly because they thought and wrote in a similar way about similar matters.[8] Scott was Byron's "buon camerado" (XII, 16). The 'noticeable difference' which Eliot discerned in the two halves of *Don Juan* corresponds closely to the advertised slippage between modes upon which Scott's fiction/reality relies.

It is more than probable that Scott found a model for his practice here not only in Shakespeare but also in Dryden whom he admired, understood and devoutly edited. If this is so, it throws some light on *Don Juan* for it is Dryden's[9] plays above all with their double-plots and, more often than not, mixed modes which provide the closest prototype for Scott's fiction. In Dryden and Scott, a blatant, apparently careless, fictionalising is part and parcel of a scrupulous, almost obsessive, concern with historical fact and understanding. Norman Abbey is just such a dramatic set-piece which, like Haidée's, Neuha's[10] or Prospero's island, observes enough of the three unities to hold together characters of markedly different kinds and blends manifest contrivance with the utmost verisimilitude.

It appears that contrasting Aurora, Adeline and Fitz-Fulke is not a straightforward matter. Adeline has far more stanzas devoted to her than either of the others but we would be wrong to suppose that she is therefore central. Her life is that which ostensibly holds sway in the Abbey. She is the presiding life of its daily appearance, whereas the Duchess and Aurora are familiars of the unapparent forces which also preside in the house. Adeline's life is, as far as she can make it, co-extensive with what she understands and can articulate. She distrusts Aurora and Fitz-Fulke because they fall outside her powers of articulation and therefore of control. Aurora's powers consist in her 'indifference' (XV, 77, 83), her quiet refusal to exercise sway. The clash between Adeline and her is almost like that between different kinds of magic:

> Perhaps she [Adeline] did not like the quiet way
> With which Aurora on those baubles look'd,
> Which charm most people in their earlier day:

(XV, 53)

> The dashing and proud air of Adeline
> Imposed not upon her [Aurora] :

(XV, 56)

Aurora's 'look' is powerful nevertheless. It is not Adeline's look of control, nor Fitz-Fulke's 'hard' look (XVI, 31) of intelligent erotic calculation, but it is disconcertingly direct. Repeatedly we are told that she 'look'd' or 'gazed' or 'surveyed' with her 'large dark eyes' (XVI, 31). Her look is related to sad knowledge together with star-like radiance:

> . . . She had something of sublime
> In eyes which sadly shone, as seraphs' shine.
> All youth — but with an aspect beyond time;
> Radiant and grave — as pitying man's decline;
> Mournful — but mournful of another's crime,
> She look'd as if she sat by Eden's door,
> And grieved for those who could return no more.

(XV, 45)

Associated with Aurora's curious gaze, here and elsewhere, is a customary posture, 'She sat' (cf. XV, 77). This posture is an emblematic counter to Adeline's domineering activity. She is a Mary to Adeline's

Martha. Her posture represents 'indifference', contemplation, but also a regal authority superior to Adeline's:

> There was awe in the homage which she drew;
> Her spirit seem'd as seated on a throne.
> Apart from the surrounding world, and strong
> In its own strength — most strange in one so young!
>
> (XV, 47)

This emblem of the sitting, gazing Aurora is completed by her smile. This occurs 'rarely' (XVI, 92), 'once or twice' (XV, 80) or very slightly (XV, 78) or even conditionally, 'she would have calmly smiled' (XV, 55), but is clearly highlighted. The qualifications are important. We are not encouraged to picture a permanently smiling face but, as in a great portrait or sculpture, we catch in Aurora's gravity the hint of a smile, and in her smile the pressure of quiet thoughtfulness. She is, marvellously, 'Radiant and grave' (XV, 45).

This indeed is a 'remarkable personage' and Eliot is right to detect her outsider character in Norman Abbey where she is, pointedly, an orphan and 'a guest' (XV, 55). However impressed, Eliot cannot account for Aurora's inclusion in the poem. Most commentators similarly do not know what to do with her.[11] Yet she is linked unmistakably with Juan, who is obsessed by her; with Adeline, and by implication all the other house guests, whose values she satirises simply by her presence, authority and gaze; above all she is linked with the house itself.

Readers of Byron's poetry learn how to grasp whole sections of his verse and relate or overlay smaller passages within them. We can see this developing particularly clearly in the cantos of *Childe Harold's Pilgrimage*, which is why it will always be the most helpful preparation for reading *Don Juan*.[12] The Norman Abbey cantos are meant to be read spatially as well as temporally. They are a design as well as a sequence. The opening description of the Abbey in Canto XIII is not a *tour de force* or a mere setting of the scene for the activities of the Duke of Dash or the 'six Miss Rawbolds'. As we have seen, the Abbey is from the outset a substantial force in its own right which cannot be held within the narrator's controlling fluency. The house and grounds have a primary life of their own not disclosed in the functions for which they are now appropriated by the present inhabitants. Aurora Raby alone is alert to this secret life of the house and is herself a sign of it. Like Fanny Price in *Mansfield Park* or Ravenswood in *The Bride of Lammer-*

moor she is, in her disregarded solitude, the real heir to a house whose true life is not comprehended by its present usurpers.

The life of Norman Abbey and of Aurora Raby is nourished by two sources quite separate in themselves but clearly joined together. The first is the ancient Catholic life of the buildings, 'An old, old monastery once,' (XIII, 55), of which Aurora is the heir:

> And deem'd that fallen worship far more dear
> Perhaps because 'twas fallen: her sires were proud
> Of deeds and days when they had fill'd the ear
> Of nations, and have never bent or bow'd
> To novel power; and as she was the last,
> She held their old faith and old feelings fast.

> (XV, 46)

The other representative of the 'old faith and old feelings' is, of course, the ghost of the Black Friar with whom, therefore, Aurora is linked.

The second source of Aurora's and Norman Abbey's hidden life does not come via a forgotten history but through their conscious present occupation of surrounding space. This is, perhaps, an odd way of putting it but the point itself is readily grasped. The Abbey was originally contrived as a co-operation between landscape and building:

> . . . it lies perhaps a little low
> Because the monks preferred a hill behind,
> To shelter their devotion from the wind.

> It stood embosom'd in a happy valley
> Crown'd by high woodlands,

> (XIII, 55, 58)

This co-operation persists in the Abbey's new identity as a mansion but is less straightforward. Initially the house appears as a monastic equivalent for Ben Jonson's Penshurst which wonderfully enfolds human life in a co-operating landscape. Natural details are gently humanised:

> . . . the Druid oak
> Stood like Caractacus

> (XIII, 56)

> The woods sloped downwards to its brink, and stood

With |their green faces fix'd upon the flood.

(XIII, 57)

Its outlet dash'd into a steep cascade,
Sparkling with foam, until again subsiding
Its shriller echoes — like, an infant made
Quiet — sank into softer ripples, gliding
Into a rivulet;

(XIII, 58)

However, as the details of the Abbey's past despoliation emerge
more clearly, the continuing co-operation of natural forces with the
extensively ruined edifice, beyond their original function, takes on an
eerie character. It is as though this secret partnership persists in spite of,
and perhaps subversive of, the present uses of the house.[13] The lake
and the church's empty, west window are particularly important here.
The lake has Aurora's clarity, depth and openness to perpetual replenishment:

Before the mansion lay a lucid lake,
Broad as transparent, deep, and freshly fed
By a river, which its soften'd way did take
In currents through the calmer water spread
Around:

(XV, 57)

Here it is as though the lake's wonderful vitality ('freshly fed/By a
river') is ensured and ceaselessly maintained by natural forces rather
than by human contrivance or for human purposes. The great, arched
window similarly, desecrated by human history, has nevertheless survived in outline and, instead of presiding over the now 'silenced quire',
is the occasion of an extraordinary natural music of its own:

A mighty window, hollow in the centre,
Shorn of its glass of thousand colourings,
Through which the deepen'd glories once could enter,
Streaming from off the sun like seraph's wings,
Now yawns all desolate: now loud, now fainter,
The gale sweeps through its fretwork, and oft sings
The owl his anthem, where the silenced quire
Lie with their hallelujahs quench'd like fire.

But in the noontide of the moon, and when
The wind is winged from one point of heaven,
There moans a strange unearthly sound, which then
Is musical — a dying accent driven
Through the huge Arch, which soars and sinks again.
Some deem it but the distant echo given
Back to the Night winds by the waterfall,
And harmonized by the old choral wall:

(XIII, 63, 64)

The effect here is both elegiac, as though Nature is singing a dirge for its desolated partner, and suggestive of immense present power. If we compare Pope's breathtaking lines in the Epistle to Burlington, which exult in Nature's resumption of an abandoned mansion:

Another age shall see the golden Ear
Imbrown the slope, and nod on the Parterre,
Deep Harvests bury all his pride has plann'd,
And laughing Ceres re-assume the land.

(173-6)

we see at once that Byron's stanzas suggest something much odder than this. The Abbey was originally built not for human pride, like Timon's villa in Pope's poem, but as a place of dialogue between heaven and earth. The daily chanting of its offices mimicked and participated in the heavenly chorus, until that is suddenly interrupted and

. . . the silenced quire
Lie with their hallelujahs quench'd like fire.

Now however, these bare ruined choirs are not simply reassumed by Nature but preserved in living sympathy with the mysterious cosmos. Moon, wind, waterfall, 'one point of heaven', Arch, 'old choral wall' combine in 'a strange unearthly sound'. It is the mutual attentiveness of the building and its surrounding space, immediate and vast, which is crucial here. Aurora is consistently presented in the same way:

The worlds beyond this world's perplexing waste
Had more of her existence for in her
There was a depth of feeling to embrace

Thoughts, boundless, deep, but silent too as Space.

(XVI, 48)

She embodies in the midst of Norman Abbey's present 'perplexing waste' the originating contemplative life of the house. Both resources of the house are united in her religious attentiveness to its spatial and historical resonances: she has something of the old house's austerity and sadness but also its sweetness, power and inexhaustible vitality. Again a comparison will make this sharper.

In Chapter XXI of *Waverley*, the hero is taken by Flora Mac-Ivor into a wild Romantic glen with a waterfall. This setting expresses both Flora's own nature and that, she claims, of the Celtic muse which 'He who wooes her must love the barren rock more than the fertile valley, and the solitude of the desert better than the festivity of the hall'. We are engaged by this splendid scene as is Edward Waverley himself, but, however intense and entrancing, it does not hold the promise of a present natural life or a comic future. It comes as no surprise that, at the end of the novel, Edward settles for the fertile valley, the festivity of the hall, and marries Rose Bradwardine. We last see Flora, emaciated, in the company of an elderly foreign nun whose convent she is about to join. This is typical of Scott's Catholic protagonists who move us by their tragic adherence to a superseded life. Their only choice is to slip out of this life, as Diana Vernon does in *Rob Roy*, and marry the hero with a future.

Aurora Raby owes a great deal to Scott's Catholic heroines and is supported, as they are, by a charged Romantic landscape. Byron's intentions are quite distinct from Scott's. Both Aurora and her supporting landscape have something of Flora Mac-Ivor's sombre nobility but they are marked too by an abundance of life. The old Gothic fountain,[14] for instance, playing within the cloistered court is fed by a spring which

> . . . gush'd through grim mouths, of granite made,
> And sparkled into basins, where it spent
> Its little torrent in a thousand bubbles,
> Like man's vain glory, and his vainer troubles.

(XIII, 65)

Here the still flowing fountain belonging to the old abbey is linked with the 'lucid lake' of stanza 57 but where that is 'freshly fed/By a river', the fountain merely spends its little torrent in an image of human transience and the vanity of the persisting house alongside ceaseless flows of water. Aurora is associated with the lake and 'deep seas'. She has her feet firmly planted in or beside deeper flows of water like the blessed man of the first psalm, a type of the contemplative life: 'And he shall be like a tree planted by the rivers of water, that bringeth forth his fruit in his season.' (Ps. 1.3). Aurora is an ideal instance of the contemplation which, as Byron wittily observes, is rarely discovered:

> And *à propos* of monks, their piety
> With sloth hath found it difficult to dwell;
> Those vegetables of the Catholic creed
> Are apt exceedingly to run to seed.
>
> (XVI, 81)

The union of attentive awareness and 'indifference' which Aurora possesses easily becomes passivity and sloth.

In the daytime, this gurgling of fountain, river, waterfall and the soaring sound of 'the huge Arch' is unheard, but in 'the moontide of the Moon' these primary sounds are unmistakably present and fearfully at odds with the present life of the house:

> The gothic chamber where he was enclosed,
> Let in the rippling sound of the lake's billow,
> With all the mystery by midnight caused;
>
> (XVI, 15)

The ghost embodies this opposition as a threatening alternative:

> Amundeville is lord by day
> But the ghost is lord at night.
>
> ('Ballad of the Black Friar')

Aurora embodies the same opposition as a kindly ('*not* stern') presence and, unlike the ghost, can be seen in the daytime, for she belongs to both past and present, religious and secular worlds. If we were to cast this in the form of a little argument we could point to the remarkable effect the ghost has on Juan. He is reduced to a silence analogous to Aurora's which specifically commends him to her:

> The ghost at least had done him this much good,
> In making him as silent as a ghost,

If in the circumstances which ensued
He gained esteem where it was worth the most.
And certainly Aurora had renewed
In him some feelings he had lately lost

(XVI, 107)

This silence is insisted upon. Juan at breakfast 'sate him pensive o'er a dish of tea,' (XVI, 30), 'all cold and silent still,' (XVI, 32). He is still much the same after dinner:

Sate silent now, his usual spirits gone:

(XVI, 105)

But Juan, sitting silent in his nook,

(XVI, 106)

Aurora attributes this later silence to a charity similar to her own which makes Juan unanxious to waste words or discuss the failings of others (XVI, 106).

Undoubtedly this silence of Juan performs many functions. It is in a way a mimic death ('all cold and silent still') from which Fitz-Fulke's glow will rouse him. A.V. Kernan claims that Fitz-Fulke's confrontation with Juan is

. . . a climatic image of the comic triumph of life over death. The illusion of a pale, bloodless world moving towards sterility and death is transformed by courage, vitality, and good chance into a living, breathing, and satisfying immediacy.[15]

In so far as this is true, Juan's own movement towards 'a pale, bloodless world' of 'sterility and death' is helpfully signalled by his silence and inertia just as he is earlier awakened from 'his damp trance' by Haidée (II, 111). That is not, however, the major significance of Juan's sudden silence. Aurora is not correct either in attributing her charity to Juan. He has, suddenly, something of her gravity but none of her radiance. Yet this checking of Juan's spirit does link him with Aurora. It corresponds to his sudden death-like illness in St Petersburg (X, 39) but is here associated with thoughtfulness and growth: 'He gained esteem where it was worth the most.' (XVI, 107). It is as though the condition of Aurora's interest in Juan is his acquisition of a reticence analogous to hers. The ghost and the old house together work this change in him. He is, like Coleridge's Wedding Guest, disabled from expected participation in human society by a remembered terror:

> And Juan too, in general behind none
> In gay remark on what he had heard and seen,
> Sate silent now, his usual spirits gone:

(XVI, 105)

He is thus placed, however crude his understanding, with Aurora in relation to the house and its day-world guests. He is attentive to its other life, fearful of the silent ghost, attracted to the silent Aurora.

Juan's silence therefore elevates him within Norman Abbey. It elevates him too within the poem. His various forms of inertia hitherto have been bound up with his physical life — sea-sick, nearly drowned, tied up as a slave, ill in St Petersburg. The unbounded narrator can relate these tales of Juan's bondage with every acknowledgement of human limitation in general but in so jauntily accomplished a fashion that we exempt the narrator from the constraints upon which he insists. Nevertheless we have seen that the narrator does acknowledge his own inarticulacy before the dead commandant ('But it was all a mystery', V, 39); and his 'lurking bias. . . To the unknown' though 'pale and struck with terror' (XIV, 6). We have seen too that the narrator is much closer to the society described in Norman Abbey than to that of earlier episodes. Thus Juan's removal from this society and his association with the superior attentiveness of Aurora turns the tables on the narrator. It is Juan who now has the metaphysical knowledge and detachment which is the source of the narrator's customary self-esteem. It is the narrator who is immersed in the social world which he details. The silence into which Juan blunders is the silence which the ever-articulate narrator skirts but never penetrates. This is an extraordinary twist in the inherited Don Juan story, for Juan's experience of terror in the civilised society to which he has now returned after his exotic adventures is more like salvation than the judgement Don Juan Tenorio eventually finds in Seville. Yet Juan is to be redirected back to Eros (for how long we do not know) by the ghost masquerade of Fitz-Fulke.

Without Aurora, these remarkable transformations would seem as farcical as the first canto and, at best, would offer no more than a stage-managed return to the kinds of confidence which the Siege and Catharine discredited. How exactly is Aurora related to the house?

In our comparision of Aurora to Scott's Flora Mac-Ivor we claimed that both were supported by 'a charged Romantic landscape'. Where Flora, however, takes Waverley to a wild glen which epitomises her proper life, Aurora is never seen in a setting of this kind. She is invariably a guest presence in the present house, representing in it the life which we may separately discern in its ruined environs. Aurora has nevertheless an unmistakable cross-reference in the design of these cantos. Above 'the huge Arch' of the abandoned church we find her counterpart:

> But in a higher niche, alone, but crown'd,
> The Virgin Mother of the God-born child,
> With her son in her blessed arms, look'd round,
> Spared by some chance when all beside was spoil'd;
> She made the earth below seem holy ground.
>
> (XIII, 61)

If we compare these lines with those about Aurora already instanced:

> There was awe in the homage which she drew;
> Her spirit seem'd as seated on a throne
> Apart from the surrounding world, and strong
> In its own strength
>
> (XV, 47)

The overlay between the two passages is exact. It is typical of Byron to insist that the Virgin Mother 'look'd round'. She does not belong to the past building alone but is actively present. The church is ruined but eerily preserves its original function: Mary looks round, human hearts are lifted, the giant shell of the building echoes still to religious music of a kind. The phrase 'look'd round' clearly links the Virgin Mother directly with the virginal Aurora who sits and looks and smiles. Both the Virgin Mother and Aurora live in immediate contact with the space or gap which the huge arch traps under the feet of Mary. Just as the Blessed Virgin sits on the edge of a celestial ruin so Aurora

> . . . look'd as if she sat by Eden's door
> And grieved for those who could return no more.
>
> (XV, 45)

Once, the great empty window was full of glass

>   . . . of thousand colourings
> Through which the deepen'd glories once could enter,
> Streaming from off the sun like Seraph's wings,

(XIII, 62)

That has gone but it is metempsychosed into Aurora's radiance:

>   . . . She had something of sublime
> In eyes which sadly shone, as seraphs' shine.

(XV, 45)

There can be no doubt that Aurora represents, in a precise and pondered way, that holiness, a specifically feminine wholeness, which the original building (dedicated to the Blessed Virgin) was designed to celebrate and, oddly, still does. If there is 'no doubt' about this, what are we to make of it?

Certainly we understand at once why T.S. Eliot was so held by Aurora and so convinced that Byron could not have maintained the poem with her in it, for Eliot faced exactly the same dilemma himself. Aurora's relationship with the guests of Norman Abbey is, in outline, identical to that of Celia with the other characters in Eliot's *The Cocktail Party*. Both exploit dramatically the inadmissibility of holiness by the modern world when it is encountered and the renewing relation of such holiness to the perplexing wastes of familiar relationships. The problem for Eliot and his audience is that *The Cocktail Party* is never more than a vehicle for its author's known designs. The problem for Byron and his readers is that Byron's designs, though far richer, are more inchoate in themselves and are not expected of him at all. Is he not busy enough attacking English Society for its snobbery and heartlessness? It would not be hard to list critical books that do not suspect Byron to have significantly greater powers of understanding than the Amundevilles.

We should insist upon this little used word 'holiness' here and not align ourselves with the prejudices of the faint-hearted or Lady Adeline:

> *Why* Adeline had this slight prejudice —
> For prejudice it was — against a creature
> *As pure as sanctity itself from* vice,
> With all the added charm of form and feature,

(XV, 52, second italics are mine)

Aurora is specifically 'holy' in a sense that Flora Mac-Ivor is not. Scott situates holiness completely within historical perspectives and is uninterested in its proper life. It is not easy to think of other successful exemplars of holiness in post-medieval English literature.[16] Byron's contemporaries, for the most part, merely play with the Gothic trappings or psychological concomitants of sanctity. But surely Byron cannot be recommending the imperatives and perspectives of Catholic Christianity as straightforwardly as do the plays of T.S. Eliot? If the answer to this question is in the negative, and it is, does it then follow that Aurora's holiness reverberates within the poem alone as a literary invention of much the same kind as the aged beadsman in Keats's *Eve of St. Agnes?*

If we try to answer this question accurately we are forced to reassert and grasp more firmly the difficult burden of previous chapters. *Don Juan* is a continuously evident fiction which, perhaps uniquely, mimics and transmits a given actuality. Both the narrator's fully displayed consciousness and Juan's succession of glowing and deathly episodes are grounded in an unknowable blankness which can be seen as meaningless or inexplicably trustworthy. This ground cannot be separately encountered apart from the structures and fictions of inherited or freshly posited fashioning. It is not, and cannot be, identical with any such fiction, with human capacity to make structures in general, nor even with human potentialities as such. In his hatred of the lie of mere fiction Byron often based his poems on historical fact in order to evade it. In *Don Juan*'s use of historical characters like Suvarrow there is something of this, but subtler, deeper strategies are also at work. The poem is about itself not in order to celebrate fictionality or solipsism but to suggest that containing space of life and fearful abyss of thought which reflexive consciousness presupposes but cannot directly face. *Don Juan* does not only celebrate its own emergence but, like all comedies, celebrates what it emerges from. The poem is open horizontally to its completion, or final incompletion, by the dialogue of historical accident and the play of Byron's structuring imagination. It is open vertically to the blank, fertile space which language, Byron's imagination and the reader's conscious life presuppose, fill and can be led to recall. The conclusion of J.J. McGann's stimulating *Don Juan in Context* makes a parallel point:

This is why imagination in *Don Juan* is not a creative but an analytic instrument. *Don Juan*'s inventions serve an intellectual (and, ultimately, moral) purpose. Nor is Byron's poem, like *The Eve of St.*

Agnes, its own reason for being. *Don Juan* does not imagine itself, as Keats's poem does, it imagines the world. It is "created" to clarify the world of men, rather than the world of poetic processes . . . *Don Juan* was specifically written to warn its age, and succeeding ages, against the solipsistic dangers latent in the new theories of poetry.[17]

The emphasis here is entirely right but Byron emerges as more neatly neo-classical than he was. *Don Juan* most certainly 'does not imagine itself' but in so far as 'it imagines the world' we are not directed exclusively to analysis and classification but also towards puzzlement, horror, laughter and reverence for the bases of its inception. Professor Gleckner has said of *Don Juan*, 'Fundamentally, it has to do not with morality or immorality but with nothingness'.[18] I cannot agree with this but 'nothingness' is a fundamental concern of the poem as I have argued in Chapter 2. 'Nothingness' in *Don Juan* is, however, not simply a static inertia or an absence of values. It is, as it were, the other face of Being. Aurora is presented as drawing sustenance from silence and space. Morality is usually grounded in forces and understanding that seem to annihilate the values which they ordain.

Aurora is thus not wholly contained within the poem like Keats's beadsman. She is trustingly open like Norman Abbey itself to a space which the poem's fiction can indicate but never fully take over. In the same way, the narrator's consciousness can never displace or fill up 'the abyss of thought', and the glow of sexual life is, but also is not, the glow of life itself. Catholic Christianity, not always treated so sympathetically in the poem, is here undoubtedly presented as an exemplar. Without it, Aurora Raby could not be as she is. Catholicism is not there for psychological, historical, atmospheric or imagistic reasons. We are not reading *The Italian, The Eve of St. Agnes* or *Christabel*. If we were told suddenly that Cantos XIII to XVIII were in fact a cunning later interpolation by Cardinal Newman disguised as Byron's own work — and in other contexts we are often asked to take such things in our stride — then received opinion would undoubtedly condemn the blatant, Catholic propaganda of the fable.[19] If, on the other hand, we are convinced that Byron belongs to 'the sceptical tradition of Montaigne, Locke and Hume' then Aurora is better left undiscussed,[20] regarded from Lady Adeline's viewpoint,[21] or glossed as one of Byron's 'ordinary Romantic Heroines'.[22] If we are right, Byron is neither Newman or Hume though he is, at the time of writing these cantos, far more sympathetic to Newman's future 'Yes' than to Hume's past 'No'.

We have already seen that the narrator claims to say no more than has been said by many before him, 'Who knew this life was not worth a potato.' (VII, 4), and that the sages he instances are sometimes religious, sometimes sceptical. The two emphases often cross over. Prime sceptics like Hume and Gibbon, for instance, were, albeit briefly, converted to Catholicism. Aurora is fashioned by a sceptic with authentic religious understanding and exists in advance, as it were, of any position that Byron could himself espouse or fully commend. But, in *Don Juan*, commended Aurora undoubtedly is.

We must not bowdlerise then Aurora's Catholicism and holiness. She emerges out of the logic of a fiction but, like some seventeenth-century Dutch portrait, bespeaks a light and shadow not only of paint and human imagination. To all this we must eventually return but *Don Juan* is falsified if we insist on it alone. Byron is at pains to enlarge, in a way to secularise, his clearly religious conception of Aurora. We do not see her at prayer, at Mass, with other Catholics. Her relationship to the Blessed Virgin and to the abbey ruins is implicit, a matter of parallel, not of explicit analogy. Christian doctrine and nomenclature are avoided. Thoughtfulness, recollection ('indifference'), quietness, solitude, charity, lucidity, attentiveness, strength, youth, purity and beauty are her hallmarks. She is manifestly in the world but not of it, yet is so in substance not in the narrator's vocabulary. Instead she is related to an author. She is 'more Shakespearian' (XVI, 48) than Adeline who admires Pope (XVI, 47), or Fitz-Fulke who once 'was seen reading the "Bath Guide" ' (XVI, 50). This explicit tribute to Shakespeare is unexpected. Byron, though steeped in Shakespeare's plays, disliked the Romantic cult of Shakespeare and publicly defended Pope. How is Aurora 'Shakespearian'?

There are three major possibilities here. The first is that Byron is associating Aurora with Shakespeare's status in a general way. She has his imaginative genius; she can sit quietly looking at the human world, transform what she sees and connect it with vast conceptions. Secondly Aurora may resemble those Shakespearian characters, Hamlet especially, who have directly encountered 'worlds beyond this world's perplexing waste' and are consistently aware of mysteries beyond Horatio's philosophy. Finally, as Professor Wilson Knight points out, she may 'have affinities with the younger heroines of Shakespeare's last period'.[23]

The evidence that Byron himself provides for Aurora's Shakespearian qualities is this:

> . . . for in her
> There was a depth of feeling to embrace
> Thoughts, boundless, deep, but silent too as Space.

(XVI, 48)

This would seem to authorise all the possibilities outlined above which are not, in any case, mutually exclusive. What may appear odd at first is the association of Shakespeare's torrent of words with Aurora's singular silence. Something more fruitful than 'negative capability'[24] is suggested by this. Aurora represents not only the heroines who draw Juan onwards through the poem but the wholeness which impels the narrator's unstoppable flow of thought and Byron's (or Shakespeare's) energies of imagination. Eros, as we last encountered it in *Don Juan*, drives us to procreate indifferently, at the mercy of the life-energies which we pursue:

> From thee we come, to thee we go, and why
> To get at thee not batter down a wall
> Or waste a world?

(IX, 56)

Aurora, 'beyond this world's perplexing waste', represents the perennial drives of fiction to imagine a world immune from this tainted cycle which, somehow, does not refuse all value to the world as it is. At the same time, she represents a religious assertion that this conviction is based on truth not fiction. Thus Aurora, linked in the most explicit way to the highest available form of religion[25] and the greatest art (Shakespeare), exists as a fiction and something more than a fiction. It is not her character nor even her significance which is primary but her being itself.

It is curious that Byron makes us grant a presumption of being to a fictional character but this is the counterpart of the ontological and existential bias of the thought and life of the whole poem which earlier chapters have demonstrated. R.B. England cautiously observes that: 'Aurora is a fictional character that he has himself created but . . . he establishes the illusion that she possesses a life independent of his mind, a life of which he is not entirely the master.'[26] We can recognise Aurora's being but we can say absolutely nothing about it. We cannot picture her consciousness nor is it made up of pictures, whereas we can articulate every feature of Adeline's complex personality but, like Juan, we come to 'doubt how much of Adeline was real;' (XVI, 96). Aurora's being is immune not only from Juan's doubt and the world's taint but also from the persistently advertised scepticism of the narrator nor, though she is fully a fiction, can she be interpreted as standing completely within a fictional word. She exists, like the poem itself, as a fiction in touch with a non-fictional given — just as Byron's or Scott's historical characters do — but in a religious and ontological not a historical sense.

If the reading we have so far given of Aurora Raby is reliable, it will be evident that a proper understanding of *Don Juan* will be hugely affected by her inclusion in it. It is not that Aurora alone is responsible for a new dimension, for we have been at pains to establish this resonance earlier in the poem by argument and analysis, but Aurora confirms this direction and brings it to the explicit attention of the reader. It must then be taken into full account. Missing her out will indicate a disinclination to treat the poem's becoming seriously. We will have substituted an essence, a prematurely fixed idea of the poem's character, for its astonishing existence. *Don Juan* is not a telling satire by a limited mind, a wonderful Shandyesque concoction, a step towards the nineteenth-century novel nor a proto-Modernist fiction disappearing into its illusory orifice. If it were any of these things, the Aurora Raby we have delineated could find no place within it.

In the end, these claims stand or fall by scrupulous and comprehensive attention to *Don Juan* itself. It is helpful, however, to enquire whether the poems which Byron was writing at the same time as the Norman Abbey cantos support or undermine our contentions.

Poems differ generically and substantially and, in any event, it would show little tact if the reader was to be asked to examine other texts in great detail at this stage. However, if *Don Juan* communicates a reality which it does not wholly use up or hide in its fictional contrivance, then we would not expect Byron's other contemporary fictions to be wholly incongruous with the sources thus revealed.

The Island is of particular interest for it was written immediately before the composition of Canto XIII,[27] and it deals with transparently similar concerns to *Don Juan*. It is worth examining in as much detail as is consonant with our larger purposes for it places Norman Abbey in an unexpectedly revealing perspective.

II

The Island is a thoughtful, cleverly structured but locally flawed poem, which modern criticism has found particularly interesting.[28] It concerns the attempt of the mutineers on the *Bounty* to leave their European legacy of law, order and technological control, represented by Bligh's ship, for the paradisal freedom of Toobonai (Tahiti). They encounter a familiar paradox of Byron's plays and tales, for the mutinous action which makes their initial freedom possible is itself murderous and egotistical. Hence, like Cain, they find that their attempt to bypass the Fall repeats it. Instead of finding paradise, they end up guilty, punished or dead.

There can be no doubt that this represents Byron's considered political, theological and psychological opinion. There is no way of avoiding the sequence which he presents. On the other hand, that is not all that can be said. Byron artfully manipulates the reader's sympathies. We respect and admire Bligh, but we share the mutineers' and islanders' horror when a naval vessel later comes to reclaim and punish the Europeans. The island itself is simultaneously mythical, untainted (I, 209-15) and actual, inconvenient (II, 481). The mutineers seek the former but bring with them a consciousness which debars them from the naturalisation which they demand.

However, one of the mutineers, Torquil, is clearly exempted from this tainting and is allowed to enter fully into the island's natural paradise. Three things enable him to accomplish, in the poem only, what is impossible for the actual mutineers whose presumed real history founds Byron's tale. Torquil is

The fair-haired offspring of the Hebrides

(II, 165)

Rocked in his cradle by the roaring wind.

(II, 167)

He half belongs to Nature and Myth already. He is not fully part of the fallen history which binds the other mutineers. He is marked too by the intensity of his love for Neuha (a Tahitian Haidée). Thirdly, he passes a test of this love which is also a symbolic rite of passage from a historical world to a natural eternity. This section is the culmination of the poem and is related both to Haidée's cave and to Aurora's Norman Abbey.

Torquil, pursued by the Royal Navy and claimed by the history, escapes in a canoe with Neuha. She guides him to 'a black rock' rising out of the sea. As the pursuers gain on them Torquil momentarily loses faith in his companion:

— "Has Neuha brought me here to die?

> Is this a place of safety, or a grave,
> And yon huge rock the tombstone of the wave?"
>
> (IV, 54-6)

At this point, his faith is tested further. Neuha

> Cried, "Torquil follow me, and fearless follow!"
> Then plunged at once into the Ocean's hollow.
>
> (IV, 59-60)

Torquil follows her without hesitation:

> He dived, and rose no more
>
> (IV, 67)

The pursuers expect to see him surface and, in time, become convinced that he is dead and a ghost:

> Some said he had not plunged into the wave
> But vanished like a corpse-light from the grave;
>
> (IV, 85-6)

Torquil has in fact made a transition of another kind. His dive is virtually a parody of religious faith and imagery.[29] It gains him a different resurrection. He has followed Neuha through an underwater cave into the inside of the hollow, black rock. There, Neuha has food prepared for him, a new fire is made from tindering material which, like Prometheus, she has brought with her (IV, 137-45), and they make love. If we have not sufficiently recognised the imagery of a natural resurrection, this is now articulated in the clearest way for us:

> Not mine to tell the rapturous caress
> Which followed wildly in that wild recess
> This tale; enough that all within that cave
> Was love, though buried strong as in the grave,
> Where Abelard, through twenty years of death,
> When Eloisa's form was lowered beneath
> Their nuptial vault, his arms outstretched, and pressed
> The kindling ashes to his kindled breast
> The waves without sang round their couch, their roar
> As much unheeded as if life were o'er:
>
> (IV, 219-28)

Two further characteristics of this 'wild recess' are important. It was discovered 'a thousand moons ago' (IV, 195) by 'a young chief' who hid the captured daughter of 'a foe' there and then claimed her as his bride. This story now belongs to song and legend. Torquil's exploit is a repetition of this archetypal tale and the sanctuary is accordingly by 'new tradition' renamed "Neuha's Cave" (IV, 414). Secondly, the interior of the cave in which new life and love are kindled is emphatically 'Gothic' (IV, 146). It is like 'some old cathedral's glimmering aisle' (IV, 133), full of 'natural sculpture' that resembles, 'a mitre' or 'a shrine' or a 'seeming crucifix'. Nature has here built 'a chapel of the seas' (IV, 157, 158, 159).

Meanwhile the naval ship ('A floating dungeon', IV, 404) returns to Europe. Neuha and Torquil are restored in triumph to the islanders' feast over which, like Juan and Haidée, they now reside. Here, however, there is no warning song, 'The isles of Greece', for history has departed with the 'sullen ship'. Instead the tale of Neuha and Torquil itself authorises 'the general revel of the night' which, in the witty and exact couplet that concludes the poem —

A night succeeded by such happy days
As only the yet infant world displays.

(IV, 419-20)

How does this tale, still in Byron's mind as he began the Norman Abbey cantos, relate to them? *The Island* has the advantage of being finished in fact and it is the kind of poem that insists upon a final full stop. It is thus far easier to interpret than the Norman Abbey section and, for the same reason, does not vex metaphysical questioning. Neuha and Torquil are free from history but cannot break out from the fabulous territory which they have gained. We may, for aesthetic, psychological or loosely 'mythical' reasons, take them seriously but only in so far as we make use of their proffered representative status.

It is evident that the instant transformation of the 'shadowy Vault' (IV, 136), which Torquil fearfully enters, into 'a new abode' (IV, 164) recalls both the double aspect of Haidée's cave (it restores Juan to life but, in Haidée's dream it is a place of deathly terrors) and the transformation of cloistered ghost into breathing woman in Norman Abbey. Neuha in the 'chapel of the seas' corresponds to Aurora and Fitz-Fulke in the ruined monastery. We can, as it happens, substantiate this by instancing an image used in Norman Abbey which appears to

come from the same source used for *The Island*. Immediately before
the ghost's first appearance in Canto XVI, the eyes of dead women
gleam at Juan from portraits in the gallery:

> . . . their eyes glance like dreams,
> On ours, or spars within some dusky cave,
> But death is imaged in their shadowy beams.
>
> (XVI, 19)

E.H. Coleridge correctly pointed out the similarity of this image to that
of Neuha's cave with its glimmering light and refers it to the passage in
Mariner's Account upon which the hollow rock fable is based.[30] Neuha
is herself compared to a 'cavern sparkling with its native spars' (II, 130).
It looks as though *The Island* uses up the religious vocabulary which it
deploys wholly for erotic purposes like some Petrarchan or Baroque
sonnet. The language of ghosts, death and resurrection, tombs and
Gothic space exists only for its own overthrow. Hence the primary
purpose of comparing *The Island* with Norman Abbey is to establish,
given their similarity of concern, Byron's consciously different purpose
in *Don Juan*. A natural resurrection of a kind is suggested in Fitz-
Fulke's flesh and ghost manifestation but that does not, as it does in
The Island, absorb the major thrust of the poem.

If this point is to be understood according to the tales themselves,
however, we will have to forsake some of this clarity before we can
regain a more durable lucidity. Byron thinks and feels through antitheses: ruined abbey, living house; Venice's 'a palace and a prison';
naval order and natural paradise. Two lines from Canto XIV express
this wonderfully well:

> And the sky shows that very ancient gray,
> The sober, sad antithesis to glowing, —
>
> (XIV, 28)

Antitheses of this kind clarify. Byron's poetry, and our interpreta-
tive procedure, rely on such oppositions. However, though they help us
to reason well and promote strong imaginative structures, they do not
fully correspond with the given, tangled character of occurences or with
the subtler movements of poetry. Byron establishes his antitheses so
that we can see clearly and feel strongly but also so that we can move
between them in puzzling ways.

Let us again take sexual glow as marking one such antithesis on whose clarity we have so much relied. Neuha glows, Aurora does not. What could be plainer? Or, if we are more precise, Neuha glows with immediate, natural life; Aurora shines with reflected spiritual life.

Neuha certainly is the apotheosis of glowing life. She is a fleshly icon:

> Voluptuous as the first approach of sleep;
> Yet full of life — for through her tropic cheek
> The blush would make its way, and all but speak;
> The sun-born blood suffused her neck, and threw
> O'er her clear nut-brown skin a lucid hue,
> Like coral reddening through the darkened wave,
> Which draws the diver to the crimson cave.

(II, 134-40)

It appears that, irrespective of the interchange of lovers, Neuha is in a permanent glow which magnetises others. This first description of her adroitly uses the simile of the diver and cave which will be expanded in the fable already discussed. The 'crimson cave' itself is a blatant sexual symbol (like Dudù's bee in the apple) which suggests the merging of sexual fear and excitement, and the identity of consciously anticipated bride and unconsciously remembered mother. If we now return to the fable itself with this passage in mind we will recognise that when

> ... Neuha took her Torquil by the hand,
> And waved along the vault her kindled brand,
> And led him into each recess, and showed
> The secret places of their new abode.

(IV, 161-4)

it is Neuha's glowing body rather than her 'kindled brand' which 'lights the vault'. The recesses and 'secret places' which she shows him too are more corporeal than adamantine. Typically, Byron is at pains to tell us that the 'black rock' was perhaps formed by some past cataclysm: 'hardened from some earth-absorbing fire,' (IV, 151). Neuha's glow reanimates the apparently long-dead rock just as Fitz-Fulke tricks her deathly disguise into life.

Aurora Raby is clearly other than this. There is no room on Toobonai for any language of the spirit or any other eternity than the all-consuming repetitions of an archetypal carnal glow. We cannot, of course, live like this. If we try to, we will experience the guilt-ridden

paradoxes that are visited as a punishing and inexplicable history upon
the consciousness of Cain and his revolutionary progeny on the *Bounty*
and elsewhere. Poetry, however, though it tells us this, also keeps alive
and feeds us with the repudiated vision and helps us to accept the intolerable divergences thus diagnosed. *The Island* should be seen in this
way alongside Keats's *Lamia* and Shelley's *The Witch of Atlas*.

There are, however, some lines from *The Island* which, surprisingly,
establish links between Neuha's glow and Aurora's spirituality:

> Then rose they [Torquil and Neuha], looking first along the skies,
> And then for light into each other's eyes,
> Wondering that Summer showed so brief a sun,
> And asking if indeed the day were done.

> And let not this seem strange: the devotee
> Lives not in earth, but in his ecstasy;
> Around him days and worlds are heedless driven,
> His Soul is gone before his dust to Heaven.
> Is Love less potent? No — his path is trod,
> Alike uplifted gloriously to God;
> Or linked to all we know of Heaven below,
> The other better self, whose joy or woe
> Is more than ours; the all-absorbing flame
> Which, kindled by another, grows the same,
> Wrapt in one blaze; the pure, yet funeral pile,
> Where gentle hearts, like Bramins, sit and smile.
> How often we forget all time, when lone,
> Admiring Nature's universal throne,
> Her woods — her wilds — her waters — the intense
> Reply of *hers* to our intelligence!

> Who thinks of self when gazing on the sky?
>   (*The Island*, 11, 366-85, 393)

In this passage, the kindled glow of Torquil and Neuha is not associated
with natural fecundity preserved by Art's unwavering outline, but is
seen as another version of the mystic's fiery ecstasy and associated with
the mysteriously filled expanses of cosmic life. It is not only this last
emphasis which recalls Aurora's space-filled consciousness but the
emblematic posture: 'Where gentle hearts, like Bramins, sit and smile.'

It would be tempting to follow this ecstatic funeral pyre of phoenix lovers backwards through Byron's poetry via *Sardanapalus* to the original fiery conclusion of *Manfred* but we must hold fast to Norman Abbey for that is where these ideas and images, profoundly reassembled, are finally articulated.[31] It will help us to do so if we single out the passage's slight but real emphasis on the orthodox alternative:[32]

> Is Love less potent? No — his path is trod,
> Alike uplifted gloriously to God;
> Or linked to all we know of Heaven below,

The implication is that we might imagine human love to be less potent as an agency of transcendence but it is not. On the other hand, it remains valid apparently to be 'uplifted gloriously to God'. This rather stiff, but unambiguous, formulation echoes another which follows the description of Neuha's glow discussed above. Byron is recoiling from that glow and acknowledging the sober, sad antithesis of 'Experience, that chill touch stone' (II, 147). Perhaps Neuha is exempt from this in the same way

> . . . as light winds pass
> O'er lakes to ruffle, not destroy, their glass,
> Whose depths unsearched, and fountains from the hill,
> Restore their surface, in itself so still,

> (II, 151-4)

But this Shelleyan[33] strategy is immediately repudiated in eight lines of rapid modulation:

> Until the Earthquake tear the Naiad's cave,
> Root up the spring, and trample on the wave,
> And crush the living waters to a mass,
> The amphibious desert of the dank morass!
> And must their fate be hers? The eternal change
> But grasps Humanity with quicker range;
> And they who fall but fall as worlds will fall,
> To rise, if just, a Spirit o'er them all.

> (II, 151-62)

We are bound to notice here the reversed relationship of the earthquake and the Naiad's cave to that presented at the end of the poem and the similarity of cadence between the last four lines and the last stanza of *Don Juan*, Canto XV ('Between two worlds'). This is not the only reversal in question. The implication here is that Neuha, a mere naiad, cannot outmanoeuvre or preserve us from the 'eternal change'. All natural resurrections are followed by a fall. The only exemption is for the spirit not the flesh, 'To rise, if just, a Spirit o'er them all.' Here is religious language tethered to religious assertion and by no means used up in its own overthrow. How are we to put these contrary indications together as we turn back to *Don Juan*? We should perhaps take a deep breath and say something like this:

The Island is a complicated poem moving between different worlds with Shakespearian adroitness. The interpretation of history, comedy and romance is as much its concern as *Don Juan's*. It is a poem with a final full stop but two endings; a tragic ending for the mutineers and a comic ending for Torquil and the islanders. The reader will, in his particular history, be on some version of H.M.S. *Bounty*, part of a dark, unacceptable but precious human order. If he seeks to break out of this community of the fallen in order to live on Neuha's isle in social liberty and permanent glow, he will end up with the bitter self-definition of the mutineers. Meanwhile, however, he can read the poem and use its perspective to criticise the civilisation which he must reluctantly endorse. That is the wisdom of the poem, the double seriousness which we attain shortly after its comic conclusion.[34] It is not the thrust of the poem, which is to realise and celebrate a wholly natural resurrection willed by our imagination as truth, like Adam's dream. Commonsense and religious intimation, however, both discredit the absolute value and possibility of such a natural resurrection even when the non-Hebridean reader is, save in his imagination, debarred from it. Moreover, comedy has to incorporate, so far as it can, objections to its universal conclusion. Hence, comparing the ecstasy of lovers to that of 'Bramins' or martyrs who 'sit and smile' amidst their funeral pyre gives a different authority to 'the new transient flame of love' (II, 336). It suggests either that spiritual love is a sublimation of erotic drives, hence not a legitimate critic of them, or that both are equally valid instances of transcendence. In addition, however, there is a brief but felt acknowledgement that the ecstasy of lovers is less valid than this. It cannot prevent the destruction of 'the Naiad's Cave' and is part of a cycle from which we can only find exemption by a spiritual resurrection. *The Island* does not balance these alternatives finely. It is overwhelmingly committed to an idyll of natural life but it does suggest some hidden interplay between the stark antitheses which it establishes.

If we now turn back to Aurora, we will find exactly the same procedure but the interplay is in the contrary direction:

And certainly Aurora had revived
In him some feelings he had lately lost
Or hardened; feelings which, perhaps ideal,
Are so divine that I must deem them real:-

The love of higher things and better days;
The unbounded hope, and heavenly ignorance
Of what is called the world, and the world's ways;
The moments when we gather from a glance
More joy than from all future pride or praise,
Which kindle manhood, but can ne'er entrance
The heart in an existence of its own,
Of which another's bosom is the zone.

Who would not sigh|Aι αι ταν|Kνθ ερειαν!
That *hath* a memory or *had* a heart?
Alas! *her* star must wane like that of Dian;
Ray fades on ray, as years on years depart.
Anacreon only had the soul to tie an
Unwithering myrtle round the unblunted dart
Of Eros; but though thou hast played us many tricks,
Still we respect thee, "Alma Venus Genetrix"!

(XVI, 107, 108, 109)

Aurora is an undoubted embodiment of spiritual life. She is presented as this here but, even at the outset, her being is not seen in its own present certainty but, at a distance, draws Juan and others as an ideal. Hence she is momentarily an occupant of that standby Romantic category, the ideal woman, who may or may not be an illusion. She is created by 'feelings . . . perhaps ideal' associated nostalgically with the remembered intensities of adolescence ('Who would not sigh'). As she thus becomes a customary, celestial pillow-fantasy for Endymions, 'Alastors' and, even Juan, she is revealed as the imagined object of 'the unblunted dart/Of Eros'. We should maintain 'respect' for the latter but Eros cannot give us eternal life 'as years on years depart'. This, though openly regretted, is covertly enjoyed. Juan goes to sleep in the next stanza full of 'those sweet bitter thoughts' (XVI, 110). We begin these lines then with a transcendent Aurora and end them with the conviction that such transcendence is only a product of the Eros – driven imagination which, though pleasureable in itself, confirms our mortality.

It should be emphasised at once that Aurora cannot be this nor do these lines set up an important alternative reading of her status.[35] Aurora is as unambiguously spiritual as Neuha is unambiguously natural. However, in the same way that Neuha is momentarily seen as an instance of the spiritual and even discredited in comparison to it, so Aurora is seen momentarily as the modified, hence unrecognised, object of Juan's usual drives and as no more than this. In the next stanza, the narrator cunningly transfers the awkward mix of these reflections, which we have associated with his own nostalgic reminiscence, back to Juan's turbulent confusion. In this fashion, we are distanced from these notions and prepared to discredit them:

> And full of sentiments, sublime as billows
> Heaving between this world and worlds beyond,
> Don Juan, when the midnight hour of pillows
> Arrived, retired to his; but to despond
> Rather than rest.
>
> (XVI, 110)

If we recall that Juan, two stanzas later, is about to meet and, pursue a ghost who turns out to be 'Alma Venus Genetrix', then the present confusion of spirit and flesh in his consciousness matches the double arousal of which he is now capable. Aurora is ultimately responsible both for his new capacity to feel spiritual fear and for his at last restored capacity for sexual arousal. The confusion of the two is essential if Juan is to remain any kind of erotic hero but the reader retains a clear sense of their distinction. It is impossible for Juan to acknowledge the puzzling admixture of the erotic in his fascination with Aurora but neither, it seems, is it now possible for him to redirect those awakened drives towards the wholly erotic terminus of the displayed Fitz-Fulke without reservation. The reader is invited to share Juan's arousal by the charmingly defrocked Duchess, laugh delightedly at the restoration of the customary gap in the text which indicates lovemaking, but then recall in the morning light that such simplifications are no longer possible. The poem cannot live by this confidence alone. The next canto is to be about orphans.

The Island, despite the blurrings we have been at pains to point out, contrasts sharply with the Norman Abbey cantos. Why did Byron write it? We can, of course, no more ascertain with certainty what went on in Byron's mind than we can determine what went on in his bed. This has not noticeably deterred the biographer nor need it substantially deflect the critic. We can at any rate establish some possibilities and probabilities. The question is a pertinent one. For if Byron could describe a natural idyll of love in *The Island*, after he had written the first twelve cantos of *Don Juan*, why could he not go on to do so in Norman Abbey?

Let us stand back a little further. Byron wrote *The Age of Bronze* immediately before *The Island*. Again there is some overlap. Canto I of *The Island* and *The Age of Bronze* were completed by 10th January, 1822. Both poems were written between Canto XII and Canto XIII of *Don Juan*. *The Age of Bronze* is a satire 'on politics, etc., etc., etc., and a review of the day in general, − in my early *English Bards* style, but a little more stilted'.[36] It is quite other than *The Island* in manner and concern. If, however, we put them both together we have a centaur more or less identical in balance to *Don Juan*. Byron has, apparently, concluded or suspended his amazing foray into drama, and in these two, very late, poems experiments by again separating the two modes of commentary and narrative upon whose juxtaposition his greatest poem relies.

The Age of Bronze is a well-conducted poem fully of witty phrases and trenchant observation. It is unlikely, however, that it will ever enjoy the attention now given to *The Island* with which it makes, at first glance, an odd comparison. For *The Age of Bronze*, though filled with despair at modern Europe, maintains that revolutionary, liberal confidence which is shown to be based on impossibilities in *The Island*. To be sure, if we read it with *The Island* in mind, we can see how that poem's vision might authorise and sustain indignation at the established order for its hostility to all kinds of natural fulfilment without necessarily suggesting that such fulfilment can easily be brought about within history. Byron intervened in Greek politics only a few months later, motivated in part by an imagined idyll. He took into account too the importance of myth, symbol, even costume, in raising morale and gaining outside support. His intervention was, however, shrewdly practical. He supported the pragmatic leader Mavrocordatos rather than the revolutionary Odysseus, and he would not have been surprised by the subsequent, scarcely idyllic, history of that inescapably Balkan polis.

The problem with *The Age of Bronze* is that, though we can read it with this perspective, the poem itself never indicates any of the paradoxes which always govern Byron's political understanding. *The Island*

is a better poem because it acknowledges that it is a simplifying fable
and indicates the values and difficulties which it cannot accommodate.
It is here that we will find the solution to our earlier quandary. Byron
can write *The Island* because he separates its fable from history. The
presumed history of Bligh and the mutineers occasions the fable and
tethers fiction to fact but the result is not the mixed mode of the
Seraglio cantos. Neuha has affinities with Haidée and Dudù but Juan
would have to be wrenched from his history in order to meet her. None
of Byron's heroines is as unmistakably mythical as Neuha, and *The
Island* is the most explicit of Byron's tales. It is almost an allegory.
Byron must therefore have known that he could not now write another
version of Juan and Haidée without making it quite clear that a natural
paradise is unreachable for the historical reader, or making this realisa-
tion the starting-point for a different kind of heroine. Hence Aurora:

> She look'd as if she sat by Eden's door,
> And grieved for those who could return no more.
>
> (XV, 45)

Aurora and Neuha are the alternatives that remain to Byron beyond
the Siege and Catharine the Great. Neither of these are Byron's 'ordinary romantic heroines' but they are conceived as a complementary pair.
Neuha is

> In growth a woman, though in years a child,
>
> (II, 124)
>
> The infant of an infant world,
>
> (II, 127)

Aurora, on the other hand, is not 'in growth a woman' but

> Early in years, and yet more infantine
> In figure,
>
> (XV, 45)

Aurora lives, however, in the midst of a non-infant world of ruins,
history and a rigid, social order like that on Bligh's ship. Neuha presides over an 'infant world' and is unknowing: 'She feared no ill,
because she knew it not.' (II, 149). Aurora is reflective and 'Sage', she
'look'd more on books than faces,' (XV, 85). The longer we hold these
two divergent figures together, the more clarity we discover in Byron's

purposes in *Don Juan* and we catch a sense of his own lucid but still developing understanding of those purposes.

Amidst the intricacies of these modulations we must hold on to a more and more discernible conclusion. Both *The Island* and Norman Abbey realise a vivid fable of natural resurrection without wholly endorsing it. In *Don Juan*, however, this fable stands in a direct, subordinate but not wholly clear relation to the spiritual reality present in Aurora and the ruined Abbey. It does not use up or simply transform the religious language which encompasses this reality. In effect this means that at the moment when an erotic centre is, for the first time for six cantos, rediscovered in *Don Juan*, it is seen as either actually or potentially displaced by a religious centre, and, in so far as it exists at all, owes its confidence to the religious intimations which we see more clearly as the ground of the narrator's thought and Juan's activities. This is to be more explicit than the poem is but is not to overstate its direction. When for instance R.F. Gleckner argues that:

Juan's "union" with the Duchess will clearly plunge him into the world's way (the ways of Catharine the Great, for example) on its own terms, thus sealing him off forever from the paradise inherent in the figure of Aurora.[37]

or Bernard Blackstone avers that 'Aurora's role is dubious:'[38] or J.J. McGann insists that Aurora 'is fated to join the company of Haidée.'[39] or E.D. Hirsch maintains that Aurora 'is there to preserve the possibility of the ideal',[40] by which he means an ideal 'of an earthly perfection', which bears witness 'to the power of Byron's persistent faith in the possibilities of life', then we may say with reasonable certainty that this is not the case. Often the best critics of Byron's poetry (and those four are clearly among the best) have half-acknowledged this. For instance, Hirsch talks of Byron's 'special sort of religious faith'.[41] Professor Wilson Knight comments that Byron is 'deeply, because essentially, Christian'[42] and he says of *Don Juan*:

As for religion, the world is at the very worst a 'glorious blunder' (XI. 3) and he in half-seriousness — and here that can mean a great deal — subscribes explicitly to orthodoxy (XI. 6); an implicit reverence is continual.[43]

M.G. Cooke remarks that Byron appears finally to endorse a position which 'psychologically and morally . . . resembles the time-honoured position of charitable asceticism'.[44] M.K. Joseph insisted similarly on 'Byron's fundamental seriousness about religion and of the part it plays in the later work'.[45] He suggested that: 'The thorough going nature of Byron's scepticism might have finally led him to orthodoxy, as he himself recognised.'[46] Joseph is echoing here the considered opinion of Shelley which we have already encountered. In a letter to Horace Smith (11th April, 1822) Shelley wrote:

> I have not the smallest influence over Lord Byron, in this particular, and if I had, I certainly should employ it to eradicate from his great mind the delusions of Christianity which, in spite of his reason, seem perpetually to recur.

Shelley's view is confirmed by an anecdote of Sir Walter Scott:

> Our sentiments agreed a good deal, except upon the subjects of religion and politics. I remember saying to him, that I really thought, that if he lived a few years he would alter his sentiments. He answered rather sharply, 'I suppose you are one of those who prophesy I will turn methodist'. I replied, 'No — I don't expect your conversion to be of such an ordinary kind. I would rather look to see you retreat upon the Catholic faith, and distinguish yourself by the austerity of your penances ... ' He smiled gravely, and seemed to allow I might be right.[47]

Don Juan itself, though usually considered irreligious by Byron's contemporaries, persuaded a reviewer in *The Literary Gazette* for 18th August, 1821 that Byron was 'half persuaded to turn Christian'.

With Byron's religious convictions in themselves we are not directly concerned. We would expect to find some consonance between mind and poem. The testimonies of Shelley and Scott, together with Byron's statements in his letters and conversation,[48] are fully in accord with the interpretation of his poetry which we have offered but it is the poetry which has made us ask questions of the life and not vice versa. There can be no doubt that the later cantos of *Don Juan* and *The Island* together indicate Byron's explicit concern with the alternatives of holiness and natural resurrection which assume clearer and clearer definition and, to some extent, even dictate the final form of his truthful navigation o'er fiction.

The *Don Juan* story is from the outset always concerned with Eros and religion. M. Tan, in his inestimable book, demonstrates that the fundamental 'matière' of the original play is religious and that this marks its subsequent history until the nineteenth century with its proliferation of prose *Don Juan*s. At this point, interest begins to shift towards 'l'érotisme et a l'érotomanie' and this coincides with 'la sécularisation de la matière'.[49] Religious motifs persist but Eros is central. A characteristic conflict of nineteenth-century versions of the story is between erotic experience and an unrealised ideal of love.

How easy it would be, by selective quotation, to present Byron's *Don Juan* as typical of this sea-change. Aurora is, as we have seen, once presented (XVI, 107-9) as blurring ideal and erotic love, at any rate in the narrator's whimsy and Juan's consciousness. This section has often been seized on by critics as though it represented the hidden truth about Aurora who can then be approximated to a familiar scenario in a wholly secular epic. However, if we concern ourselves with the adventures of any Don Juan in a way that emphasises the essentially repetitive pattern of his experience, then we are bound to set that clear pattern against the questionable nature of human existence thus illumined and also against the certain, looming boundary of Death which will bring these repetitions to an end and expose them to a clear judgement. Byron's *Don Juan* must be read in this way. If we were to lose ourselves in the felt circumstances of each of Juan's encounters then we would not do this. Instead, like good novel readers, we would be very much taken up with 'The interior of a heart'[50] (the title of Chapter XI in Hawthorne's *The Scarlet Letter*).

Is it plausible that Byron, who was always preoccupied with our complete uncertainty and the ineluctable interposition of death, would not seek out the inceptive implications of the *Don Juan* story albeit in some wholly original way? Byron's Don, like Tirso's, initially appears to have set up or be part of a pattern of escape which can go on forever but the English cantos function like Seville in the last act of *El burlador de Sevilla*; they confine Juan. He experiences fear in them and awaits a clarificatory judgement on the process of which he is the emblem. Both *Childe Harold's Pilgrimage* and *Don Juan* participate fully in the changing experience of their time whilst arresting and questioning the very motifs which they utilise. In a way, Byron's *Don Juan* does instance and help to bring about a largely secular culture in which the promptings of Eros are divinised but, properly attended to, his poem passes a not dissimilar judgement on that faulty divinisation as Tirso da Molina's play:

The nightingale that sings with the deep thorn,
Which Fable places on her breast of wail,
Is lighter far of heart and voice than those
Whose headlong passions form their proper woes.

And that's the moral of this composition,
If people would but see its real drift; —
But *that* they will not do without suspicion,
Because all gentle readers have the gift
Of closing 'gainst the light their orbs of vision;

(VI, 87-8)

Byron's originality however, his distance from Tirso's tragedy and from the pathetic psychologising of its nineteenth-century versions, is seen in the audacity with which he turns *Don Juan* into a comedy. *The Island* will again help us to see how and why this is so.

III

Don Juan is, specifically, a comedy. We have implied as much from the outset but have carefully evaded questioning the term too closely.[51] It is time to be more precise. But we must not be too precice. 'Comedy' is an inherited term frequently reinterpreted. We can use the word readily and be understood without difficulty whilst activating diverse resonances.

Comedy originates in drama and religious ritual. It is often subversive of present society but profoundly conservative in its assumption that the bonds between individuals, society, Nature and the divine are recoverable in each generation. Satirising vice, laughing at absurdity, hoping for a present future, thus converge together. Eros, potentially anarchic, a threat to the order of older generations, is often the agency of this convergence and, by and large, is to be trusted and celebrated in so far as it is so. 'Celebration' is an important word, for the restoration and renewal characteristic of comic endings is accomplished more by Dogberry's folly and Imogen's fidelity than by Adam Overdo's wisdom or Christian Fletcher's revolutionary take-over. Comedy is not a matter therefore of aspiration and make-believe. It has nothing to do with liberal idealism. Accident can be trusted to release men and women from the rough-hewn thicket of their good and bad intentions and lead them to reverence, gratitude and joy. As Suzanne Langer says,

Comedy is an art form that arises naturally where people are gathered to celebrate life ... the delight man takes in his special mental gifts that make him Lord of Creation, it is an image of human vitality holding its own in the world amid the surprises of unplanned coincidence.[52]

Comedy is typically concerned with women, society and Nature. Women are often the link between society and Nature, participating in the division between the two which often occasions the plot and, especially through marriage, they are the means of again reconciling society and Nature. Religious resonances play an implied or fully acknowledged part in this final coincidence. Comedies are playful, irreverent and convention-bound but they engage their audiences' enthusiasm for a providentially supported human life rather than for an artfully contrived fiction.[53] Comedy convinces us that despite our dark intelligence, manifest injustices and the inevitability of death, existence is a beneficent mystery that has priority over all concepts. It does not set argument against argument but finds, within an existence that cannot be contained by the intellect which arraigns it, energies that will effortlessly dispel negations and grant us more than we asked.

The comic ending offers, in one sense, an unexpected and magical transformation of rebarbitive men and material and, in another, we move to a predictable restoration that leaves us rejoicing in the inviolability and sufficiency of our present resources. We might be led, for instance, to posit separate patterns: a picaresque, low-life comedy of pure survival and, on the other hand, the transformation of the orphan/ foundling/ youngest son into the possessor of a casket (leaden or golden) of unlimited treasures and a noble bride or husband. Genres diverge, for survival stories such as *Lazarillo de Tormes* do not need an ending whereas transformation stories depend on one, but we must not exaggerate the divergence. Survival exists in the light of transformation and transformation exists for the sake of survival. One emphasises the continuity of individual life; the other celebrates the continuity of social life. Were this not so, survival would be a record of tainting. In comedy, however, a tainted audience ruefully acknowledges, laughs at and then expels all taint and is brought to recognise and claim a vision of untainted life as its own. We learn to become again like children and 'take things upon trust' (XVI, 6).

Not every comic entity will be eagerly brought to the liberal but still Procrustean bed of these defining paradoxes but most will fit it comfortably enough. If we are to pronounce that x is a comedy, it will be

sufficient if x has some of these characteristics. This will not prevent
it from being other things as well. *Wuthering Heights*, for instance, is,
profoundly, a comedy in this sense, hugely influenced by Scott and
Byron. We can say no more than 'there is an important sense in which
Wuthering Heights is a comedy', however, without denying other
important elements in it. To be a comedy in some more primary sense
than this, our x would have to be much more visibly contained within
its proper history like classical and Renaissance comedies, or find its
principal life in a major redefinition of the term. Comedy exists most
purely in its origins and in new experiments to expose and recover
those origins.

It is evident immediately that *Don Juan* is a comedy at least in the
looser sense shared with *Wuthering Heights* and that it is not a
comedy in the precise sense of a play by Aristophanes. It remains to be
seen whether it is nevertheless primarily a comedy because its principal
life redefines that term for us. We can begin at once by reminding ourselves of those major features of *Don Juan* which do not fit comic patterns.

Don Juan does not end and thus is linked more to a survival than a
transformation pattern. But it is not essentially about Juan's survival
and Juan is not a low-life character. Hence the poem does not appear to
belong to either mode.

Secondly, Don Juan leaves a trail of wrecked lives behind him
including vast numbers in the Siege of Ismail and his principal heroine
in a tomb on a Greek island. This appears to deny Helen Gardner's
law that 'comedy is not concerned with the irreversible, which is why
it must always shun the presentation of death'.[54]

Further, *Don Juan* bitterly exposes the fountain-head of erotically
renewed life in the portrait of Catharine the Great.

Again the brunt of the satire is to emphasise the divide between
social and individual life. This, if anything, is emphasised further in
the final cantos. Hence, as Karl Kroeber[55] argues, it looks as if *Don
Juan* is turning into a novel and cannot be a comedy for that portends
the convergence of social and individual life.

Finally, whether or not it resembles a novel, *Don Juan* is a poem
and comedy is a dramatic rather than a poetic genre.

To this résumé of arguments we may join the other preferred labels
— satire, epic, romance, medley — which have been attached, singly or
in pairs, to the poem, not least by Byron himself (XIV, 99).

Against this conclusion, we may put the perceptive remark of John
Wilson Croker in a letter to John Murray: 'I am agreeably disappointed

at finding 'Don Juan' very little offensive. It is by no means worse than 'Childe Harold' which it resembles as comedy does tragedy.'[56]

When we try to determine whether *Don Juan* is a comedy, the presence of elements which are not in themselves comic does not by itself tell us anything. Comedy, by its very nature, must incorporate anticomic material for that is what it has to outlast or transform. In the same way, comedy can very easily incorporate satire, and has done so from the beginning, for it will have to ridicule, gently or fiercely, the anti-comic material with which it deals. Hence the presence of satire does not necessarily challenge the hold of comedy. On the other hand, it may do so. If we remain wholly within a satiric vision then we can find no reconciliation to the world as it is or conviction of its possible transformation. If, to take an awkward case, we removed Volpone from *Volpone*, it would be hard to maintain a predominantly comic sense of Voltore, Corvino and Corbaccio. The distance separating Juvenal from Molière, Quevedo from Fielding, is not always easy to specify but it is quite easy to perceive. Sometimes, as in Shakespeare's *Merchant of Venice* or *Measure for Measure*, the difference is less perceptible and the subject of continuous debate. In fact, Byron is careful in the English cantos (the most sustained satire in the poem) to emphasise that he is not being as sharp as he might be:

My Muse, the butterfly hath but her wings,
Not stings, and flits through ether without aim,
Alighting rarely:— were she but a hornet,
Perhaps there might be vices which would mourn it.

(XIII, 89)

He makes the same point elsewhere (XIII, 8). Like Aurora, he is not 'stern' (XI, 63; XVI, 94). In a poem which contains the bitter satire on Southey and the Siege the disclaimer may seem ingenuous.[57] It is a half-truth but an important half of the truth.

What we have to concern ourselves with is not the presence or absence of non-comic modes in *Don Juan* but whether it has a central, comic life sufficiently strong to break down and recycle such recalcitrant matter.

Here we must reintroduce *The Island*. Neither Christian Fletcher nor even Ben Bunting are transformed by Byron's comedy on Neuha's island. They remain and die as they are. Nor can we say of them, as we do of Shakespeare's Malvolio or Jacques, that the comic conclusion is strengthened by their exclusion from it. We should not identify ourselves with Malvolio or Jacques and we will not finally identify ourselves with Bligh and Christian Fletcher but Bligh, Christian Fletcher and Ben Bunting typify the reader's predicament whilst Torquil and Neuha support only his fantasies. We will not recognise England in Toobonai nor will we wish to leave England and go to Tahiti for there we would repeat the experience of the mutineers.

The Island is therefore a comedy only in the sense that *Wuthering Heights* is, though we may qualify this by noting that the double ending of Emily Brontë's novel is tilted towards the tragic polarity in feeling and the comic polarity in substance whereas Byron's poem reverses those emphases.

The resurrection of Torquil, though it cannot convert everything that has preceded it into comedy, is unprecedented in Byron's poetry. Byron wrote many tales of love and everyone of them ends unhappily[58] except *The Island*. Comedy of a kind then was produced by Byron in the weeks preceding the Norman Abbey cantos but *Don Juan* cannot deal with recalcitrant matter as *The Island* does for it lacks an intended full stop and evades the fabulous. The apparently Toobonai-like society of Haidée's isle has in fact participated in Lambro's guilt and memorialises her fall. The society of Norman Abbey is an admirable target for satire but we cannot forecast its comic transformation.

We have, however, identified interrelated agencies opposed to the anti-comic society of the Abbey. These are the old house itself, the supporting landscape and its surrounding space, Aurora Raby, the ghost, night, and the glowing Duchess. Don Juan himself, so long a cypher of the narrator, is engaged by each of these. The reader again becomes interested in wonderful events whose outcome he does not automatically distrust. Once again, the poem appears to have a clue which sustains it in the dark labyrinth of its invention whilst, at the same time, Eros and a laughter untainted by sneers, connect together the antitheses upon whose separation the narrator's poised superiority depends.

This notable convergence, and Norman Abbey is a place of greater convergences than Haidée's or Neuha's island, takes place at night. The night is when Black Friar and amorous Duchess display themselves, when unearthly music sounds in the great arch and when the unattended cycle of natural life is unmistakably active. The house then vibrates with its own history and its own space.

Night has been significant in the poem prior to this for two reasons. It is the time of love-making (I, 113; II, 183; VI, 70) and of writing *Don Juan* (XV, 97). As it happens *The Island*, too, delicately incorporates night into its structure. The poem opens:

> The morning watch was come;
> . . .
> The quiet night, now dappling, 'gan to wane,
> Dividing darkness from the dawning main;

> (I, 7-8)

During this night, the mutineers have prepared their plot against the unsuspecting Bligh: 'Awake! Awake! — alas! it is too late!' (I, 52). *The Island* ends with a festal night:

> A night succeeded by such happy days
> As only the yet infant world displays!

> (IV, 419-20)

Thus the days and nights of the mutineers belong to history's sober, sad antitheses but the islanders enjoy an infant world of festal repetition. Torquil's dive into the black rock is a ritual plunge into a similitude of night from which he is awakened by Neuha's blazing life, rescued from history and death, and admitted permanently to Toobonai's natural heaven.

The part played by the island corresponds to the role of night in Norman Abbey. The mutineers cannot break through to the real life of the island and, not belonging, roam its surface until they are reclaimed by the consciousness which they have renounced and its concomitant death. This does not appear clearly at first. An early section of the poem (II, 238-71) shows the mutineers intermarrying and apparently settling down but this leads immediately into a much longer account of Torquil and Neuha. We next encounter the other mutineers in the figure of Ben Bunting, smoking a pipe, festooned with European weapons and careful to preserve European decencies by a 'somewhat scanty mat' which 'Now served for inexpressibles and hat' (II, 483). He informs Torquil that the naval ship has come for them but his unaltered appearance, fearfully comic because its incongruousness portends his exemption from a comic finale, marks the difference between the other mutineers and Torquil.[59] In the fight that follows, Ben Bunting has a companion who, in the brief interval that waits him before his death,

> Walked up and down — at times would stand, then stop

To pick a pebble up — then let it drop —
Then hurry as in haste — then quickly stop —
Then cast his eyes on his companions — then
Half whistle half a tune, and pause again —
And then his former movements would redouble,
With something between carelessness and trouble.

(III, 110-18)

These characteristics of the mutineers, together with the portrait of Christian Fletcher's bitter heroism, make plain their maddening perception of ordinary time and the persistence of a European consciousness which the 'infant world' cannot obliterate in them.

The guests of Norman Abbey are not dissimilarly placed. Like the mutineers, they are bored in their beautiful setting. They are dimly aware perhaps of the ruined past of the house and its reputed ghost who is 'lord by night' but they are trapped in a daytime world without resonance. What is the status of the world from which they are excluded? Tahiti can be found on a map but Toobonai exists only as 'the green isle' of Byron's imagination.[60] The night-time world of Norman Abbey is not fabulous or mythical in this sense. A real history, an actual space, the tangible properties of night, are present to Juan in Canto XVI both in his experience of fear and in his attraction for Aurora Raby. Everything is reversed from *The Island*. Neuha conducts Torquil to a simple, mythical world but Aurora represents knowledge, history and being in a world of bland ignorance, current gossip and frenetic activity. Torquil crosses from one world to another; Aurora represents a higher world in the world as it is. The Duchess flits from daylight to darkness. She is ignorant and trivialising but represents in Eros a primary force which, too, emerges from the mysterious inertia of night.

Byron writes in 'Detached Thoughts': 'The night too is a religious concern.'[61] The abbey's 'religious concern' has been displaced by a secularising history but night restores it and, at the same time, restores Eros to the poem. The Eros thus celebrated cannot be the untainted blessing found in an infant world. If we momentarily think so when confronted by the Duchess (and how could we not?), the morning light will disabuse us. On the other hand, what the night brings is not designated 'for the imagination only' as is Tahitian bliss. Hence it is at least possible that *Don Juan* is a comedy in a more substantial and primary way than *The Island*.

Our first objection will help us here. *Don Juan*, it seems, is not a comedy because it is neither a tale of survival nor of transformation. Juan loses zest but cannot find a larger identity. Now the normal form of comic transformation is found in marriage:

> All tragedies are finish'd by a death,
> All comedies are ended by a marriage;
> The future states of both are left to faith,
>
> (II, 9)

Juan has been found in a natural marriage of a kind with Haidée, and still recalls that bond. Round that natural marriage, a comic society was formed. However, the anti-comic Lambo returns and destroys that society instead of being permanently expelled from it or, as is the wont of older generations in comedy, being reconciled to it. We do not wholly reproach Lambro for this because the comic society has been founded, like that of *Sardanapalus*, on forgetfulness of history, and it incorporates too little.

With Aurora Raby, however, there are, for the first time in the poem, definite intimations of marriage in the customary sense. Juan himself, 'half smiling and half serious' (XV, 49), instead of rejecting Adeline's suggestions altogether singles out Aurora as a suitable bride. Adeline's intense hostility to this and evident willingness to plot against it already sets up a framework typical of the opening movements of a comic action. Adeline's omission of the orphan Aurora from her list of possible brides for Juan is reminiscent of folk and fairy tales.

It may seem inconceivable that Byron's Don Juan will marry, but coy hints of this begin as soon as Juan reaches England:

> Whether he married with the third or fourth
> Offspring of some sage, husband-hunting countess,
> Or whether with some virgin of more worth
> . . .
> Is yet within the unread events of time.
>
> (XI, 89-90)

In the next canto 'he flirted without sin' (XII, 25) but

> . . . had not seen of several hundred
> A lady altogether to his mind.
>
> (XII, 81)

Much of the satire of the London cantos has to do with marriage and marriage-making which, in this respect at least, is connected to preceding cantos. Hence Adeline's match-making manoeuvres arise out of the early cantos as well as from Byron's satire on English life. We are not unprepared then for Juan's finding 'some virgin of more worth' who will be 'altogether to his mind'. Juan's previous adventures in Russia, Seraglio and Greek Island have been in milieus which did not offer marriage as a possibility and, in any case, were the exotic setting through which a Don Juan can pass but never linger. In England, however, which Juan shows no signs of leaving after six cantos, he is subordinated to the ways of a society in which, as a diplomat, he plays a recognisable role. Juan does not travel independently or play romance adventures within this society but takes his part in the accepted social migration from metropolis to country house.

If this is beginning to sound like the novel that Karl Kroeber claims *Don Juan* turns into, it should be admitted that appearances here support his case. Nowhere is this more so than in the sustained character-portrait of Lady Adeline who dominates Cantos XIII and XIV. One again we are given a series of coy hints about a future relationship with Juan. She is described when we meet her as 'The fair most fatal Juan ever met,' and, in a proleptic vision of future events, we are told that 'Destiny and Passion spread the net . . . and caught them' (XIII, 12). This is an allusion, doubtless, to fishermen, gladiators and to Mars and Venus. Presumably Lord Henry would be in Vulcan's position of enraged husband. The narrator announces that he will tell this tale, 'And now I will proceed upon the pair.' (XIII, 13) and, in so doing, tells us that Juan and Adeline form, or will form, a pair. However, we now encounter *Don Juan*'s equivalent to Hamlet's notorious delay. A whole canto later we are told 'I think not she was *then* in love with Juan:' (XIV, 91) and, worse still:

> Whether Don Juan and chaste Adeline
> Grew friends in this or any other sense,
> Will be discuss'd hereafter, I opine:
> At present I am glad of a pretence
> To leave them hovering, as the effect is fine,
> And keeps the atrocious reader in *suspense*;
>
> (XIV, 97)

If Canto XVII is, as announced, to be about the orphan Aurora, then we are to be kept hovering longer than we may sustain suspense. The promised love-affair between Adeline and Juan seems to have been indefinitely postponed. If, eventually, it does occur, we will not, as we might have anticipated in Canto XIII, relate it to Adeline and Juan's relation with Lord Henry, English Society with its dead marriages and scandalous adulteries, or even to the sexual awakening of a woman wholly committed to social roles. We will not do this because the quite unexpected status of Aurora, Juan's revival, and the sense, given by Aurora and the ghost, that the opening description of Norman Abbey is to be picked up in our later understanding of the action, destroy Adeline's purported centrality. M.K. Joseph boldly speculates:

> As a personal guess, one might suggest that the future development of *Don Juan* was to be something like this. Juan was to be involved in a divorce, and since this could hardly be the Fitz-Filke, it must be the Lady Adeleine. The affair with the frolicsome countess was perhaps intended to precipitate the jealous concern of Lady Adeline, and thaw her dangerously "frozen" passions; a cause célèbre would follow – this is the kind of situation being prepared, for example in *Don Juan*, XIII, 14. But the real tragedy would be this, that the scandal would render impossible any marriage between Juan and Aurora Raby. That would be why Lady Adeline is "the fair most fatal Juan ever met"– she was to be the reason why Juan would lose his second, and perhaps final, chance of ideal happiness;[62]

This very intelligent guess work relies on a local misreading. If 'Destiny and Passion spread the net . . . And caught them' (XIII, 12) then the implication at this stage must be that the 'fatal' thing is the intensity of their passion rather than its effects. But Joseph is certainly right about the larger grammar of the poem. Whatever Byron's earlier intentions, the reader begins to apply the words 'the fair most fatal' to the effects of Adeline on the relationship of Juan and Aurora. Fitz-Fulke too plays her part in this for no description of Adeline's arousal subsequent to Fitz-Fulke's escapade could engage our attention as it might if it were the first reappearance of Eros in the poem since Catharine the Great.

It is possible that the announcement and then apparent avoidance of the promised affair with Adeline reveals Byron's altered tactics. He needs to recover Eros for the poem. An affair with Adeline, analogous as he very broadly hints (XIV, 100) to his own affair with Lady Frances Wedderburn Webster, exactly suits Juan's new setting. We are familiar now with Greek islands and Seraglios, here is love in an English climate.

But it is no longer possible to describe this even as he portrayed Juan's first affair with Julia which is its closest parallel. Eros in *Don Juan* must have a glowing warmth which is not wholly based on illusion nor merely on physiological or psychological mechanisms. If this last sentence is untrue, then *Don Juan* is an uncomplicated, realist novel and there would be no need for Byron to alter direction by introducing Fitz-Fulke's adventure and Aurora Raby's being. That he does so suggests a deeper plan than M.K. Joseph's or a suddenly perceived strategy which enables him to avoid the poem's concurrence with the narrator's knowing disillusion and to recover what has been lost. Which of these it was, we cannot know with certainty.[63] It is significant, however, that the earliest reference to Juan's English adventures (in a letter to Murray written before Canto VI) singles out the divorce which he causes. It is conceived as part of a series of different social tableaus of love:

> I meant to have made him a Cavalier Servente in Italy and a cause for a divorce in England — and a Sentimental "Werther faced man" in Germany — so as to show the different ridicules of the society in each of those countries — and to have displayed him gradually gaté and blasé as he grew older — as is natural. — But I had not quite fixed whether to make him end in Hell — or in an unhappy marriage, — not knowing which would be the severest.[64]

The difference between the actual and predicted modes of the poem would repay investigation and should warn us against identifying this intelligence with the whole of Byron's intelligence. We can note here that the English intention alone survives in the poem. The hints at divorce and calamity, which occur as soon as Adeline is introduced, must be linked to this otherwise effaced scheme conceived before the Siege and Russian cantos had induced a deeper malaise in the poem's development than Juan's. It is probable therefore that Aurora, Fitz-Fulke and the ghost represent an initiative which surprises their inventor but answers his deeper sense of what is now necessary in the poem. Byron's persisting coyness about the future of his characters keeps his readers guessing and allows the transformation of his original purpose:

> Above all, I beg all men to forbear
> Anticipating aught about the matter:
> They'll only make mistakes about the fair,
> And Juan too, specially the latter.

(XIV, 99)

As Byron notes, (XIV, 66), good advice is rarely heeded and we have not followed his. Instead we have tried to understand also why he gives us this advice so often at this stage in *Don Juan*.

The conditions of the restoration of what has been lost in Norman Abbey, as in *The Winter's Tale*, are a naming of the spiritual, an acceptance of loss without accompanying bitterness, and hope. Aurora Raby unambiguously represents these things. Adeline's hostility to her which, like her resentment of Fitz-Fulke, originates in a quasi-novel of unacknowledged jealousy,[65] turns into an emblematic warfare between different kinds of human being in a poem which has reabsorbed its offshoot. The reader's interest shifts away from Adeline's activities which, like Madame Bovary's, are motivated by emotional restlessness based on sexual unfulfilment:

> A something all-sufficient for the *heart*
> Is that for which the sex are always seeking;
> But how to fill up that same vacant part?
>
> (XIV, 74)

Don Juans, eager to fill this 'vacant part' and move on, are the male counterpart of this restlessness. Aurora finds another sufficiency to counter this disquiet:

> As grows a flower, thus quietly she grew,
> And kept her heart serene within its zone.
>
> (XV, 47)

She confers something of her stillness on Byron's peripatetic gigolo. Only such a transformation could return Juan and the poem to their originating comic life. Don Juan Tenorio returns from his exotic adventures to a stable society so that his tragedy may be 'finish'd by a death'; Byron's Juan appears ready for the other transforming conclusion in England.

Transformations, we have said, often involve restoration. The mutineers on the *Bounty* seek to be restored to a society once visited in the prison-house of their ship (I, 207) which embodies an innocence now claimed as primordially theirs. In comedy, low-life characters are often transformed into princes and princesses but discover to their amazement that they were originally born as such. The orphan Aurora, from her vantage-point at 'Eden's door', knows all about this but smiles. She remains miraculously in contact with pristine states whilst touched by that world's sadness which, unaccepted, finally ravages the face and serpent-like body of Christian Fletcher, as it marks Cain his ancestor (IV, 336-44). Aurora is Wordsworth's 'boy of Winander' and the mature visonary of Snowdon.[66] She is a wholly new experience for Juan but restores what he has lost (XVI, 107). She resembles 'not his lost Haidée' but is equally radiant 'in her proper sphere' (XV, 58). She is a gem where Haidée is a flower.

Some literary critics have a peculiar hostility to gems. Bernard Blackstone, for instance, complains of Aurora's coldness and says of the flower/gem antithesis, 'a comparison which tells us all we need to know'.[67] If it is essential for a heroine to have the properties of a flower, Aurora is given the necessary credentials elsewhere (XV, 43, 47). She is a flower as well as a gem. Gems sparkle but, it must be admitted, do so with extrinsic light (like 'sunny seas'), and their radiance may appear cold and hard. Flowers, superior in these respects, perform less well when it comes to the duration of their glow. Rosebuds are blithely gathered but, like the borealis race, tend to flit ere you can point their place. Even Haidée's status is, in a way, enhanced when her natural life ebbs away and she becomes like 'exquisitely chisell'd marble' (IV, 61). There is a real advantage in the gem and what it symbolises. We should not allow our modern reluctance to look beyond the natural to dictate our interpretation for Byron knew his emblems and 'the old text'. The traditional alternative to a garden paradise, whose attempted recovery renews the warm poignancy of loss, is a celestial, jewelled city which cannot be imagined. The feelings, even of Milton, more naturally cluster round vivid imaginings of an abandoned garden, like Haidée's isle 'all desolate and bare' (IV, 72), than the substance of things hoped for, an apprehended but not experienced wholeness of life. Only Dante perhaps could convince us of the superior strength and sweetness of a finally unimaginable *Paradiso* to the denser experience of his *Inferno*. Is not the *Divine Comedy* a comedy, irrespective of whether we believe that the picaresque Florentine is himself permanently transformed by the vision which finally stills his sequential consciousness and restores what he has lost in a different mode. The often mentioned smile of Beatrice and her eyes radiant with reflected light, may have influenced Byron's portrait of Aurora. Byron, we say at once, is creating a human comedy, not a divine one.[68] Nevertheless Aurora acts in this human comedy as a terminus of a special kind who, if Adeline is 'the fair most fatal Juan e'er met', cannot be surpassed in Juan's history. Byron knows that she will not draw our imagination after her in the same way that Haidée did, for her poignancy is of a different kind. She cannot be forced to re-enact her bright experience in a dark dream and remember what she has forgotten since Aurora's radiance accepts and is nourished by darkness and a remembered history. On the other hand, Aurora has no human father to cherish and forget. Like Catharine, Aurora is womanhood without the restraining interpolations of father or husband. She draws men to her and through her to the forces with which she is intimate but to opposite effect. Similarly, both her radiance and her gravity are unalterable because they take fully into account the agencies which threaten them. It is this steadiness which enrages the 'mobile' Lady Adeline and attracts Juan who has had a sufficiency of flowers. It is not that flowers are rejected but their celebration is linked too closely with poignancy and loss, 'sweet-bitter thoughts', for comedy's comfort. Haidée cannot be restored by another mortal flower.

Juan's attraction to Aurora restores something else that has been lost. At the beginning of the poem, when Juan first falls in love with Julia, he is suddenly rendered

> Silent and pensive, idle, restless, slow,
> His home deserted for the lonely wood,
>
> (I, 87)

In the 'leafy nooks' of this adjacent landscape Juan is aware also of its puzzling openness to unimaginable spaces:

> . . . of the many bars
> To perfect knowledge of the boundless skies;
>
> (I, 92)

The narrator makes fun here of Juan, Wordsworth and adolescence in an epigram which appears to|settle the matter:

> If *you* think 'twas philosophy that this did,
> I can't help thinking puberty assisted.
>
> (I, 93)

On all future occasions, as we have seen, Juan's tumult is bounded and directed by physical proximity to a woman. It cannot acquire a surrogate life of its own.

The effect of Aurora on Juan, however, is not dissimilar to that of Julia but the narrator does not seek to destroy it. For Juan's love-making with Julia in Seville placates and uses up his metaphysical tumult which thus appears to be, as the narrator claims, a by-product of puberty. Moreover, Julia is, less excusably, prey to a similar self-deception. Aurora Raby, on the other hand, the initiator of Juan's new thoughtfulness, possesses in a serene and apparently understood form the same intimations that she causes. The glow of Fitz-Fulke does not obliterate or use up this different intensity, though we have seen in Juan's consciousness, just before his encounter with the Duchess, a confused blend of Eros and spirituality.

Hence we must say that Aurora, beyond and before the onrush of sexuality, somehow restores to Juan both the sexual passion associated with Haidée and a purity which is the condition of other kinds of acknowledgement. In the design of these cantos, these things are clearly demarcated but they are blurred in Juan himself. Aurora represents the survival of innocence ('in growth a child'), the sad fruits of pondered experience ('so very sage') and a transforming attention to a far more deeply interfused immediacy. She is, in ideal form, where Juan has come from and what he might attain. She represents too that blend of fiction and real, trusted space which the poem discloses as its own proper life and to which the narrator is brought to say 'Yes'. This is not a familiar Romance or Romantic ideal but a discovery in the midst of satire, farce and festivity of an indestructible spiritual reality on which comedy's celebration of the contingent rests. *Don Juan* ends, like any comedy, with a joyously recovered starting point.

It would smack of hubris to insert a *Quod Erat Demonstrandum* at this point but the main outline of our argument should now be clear. We should at any rate be able to deal with most of the objections to *Don Juan* as comedy that we earlier listed.

Haidée's death can be fully accepted because Aurora restores more than has been lost. For Aurora not only represents an equivalent radiance to Haidée but one that already incorporates death and a dark history, and thus cannot be threatened by them in the same way. Similarly, though Aurora cannot be used as a glib antidote to the deaths of Ismail, she does represent a wholly different way of transforming the wastes of history into an unbounded life than Catharine the Great.

It is inaccurate also to place the secondary, social life of Norman Abbey alongside the primary life of an individual and argue that *Don Juan* is therefore turning into a novel. Byron's characterisation is magnificent but he is closer to Chaucer[69] then he is to George Eliot. He is concerned far more with the energies and forces which underly individual and social life than he is with the interior of a heart. Consider, for instance, the names that he uses in the last section of the poem.

Aurora Raby is awe, dawn, ray and baby.[70] Adeline picks up the latter as a pejorative but we are instructed to interpret it as 'young', 'innocent' and 'child'. The Duchess of Fitz-Fulke is as transparently named as Congreve's Lady Wishfort. Adeline Amundeville presides aristocratically over Worldly Town.[71] Our wayfarer in this emblematic territory is not Bunyan's Christian but our damnable friend Don Juan. What is portended here is not nineteenth-century tensions between individual and social life but the perennially comic intimations of a wholly renovated human life, whether naturally or supernaturally based. Byron's satire comes from this never yielded intimation but his refusal to yield it takes him in the end either to the splendid but merely imagined territory of Neuha's island or to the brink of Aurora's orthodoxy. If he had crossed that brink he would not have written *The Island*, but in the last cantos of *Don Juan* he bases a knowingly different comedy on the religious foundations that underlie archetypal comedy and the original *Don Juan*.

That Byron was aware of this is certain but that he had this degree of explicit understanding we may doubt. Aurora is an answer to the literary and religious question: 'On what foundation can a comic reading of life be based?' The question can be felt in Byron's biography and underlies not only *Don Juan* but also *Beppo*, *The Vision of Judgement* and *The Island* which were written whilst Byron was also fashioning his deliberately traditional, but also experimental, tragedies. *Don Juan* is the record of his engagement with this problem and his solution of it.

We may associate Byron's ability to redefine but still use the fundamental modes of Western Literature with his reiterated sense that his contemporaries were not transmitting usable idioms. *The Excursion*, *Prometheus Unbound*, Blake's Prophetic Books, for instance, have magnificent passages but they do not work. The Victorians inherited a diction from Keats, some metrical forms from Shelley and a bias to 'the lyric' and 'narrative verse', as the only poetic genres that functioned. Byron's worries about what would occur in English poetry after his death were fully justified. *Don Juan* was designed to offer different possibilities for the future but it was left to Pushkin to make something of them.

Romantic poetry is, of course, notorious for the indeterminacy of its genres. An important factor here is the conclusion which often determines genre more than mode does. It is unusual for the conclusion of long Romantic poems in English to be as crucial as they might be. The

last book of *The Prelude* is superb but no one reads the poem for the
end which it reaches but rather for the central imagined experience continually summoned for definition throughout. By the end of Keats's
odes or *The Eve of St. Agnes*, an ambiguous something has ceased, but
no amount of inspecting Beauty and Truth will give us a verdict on or
represent some further development of that ambiguous entity. Readers
of *The Ancient Mariner* are no better placed. Though the journey stops
and a moral is given, it is the centre which holds us.

This is a familiar diagnosis and may be turned into praise but it is
not helpful to readers of Byron's poetry. The last cantos of *Childe
Harold's Pilgrimage* and *Don Juan*, the full stops at the end of *Beppo*,
the *Vision of Judgement* and the three tragedies, fully determine the
whole which they conclude. Byron wrote to Murray: 'You have
destroyed the whole effect and moral of the poem, by omitting the last
line of Manfred's speaking'.[72] The comment reveals Byron's concern for
his endings. We cannot make sense of *Don Juan* unless we take its final
cantos as a clarifying development of the whole poem. Comedy is invariably teleological. *Don Juan* always was, whatever it becomes.

In this important respect, its closest counterpart is not in English
Romantic[73] poetry at all but in the major work of Byron's admired and
admiring contemporary Goethe. Goethe's *Faust* reinterprets the story
of Don Juan Tenorio's contemporary and, also, turns a tragedy into the
semblance of comedy.

IV

The relationship of Byron to Goethe has been extensively and sensibly
examined.[74] There are two points nevertheless arising out of their comparison which will enable us to clarify our argument much as we invoked Hume at the end of Chapter 2. These two issues are the use of
Christian symbols and structures in secular fictions and the interplay
between north and south represented in Goethe's Euphorion.

Euphorion is the child of Faust and Helen in Part II of *Faust*. He is,
in part, a tribute to the recently dead Byron. Euphorion is the product
of a northern, introspective culture and a southern culture enamoured
of natural life. He is seen attempting to rape a woman, striving beyond
bounds, and eventually falling like Icarus. However, his brief life has
united Faust's intellectual energy with Helen's native country and thus
set about the liberation of Greece from the Turks. To this heady brew,
we must add Goethe's personal transformation by his own visit to Italy

about the time of Byron's birth which he records in his *Italian Journey*.

For Goethe, Italy and the Italians seem to have represented a more attainable version of what the mutineers sought on Neuha's Isle. The *Italian Journey*, it is true, recounts paintings seen, learned conversations, and churches visited, but all these are presented as dramatically intensifying an idyll of present existence. The darker resonances of Italian history and life, which engage Byron in Canto IV of *Childe Harold's Pilgrimage* and in his Venetian plays, do not interest Goethe. He is clearly intrigued by Catholicism but, though figures like St Philip Neri evade his fascinated attempt to transform them into enlightened German seers, he can for the most part turn Catholicism into a useful device for appeasing legitimate, popular demand for a mythologised, yearly cycle which nevertheless suggests some basic spiritual truths. These basic truths are Goethe's version of the high-minded commonplaces of eighteenth-century natural religion.

Byron intermittently voiced not dissimilar convictions and, like Goethe, found in Italy 'the garden of the world' (*Childe Harold*, IV, 26). Goethe assumed that Byron was travelling in much the same direction as himself though at a slower pace. It remains customary to nod to Byron's Calvinist upbringing and, with varying degrees of emphasis, to allow for its influence even in Byron's later life. Goethe, as we saw in Chapter 1, took for granted that Byron's *Cain* was written to free himself from the Christian doctrines imbibed earlier.

This easy reasonableness denies what was obvious to the disinterested witness of Scott and Shelley and should be apparent to the reader of *Beppo*, *The Vision of Judgement*, *Cain*, *Heaven and Earth*, *The Deformed Transformed* and *Don Juan*, that Byron developed and changed emphasis in religious matters just as he did in politics. Religion was not a recalled experience to him but a present problem bound up with an enigmatic future. He called himself, and was called by Shelley, a 'pilgrim of eternity'. It was obvious to Dr James Kennedy, with whom Byron had his famous conversations on religion,[75] that Byron was not a convinced, believing Christian. It was equally obvious to the onlookers of that debate that Byron brought to it a life-long preoccupation with religious evidence and belief. As always, Byron's jokes are instructive. He pretended that he was already converted by Kennedy and exclaimed:

Oh! I shall begin the 17th Canto of
Don Juan a changed man.[76]

The Christian religion presented by Dr Kennedy, familiar to Byron from his youth, centred on the rational and moral exposition of the Bible. There can be no doubt, however, that Byron's sojourn in Italy had made real to him the different life of southern Catholicism.[77] This blended or juxtaposed asceticism, an acceptance of natural pleasures, esoteric symbols and tangible sacraments,[78] vulgarity and the sublime. It also recognised and promoted in the cult of Our Lady a distinctively feminine icon of spiritual life. The change from his 'moderate Presbyterian' upbringing (XV, 91) to life with a Catholic mistress who dosed him with Dante is as dramatic as anything that happened to Goethe. Byron was not allowed to educate his daughter by his estranged wife but he did give Allegra, his natural daugher, an Italian convent education: 'It is, besides, my wish that she should be a Roman Catholic'.[79] He was determined that Allegra should not be brought up in the atheistic rationalism of Shelley and his circle.[80] It is possible that there is some affinity between Allegra who died in 1822 aged five and, in that sense, remained an infant, with the creation of Aurora less than a year later. It is curious that Shelley, who certainly fictionalised the real Allegra in *Julian and Maddalo*, calls her:

A serious, subtle, and yet gentle being,
Graceful without design and unforeseeing,
With — oh speak not of her eyes! — which seem
Twin mirrors of Italian Heaven, yet gleam
With such deep meaning.

(145-9)

and then, at the end of the poem, imagines her now 'become A woman . . . Like one of Shakespeare's women' (592). The Shelley circle called the young Allegra 'Alba, or the Dawn' and introduced her to Byron with this name.

The oddness of Byron, and the difficulty of dealing with him, has always been attributed to the inseparability of Byron's life and work. It is only comparatively recently that his poetry has received extensive attention without respect to his extraordinary life. Yet certain customary kinds of interconnection do not obtain. Keats's famous line in the 'Ode to a Nightingale', 'Where youth grows pale, and spectre-thin, and dies;' still carries the famous annotation that Keats's brother Tom had just died before the line was written.[81] Faust's betrayal of Gretchen is always, and naturally, related to Goethe's abandonment of Friederike Brion. Who does not know that the author of *The Ancient*

Mariner had recurrent nightmares, took opium and had real or feigned visitors from Porlock? Not so the reader of Byron's verse, who has no particular sense of whether Byron changed his mind about anything and does not envisage a separate but interpolating biography. The comparison we drew earlier, for instance, between Lady Adeline and Lady Frances Wedderburn Webster, is not a familiar one. I tried once to see if the death and cremation of Shelley, an event which undoubtedly moved Byron, surfaced in the poetry written at that time and discovered that the stanzas in *Don Juan* on death, addressed to a skeleton (IX, 11-12), were indeed written then. Whether that event played any part in their conception is impossible to know. Certainly, if it did, it is well effaced, could not intrude on a reader's consciousness and should not be mentioned by a zealous annotator. In the same way, emphatically, Aurora Raby should not recall Allegra to our mind whilst reading *Don Juan*, though I think it possible that she is a response to Shelley's version of Allegra in *Julian and Maddalo*[82] and probable that she represents Byron's alternative vision to Shelley's sequence of idealised heroines. Byron's verse cannot be got at in this way for he incorporates history into fiction explicitly and cares little for the critical sleuth who, like Byron's friend Hobhouse, is moved to produce *Historical Illustrations* to Byron's poetry.[83] Byron's advice is to the point:

> And recollect the work is only fiction
> And that I sing of neither mine nor me,
> Though every scribe, in some slight turn of diction,
> Will hint allusions never meant. N'er doubt
> *This* — when I speak, I *don't hint*, but *speak out*.
>
> (XI, 88)

The conclusion is true but the premiss is only half-true for, of course, 'my Muse by no means deals in fiction' (XIV, 13).

The modern photographs of Newstead Abbey, for example, which are included in this book are of buildings inside and outside *Don Juan*. Many of Byron's contemporaries wrote about or painted ruined abbeys but Byron lived in one. He did not build it like Beckford or Walter Scott, he inherited a Gothic ruin. If we read Mme. de Staël's *Corinne* (1807), we are taken aback by the closeness of the fictional Oswald to the real Lord Byron. Fictions break into the life of Byron and his life is a supreme fiction for others. We should not dissolve these peculiarities by dismissing Byron as 'theatrical' in a neo-Puritan cant, nor, conversely, claim Byron's support for the present cult of fictionality

über alles.

The forms of fictional and non-fictional life are similar, often identical. Both are kept going by plots, happy endings, coincidence, new characters, misfortunes, deaths and marriage. Artists fashion their art from their experience and audiences fashion their experiences out of art. Both arise out of an unknowable blankness disclosed or forgotten in the intervening shapes. The status and controllability of these forms, however, is not the same. The arch of Newstead Abbey sounds, if at all, when it pleases. The arch of Norman Abbey sings at Byron's direction and ever in the ears of his readers. Yet if we were to hear Newstead Abbey's 'unearthly sound', we would also be hearing what the guests in Norman Abbey could hear. This is not because Newstead Abbey is a real building just as Catharine the Great is a historical personage. The photographs in this book are not annotatory in function. They are not simply modern pictures of the buildings and statue once used by Lord Byron as the basis of his fictions for, certainly, the buildings in the photographs, though modified by later owners, are still receptive to whatever Norman Abbey was in contact with, if we are convinced by the poem that Norman Abbey exists in real space. Any visitor to Newstead Abbey who knows his Byron is alerted to the disparity between the listening building and its declared use. A more reassuring effect would be produced by substituting for these photographs some pictures of Newstead Abbey in Byron's time.

Byron was peculiarly sensitive to the baffling emergence of thoughts and living forms:

> But words are things, and a small drop of ink,
> Falling like dew, upon a thought, produces
> That which makes thousands, perhaps millions, think;

(III, 88)

Random and inexplicable initiatives shape themselves into intelligibility and history, thus undermining either the randomness of the random or the intelligibility of the intelligible. Napoleon's meteoric career fascinated Byron for this reason. *Don Juan* is a mimesis of this conundrum but does not stand apart from it. Though the poem is more controllable than the world which it presupposes, Byron yields much of his authorial advantage and, as it were, allows his improvisations to stand just as we have to in our reluctantly moral lives. Byron's claim is not literally true but the spirit of it is confirmed by the poem:

> . . . there's no servility
> In mind irregularity of chime,
> Which rings whats uppermost of new or hoary,
> Just as I feel the Improvvisatore.
>
> (XV, 20)

Goethe's activity as an author is quite different. His art is always a *bildungsroman*. He constructed *Faust* over the course of his life just as Byron fashioned *Childe Harold's Pilgrimage* and *Don Juan* in the course of his, but we see Goethe transferring material from one to the other. Thus we can say of Goethe that his sojourn in Italy opened his eyes to the wholeness of southern culture and that his revalued version of Faust's love for Helen derives from this. Southern culture can be recognised here clearly and separately in Goethe's non-fictional account, in his altered subjectivity, and in his fiction. We encounter these fully formed and are not reminded of their puzzling emergence.

In much the same way, we notice Christian myth used as such in *Faust*. We are not surprised to learn of Goethe's disengagement from the myth which he uses and may be edified by Goethe's oecumenical endorsement of the coincidence of his aesthetic and moral purposes with the substance of that myth:

"In these lines" said he, "is contained the key to Faust's salvation. In Faust himself there is an activity that becomes constantly higher and purer to the end, and from above there is eternal love coming to his aid. This harmonizes perfectly with our religious views; according to which we can obtain heavenly bliss, not through our strength alone, but with the assistance of divine grace. "You will confess that the conclusion, where the redeemed soul is carried up, was difficult to manage; and that amid such supersensual matters about which we scarcely have even an intimation, I might easily have lost myself in the vague – if I had not, by means of sharply-drawn figures from the Christian Church, given my poetical design a desirable form and substance".[84]

Similarly Goethe, like Byron, relies on the figure of the Blessed Virgin at the end of *Faust* and uses her to represent a fusion of the practical, erotic and spiritual agencies which draw men (genus and gender) 'Upward and on!'[85]

All this would be a great deal clearer if Goethe was more puzzled by what he was doing. As it is, we encounter in *Faust* Part II a mass of

mutinous material press-ganged into the service of one or two controlling ideas much as Goethe the geologist or botanist approached and
classified the heterogeneous but unifiable world of nature.

The original Faust story, like *El burlador de Sevilla*, is, however, an
existential fable. The character of the heroes is not determined by the
essence they defiantly choose but by the death which claims their existence and fixes the meaning of it for them. The audience is horror-struck
and fascinated by this because the death that claims Faust and Don
Juan Tenorio is not harmlessly contained within the fiction but also
intervenes and fixes the character of their non-fictional lives too.

Goethe draws the teeth of this dangerous puppet-show by taking
existence out of it altogether. The audience is no longer horror-struck
for it is now concerned with edifying meanings. The audience is flatt-
tered to discover that it is permanently superior to the naïve fable
whose outline Goethe preserves, categorises as myth and, whatever he
says to Eckermann, reverses.

It should be clear that if Byron transforms the Don Juan story into
a comedy, he is not performing Goethe's manoeuvres. For Byron is at
pains to relate the eros of his fiction to Eros ('is it not *life*?'), to relate
the thought of his fiction to that abyss which permanently confronts
the reader, and to relate the existence of his poem both to Byron's
actual, about-to-be-terminated existence and to the inexplicably recurring patterns of comic life. The Blessed Virgin who sits enthroned above
Norman Abbey is not Byron's or Goethe's Blessed Virgin. She is the
Blessed Virgin. We may accord her what status we please but she does
not lie wholly within Byron's fictional jurisdiction ready to buttress
a selected meaning, any more than Byron's own existence does. Byron,
of course, writes the poem and means it but, as in any comedy, much
of his meaning is given by the forms he chooses and is referred back to
the life which gives rise to and lives in those forms. The narrator, at
least at the beginning, sits in judgement upon the adventures which he
recounts but we are not in the same position as the audience of Goethe's
Faust and cannot be so. We are directed via paradox, reversal and
laughter to recognition rather than to knowledge or experience.

It is for this reason that Byron is at pains to suggest and call attention to the being of Aurora, his comic terminus, rather than to her
actions, character or significance. Aurora is Byron's Euphorion but we
do not see through her and read off what she means. Or, we might say,
that the suggestion of Juan's marriage to Aurora is an equivalent for
Goethe's reversal of the traditional emblem of Faust and Helen.
Goethe's Faust has to recognise in Helen a natural wholeness of life

denied to anxious, northern Protestants like himself or Christian
Fletcher. But southern Juan stands in no need of this knowledge. It is
not the spiritual who make spiritual quests. Holiness stays put, it is the
peregrinating flesh which unwittingly seeks it. Out of this quest, Byron
can make his comedy, where Goethe seems to found Part II of *Faust* on
the opposed conviction.

Byron's emblems too are quite other than Goethe's. He makes some
play with England's northern climate and the presence in it of the
Spanish Juan, but this is not the major theme that it is in Goethe.
Beppo exploits the contrast between the author's English audience and
present, Italian location to fine effect and much more consistently. If
we look back to the 'Ave Maria' stanzas (III, 102-3), we find there too
a romantic, English conception of Italian religion, landscape and
women offered back to an English audience.[86] In Norman Abbey, how-
ever, it is Byron's memory of a still remaining, English, statue of the
Blessed Virgin and the saintly but wholly indigenous presence of
Aurora Raby who beckons both to cold English hearts and warmer
Spanish ones in that cool but vital landscape. We are not directed to set
Juan against the environment he encounters. Instead that environment
is given to us and to Juan in stages. First it is a lovely ruin, then
Adeline's house and that of her guests, then Aurora's, the ghost's and
Fitz-Fulke's. We do not contemplate these shifts with a keen con-
ceptual eye but are drawn into the intelligible trauma of the poem's
comic renewal. That it is renewed is more important than how or why
because the priority of existence over concepts is an integral tenet of
comedy, as we have seen. Byron can only grant the imagination's
warrant for the happy days and nights of his comic islanders on Toobonai. That is not enough. This priority of existence over meanings
evidenced in comic endings is transferred to the real process of the un-
concluded *Don Juan*, and when we see, in what turn out to be the concluding cantos, this process together with its terminus in a peculiarly
exposed way, we react with fear, laughter, relief, and recognition.
Goethe, perhaps influenced by *Don Juan* which he much admired,
played for some laughs in *Faust* Part II but his poem is not existential
and represents an idea of comedy rather than a realised comic life.

V

Aurora is untainted and the terminus of Byron's comedy, whatever
happens to it in the future, because she alone can again connect Juan

and the poem trustingly to their existence and restore what has been lost.[87] She displaces Adeline, either as a sudden invention or a considered scheme on Byron's part, because Adeline can only offer a repetion of Juan's first, erotic experience with Julia which, as a repetition, cannot even attain the value of its original, nor can it eradicate the taintings that Catharine the Great has attached to Eros. To wrench the poem away from a wholly religious direction, Byron provides in the Duchess of Fitz-Fulke a fleshly counterpart to Aurora who, from an opposite perspective to the latter, makes Adeline appear pallid and unreal. His task is to recover convincingly the glow of Eros in the poem but not to displace Aurora on whom, obliquely, this recovery now depends. If possible a connection should be made between the natural resurrection of Eros and the life of the spirit but not in such a way as to blur the two, except for a single moment's laughter. It should be apparent that this is description rather than prescription. The sheer brilliance of Byron's imaginative manoeuvres towards the end of *Don Juan* cannot be over-stated. At the precise moment, for example, when Juan and the reader discover that the ghost is a woman, we are suddenly reminded of the night landscape:

A red lip, with two rows of pearl beneath,
Gleamed forth, as though the casement's ivy shroud
The moon peeped, just escaped from a grey cloud.

(XVI, 121)

All the spiritual resonances of the house at night are at once actively present and, momentarily, subordinated by the playful 'peeped' and salutary 'escaped' to the glowing antithesis of the flesh. Only Wordsworth, amongst Byron's British contemporaries, does anything of comparable depth and subtlety to the Norman Abbey section[88] and we may be reminded of Wordsworth by a peculiar feature of the last cantos.

If Aurora is so unmitigated an exemplar, how can she possibly survive in a poem notorious for its savaging of consolatory ideals and unremittingly ironic in mode? In Haidée's case, a powerful, positive portrait includes several negative elements. Aurora is young and old, inexperienced and wise, flower and gem, associated with and wholly distinct from Eros, but none of these things is bad. Even the tincture of Eros, suspected at one point by Lady Adeline, and presented as not altogether admirable in Juan's confused feelings for Aurora, is wholly purified in her consciousness, 'Aurora's spirit was not of that kind.' (XV, 81).

One simple explanation could be that cynicism and sentimental idealism go hand in hand. Heine, Musset, Keats and Shelley veer between the viewpoint of Blake's clod and his pebble. Byron's Romantic irony,[89] on this view, is a protective mask, analogous to that of the Byronic hero, which hides a vulnerable heart. Irving Babbit avers that 'Byron's irony is prevailingly sentimental'.[90] Whatever larger truth this specious simplification offers, it certainly will not do for Aurora. If we compare her, for instance, with Medora in *The Corsair*, who is little more than a projection of one suppressed feminine need in Contad's personality as Gulnare is of another, it is quite clear that Aurora's being is autonomous. She intervenes in the life of the poem. She represents the sweet force of the old abbey but is not one with it as Medora or Neuha or Shelley's Emily[91] are with their imaginary islands. Nothing in the description of Aurora marks her as insubstantial or liable to fade. Unlike the dream objects of Keats's *Endymion*, she is there in the morning. Unlike his Lamia, she can outstare Apollonius, Corinth and Regency society. The verse that establishes Aurora's presence is more assured in the tone of its encomiums than even that of Haidée. Haidée is 'ripe and real' in comparison with the 'stone ideal' of sculptors (II, 118) but she is also 'like a vision' (III, 76) and like a nymph 'born from out a rill' (IV, 15). Her ripeness and reality are not in question but her ideality is. Lambro's return, presaged by her dark dream, separates the two and Haidée becomes a true fusion of them only by death's alteration (IV, 61, 70, 71). No one in Byron's verse is described like this,

> . . . in her
> There was a depth of feeling to embrace
> Thoughts, boundless, deep, but silent too as Space.
>
> (XVI, 48)

These words are oddly reminiscent of Wordsworth's famous lines on Isaac Newton[92] but are here allied specifically with holiness, stillness, being and womanhood rather than with the sustained movement of abstract thought. Aurora's depth of feeling 'embraces', that is to say has a larger coverage than and is united lovingly with boundless thought. Space itself, conterminous with this thought, is embraced by another depth in contact with 'worlds beyond this world's perplexing waste'. Aurora sees the Space shown to Cain by Lucifer as wastes of Death but Aurora's 'deep calleth unto deep' (Ps. 42) and she is renewed, where Cain turns inward in murderous self-hate. The death which Cain first brings into the world, and becomes Catharine the Great's minion and Haidée's destroyer, is the source of Aurora's untroubled gravity and her enigmatic radiance.

The quality of Byron's verse clearly should not be overlooked as one of the agencies that establish Aurora's authority and exempt her from the poem's reflex ironies but how can Aurora's exceptional being be lodged reverently within Byron's iconoclastic rhymes? Wordsworth faces an analogous problem often enough in his blank-verse poems when he has to modulate between ordinary and extraordinary modes of conscious being in such a way as to leave both intact but connected. In perhaps the most celebrated example, although there are many such, he interposes a saving doubt in order to distance us from it:

> ... If this
> Be but a vain belief, yet oh! how oft,[93]

By articulating a common-sense objection to the existence of unknown modes of being, Wordsworth assures us of his good sense whilst simultaneously renewing our confidence in his grasp of the transcendent. It could be but it is not a vain belief.

Byron's version of this device is to present alternative ways of seeing Aurora. First we are presented with an unqualified and exalted portrait. Lady Adeline, however, when she sneers at Aurora, accepts the vocabulary already applied to her in the poem and reads it off in the devil's sense:

> She marvell'd "what he saw in such a baby
> As that prim, silent, cold Aurora Raby?"

> (XV, 49)

There is nothing slanderous in this. It is an alternative way of presenting the facts about Aurora which, if true, would make a vain belief of their earlier interpretation. Thus the poem transfers the capacity to qualify or deride what is turned up by the narrative from the narrator to a character within the poem. This is new in *Don Juan* and requires explanation, for it means that the poem itself is not directly implicated in the aspersions cast on Aurora. It is a misreading for example to suggest, as R.B. England does, that 'we are sometimes made to suspect that Byron's tongue is in his cheek when he describes Aurora'.[94] Professor England perhaps has in mind a phenomenon which we should interpret in a different way. What does the narrator do after Adeline's outburst? We find a number of interjections which put before us the original view of Aurora and Adeline's version as alternatives:

> Such was her coldness or her self-possession.
>
> (XV, 57)
>
> The devil was in the girl! Could it be pride?
> Or modesty, or absence, or inanity?
> Heaven knows! But Adeline's malicious eyes
> Sparkled with her successful prophecies,
>
> (XV, 78)

If these lines are read in context there can be no doubt whatever which version is correct. It is self-possession, it is not coldness. It is modesty, it is not pride. The negative view is, in any case, rendered suspect by its association with the 'malicious' Adeline whose judgement is not to be considered reliable:

> Adeline, no deep judge of character,
> Was apt to add a colouring from her own.
>
> (XV, 17)

However, the presence of this negative reading of Aurora's character, like the single licensed ridicule tolerated at a Roman funeral, assists us in accepting an astonishing exalted one and should help us not to set gems against flowers as though our own vitality was vindicated by the natural preference. Nor should we say that Byron allows both possibilities to coexist in some rich, literary mixture. There is only one way to take Aurora Raby.

It is in this fashion that *Don Juan* can allow the reader's inevitable doubt into Norman Abbey but enlists it for Aurora's sure celebration. The negative way of seeing Aurora is forcibly articulated but neither endorsed nor granted equivalent status to the positive one. Yet much of the poem has been spent in balancing intellectually centred doubt against the irresistible onrush of events. What has happened to exempt Aurora from the narrator's banter?

We have seen that the interplay of absolute doubt and absolute confidence which controls both the poem and our reaction to the life which it discloses is, with increasing explicitness, found to be a religious matter. The poem is always an exemplum in this debate but, in its final cantos, knows itself to be so. Let us for, the last time in this study, try to catch the narrator's and the poem's constantly adjusted procedures. The 'she' in the first line is Byron's muse:

4

But of all truths which she has told, the most
True is that which she is about to tell.
I said it was a story of a ghost —
What then? I only know it so befell.
Have you explored the limits of the coast,
Where all the dwellers of the earth must dwell?
'Tis time to strike such puny doubters dumb as
The sceptics who would not believe Columbus.

5

Some people would impose now with authority,
Turpin's or Monmouth Geoffrey's Chronicle;
Men whose historical superiority
Is always greatest at a miracle.
But Saint Augustine has the great priority,
Who bids all men believe the impossible,
Because 'tis so who nibble, scribble, quibble, he
Quiets at once with "*quia* impossibile".

6

And therefore, mortals, cavil not at all;
Believe: — if 'tis improbable, you *must*;
And if it is impossible, you *shall*:
'Tis always best to take things upon trust.
I do not speak profanely, to recall
Those holier mysteries, which the wise and just
Receive as gospel, and which grow more rooted,
As all truths must, the more they are disputed.

7

I merely mean to say what Johnson said,
That in the course of some six thousand years,
All nations have believed that from the dead
A visitant at interval appears;
And what is strangest upon this strange head,
Is, that whatever bar the reason rears
'Gainst such belief, there's something stronger still
In its behalf, let those deny who will.

(XVI, 4-7)

It is an easy matter to stifle the delicate bravura of these stanzas by ponderous elucidation but then it is as easy to miss the gravity of Byron's radiant foolery. The status of fiction in general, and Byron's in particular, the existence of ghosts and the truth/absurdity of religious belief are all woven together. The reader is invited mock-seriously and seriously to believe in the fiction, in ghosts and, by implication, in the illogical logic of faith. The stanzas bewilder us by their incongruous mixture of material and by the incompatibility of the tone with the proffered advice. We can perhaps go some way to reconciling these things by seeing the stanzas as a parody of the introductory devices used by the skilled teller of ghost stories. This begins in the last stanzas of Canto XV ('Grim reader! Did you ever see a ghost?'). We expect a certain amount of banter and mock-assertions of truth-telling from such a one and, for our part, will co-operate by laughter, suspending disbelief and, even, activating sufficient belief for the fiction to frighten us beyond its immediate duration. All this is familiar, and the narrator's insistence that we remember the errors of excessive scepticism ('who would not believe Columbus'), excessive credulity ('Monmouth Geoffrey's Chronicle') and of orthodox belief ('believe the impossible') might suggest a reliable speaker who, if he asks us to accept anything abnormal, will do so only for something that 'All nations have believed'. In this way, the stanzas may appear to testify both to Byron's narrative skills and to the narrator's good sense. Editors comment approvingly on Byron's use of Tertullian's (*not* Augustine's) tract: 'He used it here and in the next stanza to mock irrational extremes'.[95]

All this is perfectly true so far as it goes. Tertullian/Augustine is mocked, as are excesses of scepticism and credulity, but we are not left with the golden mean beloved of Satirists and, more especially, of their cautious commentators. There is no golden mean 'Between two worlds'. Let us try to follow the narrator's logic.

He is going to tell us a ghost story which is true because he can vouch for it. We are not to doubt it because human beings do not know everything and have often been proved wrong when they try to deny matters beyond their own experience. He then changes tack and mocks the acceptance he has recommended by overstating it. In any case, he argues, many famous historical records depend upon outrageous miracles and, even better, Augustine asks us to believe religious truths precisely because they are impossible. Hence we should have no difficulty in accepting a mere ghost story.

The narrator then steps out of this guise and recommends the religious belief, or some version of it, which he has just pilloried. The suddenness of this modulation (the last four lines of stanza 6) take us by surprise and, though generally cogent, leave us unsure of ourselves. We do not know what the 'holier mysteries' are holier than. Is it than the sort of extras that Augustine asks us to believe, hence a recommendation of a liberal, no-nonsense Christianity? That would give us a golden mean in religious belief. The Trinity, however, and Christ's Resurrection would obviously be such extras and it would be odd to specify the putatively rational remainder as 'holier mysteries' to be received 'as gospel' and imply that this Highest Common Factor in believers and deists is, of all things, continually disputed. We would have to say perhaps that, whilst there has always been dispute about Christian beliefs, certain basic doctrines survive and, because they are seen to do so, become 'more rooted' by their very disputation. 'The wise and just' here would refer to a special group within Christianity who discern these basic truths. The alternative is to take 'holier mysteries' to refer to the basic doctrines of orthodox Christianity, to exempt them from the narrator's banter, and to make them 'holier' than the present mystery of Byron's ghost fiction. Byron, in this way, would present a startling analogy which mingles reverence and irreverence in similar fashion to his famous letter to Moore[96] and then distance himself from the flippancy of his own commingling. This alternative does not dispose of difficulties for it is the basic paradoxes of Christianity (Incarnation, Redemption, Resurrection, Trinity) which are recommended by the 'quia impossibile'.[97] Hence we are being asked to laugh at and soberly accept the mysteries of faith. The last two lines of stanza 6, which must be read straight in the first interpretation, have a slightly ironical tinge in the second for they make us picture the tenacity with which religious beliefs are maintained despite, and perhaps because of, their incessant disputation.

Which of these two interpretations is right? Both cannot be and the difference between them is a crucial one.

It would not be hard to find quotations from Byron that would authorise the first version as, at least, a possible view of his. Further the narrator often suddenly veers away from betraying intimations of orthodox doctrine. He does so in Canto III after the stanzas associating the Italian evening with the Blessed Virgin:

Ave Maria! may our spirits dare
Look up to thine and to thy Son's above!

(III, 103)

He counters this explicitness immediately by a knowingness like Goethe's:

> Some kinder casuists are pleased to say,
> In nameless print — that I have no devotion;
> But set those persons down with me to pray,
> And you shall see who has the properest notion
> Of getting into Heaven the shortest way;
> My altars are the mountains and the ocean,
> Earth, air, stars, — all that springs from the great Whole,
> Who hath produced, and will receive the soul.
>
> (III, 104)

Byron does exactly the same manoeuvre, on a reduced scale, after the lines on the Norman Abbey statue of Our Lady[98] when he immediately acknowledges, generalises and weakens the effect in another version of 'If this/Be but a vain belief':

> But in a higher niche, alone, but crown'd,
> The Virgin Mother of the God-born child,
> With her son in her blessed arms, look'd around,
> Spared by some chance when all beside was spoil'd;
> She made the earth below seem holy ground.
> This may be superstition, weak or wild,
> But even the faintest relics of a shrine
> Of any worship, wake some thought divine.
>
> (XIII, 61)

It would appear then that the last four lines of stanza 6 (XVI) could be plausibly interpreted in a sense which demotes orthodoxy and prefers possible to impossible beliefs. Our concern is not with the beliefs in themselves but with their role in *Don Juan* and the correct interpretation of these revealing stanzas. However, the fact that the argument is possible derives from the presence in Byron himself, as well as his Protean narrator, of centres of belief and unbelief together with some rational accommodation of the gap between them. We encounter all these in *Don Juan*. They are the alternatives proposed by Byron's history. What matters to us is the whole movement of mind and poem.

If we look yet more carefully at these stanzas and take stanza 7 into account we must notice that the last lines of stanza 6 are part of a flow of voice which continues into the next stanza. 'I do not speak profanely' (6) is continued by 'I merely mean to say' (7). But the voice cannot continue thus if the second half of stanza 6 is an aside. Moreover, the claim that ghosts exist cannot be something much easier to swallow ('I merely mean to say') than the sentiments and moral commonplaces of a rationalised Christianity which do not involve paradox, miracles or abnormal occurrences. Goethe expected his audience to acquiesce piously in the rational religion of his secularised *Faust* and they usually oblige. It would be odd to instance Samuel Johnson too ('what Johnson said') for this belief in ghosts immediately after a rejection of orthodox Christianity for, as Byron well knew, Johnson was as committed to orthodox Christianity as he was fascinated by ghosts. Finally, though Byron stresses the universality of ghost stories ('All nations have believed'), he also stresses the oddities involved ('what is strangest upon this strange head') and the ability of 'something stronger still' to overrule the arguments of reason. This would make no sense after the 'holier mysteries' passage if that recommended a sensible whittling down of orthodoxy to the rationally 'possible'. Hence we can be certain that the second interpretation of stanza 6 is correct.[99] Difficulties of this kind are not uncommon in literary criticism for when we talk about particular words, as we must, we arrest their flow. Moreover, Byron's centre of belief is intimately bound up with his doubt so that if we find the one we are likely to find the other. Doubters are usually less keen on this undoubted truism than believers.

Let us, with the 'holier mysteries' passage indisputably in place, now try to state the remarkable implications of these four stanzas. It is important to get them right for they introduce the final action of *Don Juan*.

The narrator's argument is an outrageous one because the tone belies the recommendation:

And therefore, mortals, cavil not at all;
Believe:- if 'tis improbable, you *must*;
And if it is impossible, you *shall*:

Disparity between tone and matter is, of course, the life and soul of the poem. The difficulty here is that whilst we normally defer to the tone when the two diverge, here the recommendation to believe the coming ghost story is the only one available to us and we will in fact take it.[100] If that is so then all the analogies hold. Fictions believed in are the truth. The impossible is certain.

Byron undoubtedly parodies the inception of religious belief here just as he parodies the Ten Commandments in Canto I (205-6) but his purpose is not primarily satirical at all. These stanzas arise out of the narrator's ruminations about fiction, truth and ghosts at the end of Canto XV and the beginning of Canto XVI. Byron, as a writer, always has to ask for the reader's answering belief in his narrations but telling a ghost story is a particularly blatant instance of this. The reader's reception of such a story could be seen as a characteristic instance of human credulity or as disclosing underlying analogies between imagination, belief and reality. Columbus told a story. So do the gospels. So do 'those holier mysteries' received 'as gospel'. 'Philosophy' would reject these analogies but does not have the 'clue' of reality. 'Religion' does have this 'clue' and accepts the analogies and connections which the poem lives by. Belief is therefore inescapable but remains absurd for the palpable incongruity of what is unified by it persists. In this way, Byron's ghost story is a trap to catch the conscience of the reader for it makes the problems of belief ('Yes' or 'No'), which are so central to the poem's continuity, and, separately, so grave in themselves, into the familiar, opening patter of a story-teller. Byron's tone makes it impossible for us to take this gravely yet we are forced, like Juan, into complicity with belief. The poem itself is presented as a story improvised in the long streches of the night (XV, 97).

The analogies between faith and fiction are made explicitly for us and then instantly withdrawn: 'I do not speak profanely,'. Without this withdrawal, the analogies would make faith a version of fiction rather than balancing the two or suggesting the reverse emphasis. We have simultaneously then to detect the opening patter of a ghost story, respect our emerging will to believe it and the connivance of reason at 'something stronger still'. In the same way, religious faith is incredible and we can detect the manoeuvres designed to outwit scepticism ('*quia impossibile*') but, at the same time, these 'holier mysteries' grow 'more rooted' by the counter-energy raised by their disputation.[101] Laughter, unease, poise, absurdity and reverence coexist in Aristophanic interplay here. Religious faith is ridiculed and reasserted just as a ghost story is mocked but attended to and Truth 'must often navigate o'er fiction' (XV, 88). Professor McGann offers a helpful analogy:

Unamuno argues in *The Tragic Sense of Life* that all religions and transcendental experience demands a prior experience of absolute skepticism. Stripped of all humanly definable reasons for hope, man, Unamuno says, cries out that his highest longing must nevertheless be true. *Certum est quia impossibile est.* This idea erupts with extraordinary vigor in the last four cantos of *Don Juan.*[102]

I have tried to keep track of this eruption here.

What happens if we do believe the ghost story? We can easily read off the dazzling sequence of answers to this question. At first our faith in ghosts is rewarded by a real 'visitant' from the dead. Next our comic faith is rewarded by the reappearance of Eros in the midst of a ghost story. Then we find ourselves sceptical about ghosts (the first ghost) but also about Eros (Fitz-Fulke at breakfast). Finally reflection restores to us the reality of the first ghost (and therefore fiction's truth). Juan is understandably exhausted by this sequence (XVII, 14) but the reader is exhilirated by the rightness of the movement and by a marvellous sense of renewed comic purpose in it all.

Aurora plays no part in the doings of these two nights when Juan encounters Death and Life. She is the dawn[103] 'upon the horizon's verge' situated 'Twixt night and morn' (XV, 99). Without Aurora, however, these opposites would have neither separate definition nor necessary connection in Norman Abbey. If we remind ourselves of the major crisis in *Don Juan* where, we have insisted,[104] comedy is lost in a betraying parody of its sustaining confidence, Catharine the Great sees Juan for the first time, fresh from war, and her consciousness modulates instantly from slaughter to sex:

> Oh Catharine! (for of all interjections
> To thee both *oh*! and *ah*! belong of right
> In love and war) how odd are the connections
> Of human thoughts, which jostle in their flight!
>
> (IX, 65)

Catharine causes the same modulation in others. She presides over a world where Death and Life have lost all determinacy, in which sexual and mortal terminations produce almost identical 'interjections' in automatic throats.[105] In Norman Abbey, on the other hand, the cold ghost and the warm duchess are held together by night and are connected in Juan's aroused consciousness but there is no denying the difference when 'Ah! changes into 'Oh!'. Without Aurora, the ghost would be a gothic stage-prop in a mental theatre but Aurora associates him with a still living history and the reverberation of unimaginable spaces. Without Aurora, the Duchess would be a farcical *intrigante* but Aurora parallels Fitz-Fulke's perpetual play with her own different absorption in an immediate plenitude and associates her with innocence. The Eros and Agape juxtaposed so stridently in Fitz-Fulke's disguise are reconciled in Aurora's feminine grace. Juan's head spins with ghosts, flesh and spirit in a world apart from the contrivances of Lady Adeline, who has stemmed every natural and spiritual force in her being and must therefore be hostile to both Fitz-Fulke and Aurora. Nevertheless, like the time-serving Greek poet of Canto III, Lady Adeline can sing a song that honours what she cannot acknowledge.

Aurora is a guide to the reader of the last cantos. Catharine gave back to the reader an exact indication of where he now feared that the poem had to go. Aurora does the same but confirms his best hopes for the poem. Both women surprise us by the extreme clarity of their articulation but confirm the development we have already discerned. Both live their version of a wholly comic existence for, in essence, comedy looks straight at death for the reassertion of 'Life's strange principle'. Catherine inexhaustibly replenishes the men whom she wears out by sex and dooms to death. She finds these renewing energies in herself and Nature. Aurora finds quite other energies beyond the self and its immersion in the rhythms of natural life. Therefore, though she grieves for those who are bound by history and the natural cycle, she can locate a finer 'indifference' than Catharine's. Aurora sits and smiles. She can do so not solely because she has some measure of exemption but because history and the natural cycle themselves do not represent the whole of reality. There are worlds beyond 'this world's perplexing waste'. History and Nature cannot therefore completely hide the untainted sources 'beyond time' (XV, 45) which press in, unregarded, upon the inhabitants of Norman Abbey and touch the poem itself.

If we consider *Don Juan* as a whole and the emphases which we separated in 'The Narrator's Cantos' and 'The Amorous Sphere', it is apparent that Aurora's being and knowledge arise as much from the narrator's persistence in exploring the invisible boundaries between Nothing and Being, to which Aurora is an answer, as from the separate development of Juan and his exploration of differing exemplars of the amorous sphere. We could put the same point in a different perspective. Aurora is shaped and made possible both by Byron's own conscious propinquity to orthodox belief and by the logic of comedy itself whose ultimate resources of hope he is forced to probe and disclose. These things are quite separate in themselves, and so the scholarly critic will need to follow different routes in order to unturn them,[106] but they coincide in the author (who is also a man) and in the recognition of the reader (who does other things than read).

Because Aurora arises in this way out of both narrative and commentary, she can maintain a knowledge superior to the knowingness of the narrator and cannot be challenged by him or anyone else. She can be envied, hated or misunderstood by other characters but she cannot be |the poem's own object of satirical attention for she is the realised ideal from which satire takes its energy and authority. She lives within the poem and engages with Juan but she is also a detached spectator like the narrator though with a deeper vision than he. Aurora therefore reconciles the satirical and romance thrusts of the poem by making visible within *Don Juan* the comic containment implicit in its process.

Like the good listener to a ghost story, Aurora lives by the narrator's absurd but not withdrawn advice: 'Tis always best to take things upon trust'. (XVI, 6). Juan has always lived unthinkingly like this but, in the latter half of the poem, he is checked in this confidence. Aurora 'revives' in him the capacity to move forward but bewilders and fascinates him too by the steadiness with which she contemplates the turn of events. In the two ghost experiences, Juan encounters, in extreme and separated form, the properties of Life and Death which merge in Aurora's resilient tranquillity. We could say that the whole poem lives by the advice 'to take things upon trust' but it also ridicules, redefines, celebrates, loses and recovers confidence in this comic wisdom. In the process, *Don Juan* has to change profoundly in order to stay the same and surmount the ceaseless shocks to its purported comic hold.

One by one, we find the basic devices of comic ebullience named in the poem. In a contained comic drama, any one of these might work on several occasions but *Don Juan* depends upon them working indefinitely. In effect, this involves going behind ransacked comic devices in order to establish an imperishable and trusting hold upon a life that remains fleshly and contingent. It depends too on referring the temporary eruptions of laughter to the final, undeviating radiance of a smile. By the end of the poem, this hold has been found and, in Aurora Raby, named and recognised.

Notes

1. William Hazlitt, *The Spirit of the Age* (London, 1910), p. 241. n. 1.

2. E.g. 'Byron intended that the chief interest of his poem should not be in the hero's living and dying his death "but in the poet's writing the poem." ' Hermione de Almeida, *Byron and Joyce through Homer* (London, 1981), p. 142.

3. William Hazlitt, 'Mind and Motive' in *Winterslow* (London, 1902), pp. 95-6.

4. Hazlitt claims that Byron 'raises our hopes and our belief in goodness to Heaven only to dash them to the earth again' (*The Spirit of the Age*, p. 241) as

though Byron is the cynic and he the believer but 'belief' here is a trigger-word for a vague, liberal optimism.

5. T.S. Eliot, 'Byron' in M.H. Abrams (ed.), *English Romantic Poets* (Oxford, 1960), p. 207.

6. Ibid., pp. 207, 208.

7. Ibid., p. 206.

8. Kroeber notes that 'Byron moves from simple narrative organization towards narrative arrangements more like those of the *Waverley* novels than those of *The Excursion*'. Karl Kroeber, *Romantic Narrative Art* (London, 1966), pp. 136-7.

9. Dryden's plays usually appear in relation to Byron's *Don Juan*, if at all, as an end note, because Byron's lines on the old women who regret their failure to be raped after the Siege (VIII, 132) are closely parallel to a passage in Dryden's *The Spanish Friar* (I, ii). *The Spanish Friar* has a double plot and mixes modes with a vengeance.

10. Neuha is the heroine of Byron's *The Island*. She is discussed extensively in section II of this chapter.

11. The most blatant instance of this is C.N. Stavrou's article 'Religion in Byron's *Don Juan*', *Studies in English Literature*, vol III, 1963, pp. 567-95. Stavrou contrives not to mention Aurora Raby at all. This comes as little surprise to the reader for Stavrou appears to have as limited a sense of religion as he has of *Don Juan*. The article is still regularly cited (e.g. *Lord Byron: Don Juan*, T.G. Steffan, E. Steffan and W.W. Pratt (eds.) (Harmondsworth, 1973) p. 31) as though it were authoritative.

12. E.D. Hirsch, 'Byron and the Terrestrial Paradise' in F.W. Hilles and H. Bloom (eds.), *From Sensibility to Romanticism* (New York, 1965) pp. 467-8, lambasts those critics who regard *Don Juan* as quite other than *Childe Harold*. The critics who take *Childe Harold* seriously (e.g. M.K. Joseph, J.J. McGann) give the best accounts of *Don Juan*.

13. R.B. England observes that 'whereas Pope's description of the natural scene in "Windsor Forest" leads to an emphasis on a commensurate harmony in English civilisation, the civilisation that makes its home at Norman Abbey comes to be characterised above all by its desultory fragmentation'. *Byron's Don Juan and Eighteenth-Century Literature* (London, 1975), p. 32.

14. The Gothic fountain of Newstead Abbey is a mixture of Gothic and eighteenth-century details (*Byron's Don Juan: A Variorum Edition*, T.G. Steffan and W.W. Pratt (eds) (4 vols., Austin, Texas, 1957), vol. IV, p. 250).

15. A.V. Kernan, *The Plot of Satire*, (New Haven and London, 1965), p. 199.

16. Byron's account of Norman Abbey's partnership with Nature is quite distinct from Wordsworth's version of the ruined St Mary's Abbey, York in Book II of *The Prelude*. There too we find a 'holy scene', natural music and a kind of eternity, but this is simply caused by Nature reassuming the edifice.

17. J.J. McGann, *Don Juan in Context* (London, 1976), p. 165.

18. R.F. Gleckner, *Byron and the Ruins of Paradise* (Baltimore, 1967), p. 232.

19. D.G. James in *The Romantic Comedy* (London, 1948), pp. 253-70, first drew the attention of readers of Romantic poetry to Newman's two essays 'The Mission of St. Benedict' and 'The Benedictine Schools' in *Historical Sketches*, vol. II (London, 1873). Newman's early Benedictines, like Aurora, mourn, watch and avoid a life of undertakings. Newman was unsympathetic to the Gothic. Cistercian subjugation of landscape and the speculations of Abelard and Scholasticism were perhaps the counterpart of Victorian engineering and liberal controversy. His scattered references to Byron are unenthusiastic but he would have liked the unpretentious character of Norman Abbey and its acceptance of an adjacent landscape. Aurora's steadiness, like that of Newman's Benedictines, is

set against the remorseless speculations of the narrator and the heartless undertakings of the house which include a plan by 'a modern Goth' to rebuild the Abbey (XVI, 5-9). Newman saw the Benedictine golden age as the innocent childhood of Christian Europe which, nevertheless, understood and accepted patience, mourning and wisdom. Aurora is very close to this conception. D.G. James suggests its connections, however, with Wordsworth's children, solitaries and quiet, working communities.

20. E.g. Brian Wilkie, *Romantic Poets and Epic Tradition* (Madison and Milwaukee, 1965).

21. E.g. Bernard Blackstone, *Byron: A Survey* (London, 1975), p. 319.

22. Gleckner, *Byron*, p. 342.

23. G. Wilson Knight, *Poets of Action* (London, 1967), p. 253. We should not confine the relationship to Shakespeare's late plays. Aurora resembles Portia and the religious tonings of landscape at Belmont presage Norman Abbey.

24. Wilkie (*Romantic Poets*, p. 223) is clear that Byron preaches and *Don Juan* exemplifies negative capability. Negative capability, however, necessarily freezes the antitheses which it juxtaposes. Byron's poem, on the other hand, lives, moves and grows. It does not terminate in an aesthetic stasis or suggest the equivalence of the phenomena which it handles.

25. Byron said that he looked upon Catholicism 'as the best religion, as it is assuredly the oldest of the various branches of Christianity'. Leslie Marchand, *Byron: A Biography* (3 vols., London, 1957), vol. II, p. 905.

26. England, *Don Juan*, p. 169.

27. 'The first canto of *The Island* was finished January 10, 1823. . . and may reasonably conjecture that a somewhat illegible date affixed to the fourth canto, stands for February 14, 1823. The M.S. had been received in London before April 9.' (*The Works of Lord Byron: Poetry*, E.H. Coleridege (ed.) (7 vols., London, 1898-1904), vol. V, p. 581). 'Byron began the first draft of Canto XIII (Tn) at Genoa on 12 February 1823 and completed it on 19 February 1823.' *Don Juan*, Steffan, Steffan and Pratt (eds.), p. 713). 'Byron began the first draft (B) of Canto XIV at Genoa on 23 February 1823 and finished it on 4 March. (Ibid., p. 723).

28. *The Island* has in the last 25 years come to be widely accepted by readers and critics of Byron's poetry as one of his most important poems though it is still not as well known as it should be by readers and critics in general. Hirsch, McGann, Blackstone, Joseph and others write well about *The Island*. See also Paul D. Fleck, 'Romance in "The Island" ', *The Byron Journal*, vol. 3, pp. 4-23.

29. McGann, *Don Juan*, p. 198 has a fine commentary on the religious metaphors of *The Island*.

30. See *Works*, vol. VI, p. 577 n.1 and *Works*, vol. V, pp. 629-30.

31. For the same reason, I will not examine the earlier passage in *The Island* (II, 111-13) which also compares lovers to martyrs 'who revel in their funeral pyre'.

32. Hirsch in Hilles and Bloom (eds.), *From Sensibility*, p. 485 n. 19 comments intelligently on these lines although he sees them as a typical form of Romantic 'spilt religion'.

33. See *The Witch of Atlas*, LXIII.

34. J.J. McGann in *The Romantic Ideology* (Chicago, 1983) criticises Romantic literature and current criticism for largely ignoring this wisdom and defending illusion.

35. It is interesting that those critics (e.g. Hirsch, Gleckner, Mellor) who wish to see Aurora as one instance amongst others of a love ideal invariably dwell on this passage.

36. *Works*, vol. V, p. 537.

37. Gleckner, *Byron*, p. 342 n. 18.

38. Blackstone, *Byron*, p. 319.

39. J.J. McGann, *Fiery Dust* (Chicago, 1968) p. 200.

40. Hirsch in Hilles and Bloom (eds.), *From Sensibility*, p. 477.

41. Ibid., p. 472

42. Wilson Knight, *Poets of Action*, p. 263.

43. Ibid., p. 255.

44. M.G. Cooke, *The Blind Man Traces the Circle* (Princeton, 1969), p. 212.
Professor Cooke's lucid and intelligent study mentions Aurora only once in
passing. His comment here does not refer to *Don Juan* but to *The Island* and
'On This Day I complete my Thirty-Sixth Year'. In his later work, *Acts of Inclusion* (Yale University Press, New Haven, 1979), Cooke has some shrewd comments
on Aurora (see pp. 231, 241) but can disown his insights elsewhere (e.g. p. 232)
perhaps because they seem to be at variance with his working assumptions..

45. M.K. Joseph, *Byron the Poet* (London, 1964), p. 305.

46. Ibid., p. 308.

47. Marchand, *Byron*, vol. II, p. 529.

48. E.g. 'When I turn thirty – I will turn devout – I feel a great vocation that
way in Catholic churches'. (Byron's *Letters and Journals*, Leslie Marchand (ed.)
(12 vols., London, 1973-81), vol. 5, p. 208, to Murray, 9th April, 1817). 'I have
often wished I had been borne a Catholic' (*Medwin's Conversations of Lord
Byron*, Ernest J. Lovell, Jr. (ed.) (Princeton, 1966), p. 80). 'Incline very much,
myself, to the Catholic doctrines' (*Letters and Journals*, vol. 9, p. 118, to Moore,
8th March, 1822). There is more evidence of this kind but also, of course, there is
evidence of Byron's unbelief and of his moralised Deism. There can be no doubt,
however, of Byron's closeness to orthodox belief and his own knowledge of his
persistence on the perimeters of religious faith. We could ascertain this from his
poetry alone but there is no good reason for disregarding his biography as wholly
other than his poems. E.M. Marjarum, *Byron as Sceptic and Believer* (Princeton,
1939) remains the standard work. W.J. Calvert, *Byron: Romantic Paradox*
(Chapel Hill, N.C., 1935), stresses Byron's Calvinism. John Cunningham, *The
Poetics of Byron's Comedy in Don Juan* (Salzburg, 1982) writes with insight and
warmth about the religious character of *Don Juan*. See also Steve Ellis, *Dante and
English Poetry* (Cambridge, 1983), (p. 83) and C.M. Woodhouse, The Religion of
an Agnostic' in *The Byron Journal*, vol. 6, 1978, pp. 26-33. By far the best
account of Byron's religious views, however, is to be found in McGann's brilliant
summary in *Fiery Dust* (pp. 247-55) which establishes 'The strange marriage of
Socinianism and Catholicism in Byron's thought' (p. 254) and downplays the
importance of Byron's Calvinism. Even McGann's argument is, arguably, too
clear-cut at first and then too vague in its final suggestions. For Stavrou, 'Religion
in Byron's *Don Juan*' see note 12 above. See also David Leigh, S.J., 'Infelix Culpa:
Poetry and the Skeptic Faith in *Don Juan*' in *Keats-Shelley Journal*, vol. XXVIII,
1979, pp. 120-38.

49. H.G. Tan, *La matière de Don Juan et les genres littéraires* (Leyde, 1976)
p. 39.

50. Byron claims that the 'history of a heart' (XIV, 21) is one of the things
that he can 'easily sketch' in *Don Juan*.

51. G.R. Elliot, 'Byron and the Comic Spirit' in *Publications of the Modern
Languages Association*, vol. 39, December, 1924, pp. 897-909 argues that
Byron's 'proper genius' was the comic spirit but *Don Juan* is only touched here
and there by it. *Sardanapalus*, on the other hand, is a pure comedy. Kernan's
analysis of *Don Juan*'s comedy (*Satire*, pp. 185-99) has been, properly, very influential. He sees it as in tension with the 'satire and 'tragic' 'portions' of the poem
but takes no account of *Don Juan*'s development. See also Cunningham's percep-

tive commentary in *The Poetics of Byron's Comedy in Don Juan*, though we lose sight of the title in massed details. Helen Gardner, 'Don Juan', *London Magazine*, vol. 7, 1958, p. 63, wrote: . . . 'the underlying impulse of the poem is not satiric, it began as a farce and developed into comedy'.

52. Suzanne Langer, *Feeling and Form* (London, 1953), pp. 331-2.

53. H.J. Rose, for example, comments on 'the utter lack of respect' shown in many Greek Old Comedies to the gods and warns us that this 'does not signify lack of belief in them, or even of reverence'. H.J. Rose, *A Handbook of Greek Literature* (Dutton paperback, New York, 1960), p. 219. C.L. Barber, *Shakespeare's Festive Comedy* (Princeton, 1972), p. 160 emphasises the association of scepticism with the positive meanings of *A Midsummer Night's Dream*. Leo Salingar (*Shakespeare and the Tradition of Comedy*, London, 1974) argues that comedy is written 'at a time and place of deep political change – partly under the stress of war – and of incessant public discussion. Hence the dualism of Old Comedy is complicated further, it includes attitudes of belief and unbelief, rationalism and magic, as well as the two planes of contemporaneity and the mythical. And hence the plays of Aristophanes are thoroughly imbued with irony, with the awareness of the multiple, but in part conflicting, interpretations and possibilities' (p. 94) and he claims that Aristophanic comedy, unlike tragedy, 'insists on the reality of the present moment, even while practising its own form of "deceit". It offers illusion without wish-fulfilment and wish-fulfilment without illusion. The trickster-hero is a projection of the 'ingenious' poet' (p. 104). It would be hard to find more apposite comment for *Don Juan*. It is relevant also to *Don Juan*'s claim to be fiction and truth that Old Comedy alludes to contemporary historical characters by name whereas New Comedy always uses fictional characters. Byron intermingles these like Scott and Shakespeare.

54. Helen Gardner, *'As You Like It'* in John Garrett (ed.), *More Talking of Shakespeare* (London, 1959), p. 22.

55. Kroeber, *Romantic Narrative*, pp. 135-67.

56. 18th July, 1819. The letter is partly reprinted in Theodore Redpath, *The Young Romantics and Critical Opinion 1807-1824* (London, 1973), p. 249.

57. We could probe further here for Barber (*Festive Comedy*, p. 7) in an argument based on F.M. Cornford's *The Origins of Attic Comedy* (Cambridge, 1934) asserts that 'invocation and abuse were the basic gestures of a nature worship behind Aristophanes' union of poetry and railing.' Byron's flyting dedication ι of *Don Juan* to Southey may be covertly in league with and help to inaugurate the comic humour which it appears to deny.

58. To be strictly accurate we should acknowledge that *Sardanapalus* ends in a funeral pyre of love which can be read as defeat and victory. *Beppo* also, a love-story of a kind, ends comically. Neither of these invalidates the point.

59. E.H. Coleridge wishes that Byron had removed the lines on Ben Bunting (*Works*, vol. V, p. 615 n.1), but they are, surely essential to it.

60. See *Works*, vol. V, pp. 582-3. Byron turns 'Tahiti into Toobonai (Tubuai)' and transports 'Toobonai from one archipelago to another – from the Society to the Friendly Islands'.

61. 'Detached Thoughts', 100, in *Letters and Journals*, vol. 9, p. 46.

62. Joseph, *Byron*, p. 186.

63. It may be that the suddenness of Aurora's appearance and of the ghost episodes is designed to persuade the reader that, despite the more stable framework of the final cantos which implies much greater planning by the author, the poem is still capable of exactly the same narrative surprises as ever.

64. *Letters and Journals*, vol. 8, p. 77, to Murray, 16th February, 1821.

65. Or perhaps a hybrid like Pushkin's *Eugene Onegin* which is shaped by Byron's poem and by prose fictions.

66. Wordsworth, *The Prelude* (1850), Bk V, 364-425. Wordsworth inter-
polated some lines on the Winander village church (not in the 1800 publication
of the passage) the vocabulary of which links his conception clearly to Byron's:

> That self-same village church; I see her sit
> (The thronèd Lady whom erewhile we hailed)
> On her green hill, forgetful of this Boy
> Who slumbers at her feet.
>
> (V, 399-402)

67. Blackstone, *Byron*, p. 319. Kernan, *Satire*, p. 190 n. 11 also takes for
granted the superiority of the flower to the gem. Not all readers share the opinion
that Aurora is downgraded by the comparison. G. Wilson Knight in *The Starlit
Dome* (London, 1941, Oxford paperback, 1971) p. 101 has a fine sentence on
this passage, and Joseph (*Byron*, p. 247) notes, with Perdita's excellent logic, that
gems are a refined version of Nature. It is perhaps significant that Byron originally described Neuha as:

> And she herself the daughter of the Seas
> As full of gems and energy as these.
>
> (*Works*, vol. V, p. 604 n.i)

and then altered the second line to 'Herself a Billow in her energies'.

68. 'You have so many "*divine*" poems, is it nothing to have written a *Human*
one.' (*Letters and Journals*, vol. 6, p. 105, to Murray 6th April, 1819). Byron's
'*Human* one' is always taken as referring to *Don Juan* but in the context it must
be a reference to *Childe Harold*.

69. Byron's characters resemble Chaucer's in their typical and emblematic
character but, like his, have presence and are not simply counters for concepts. In
other ways too, of course, Byron's art resembles Chaucer's. This comment could
be wholly applied to the author of *Don Juan*: 'One of Chaucer's familiar preferences is that he is a versifier utterly devoted to simplicity of meaning for the
reason that he considers himself, apparently, utterly incapable of complexity. He
defines his poetic mission as the reporting of facts in tolerable verse, and he
implies that that's hard enough to do.' E. Talbot Donaldson, *Speaking of Chaucer*
(London, 1970), p. 84.

70. See T.L. Ashton, 'Naming Byron's Aurora Raby', *English Language Notes*,
vol. VII, no. 2, December, 1969, pp. 114-20.

71. The Song of the Black Friar tells us that Amundeville is 'lord of the hill'
which may suggest that 'munde' here means 'mound'. It can do so and still
obviously recall 'mundus' ('le monde') equals 'world'.

72. *Works*, vol. IV, p. 136.

73. A more obvious example, but not in verse, is Scott's novels which have to
be interpreted wholly through their endings.

74. Notably E.M. Butler, *Byron and Goethe* (London, 1956); see also
G. Steiner, *The Death of Tragedy* (London, 1961, paperback, 1963), pp. 198-202.

75. James Kennedy, *Conversations on Religion with Lord Byron* (London,
1830).

76. Marchand, *Byron*, vol. III, p. 1127. The joke is reminiscent of stanza 94 of
Canto XV.

77. Joseph, *Byron*, p. 308 concurs: 'In spite of his awareness of corruptions
of Italian society, his residence in Italy caused him to modify his earlier stock
response and gave him a considerable regard for the older religion.' See also
McGann, *Fiery Dust*, p. 254.

78. 'As I said before, I am really a great admirer of tangible religion. . . What

with incense, pictures, statues, confession, absolution, − there is something sensible to grasp at. Besides it leaves no possibility of doubt; for those who swallow their Deity, really and truly, in transubstantiation, can hardly find any thing else otherwise than easy of digestion.

I am afraid that this sound flippant, but I don't mean it to be so; only my turn of mind is so given to taking things in the absurd point of view, that it breaks out in spite of me every now and then. Still, I do assure you that I am a very good Christian. Whether you will believe me in this, I do not know . . .' *Letters and Journals*, vol. 9, p. 122, to Moore, 8th March, 1822. We may compare with this well-known letter some rejected lines from *The Island*:

> . . . "Ho! the dram"
> Rebellion's sacrament, and paschal lamb.
> (A broken metaphor of flesh for wine
> But Catholics know the Exchange is none of mine.
> > (*Works*, vol. V, p. 592 n.i)

These verses and Byron's letter to Moore are curiously reminiscent of Dryden's fascinated blasphemies about transubstantiation, in *Absalom and Achitophel* and elsewhere, before he became a Catholic:

> The *Egyptian* rites the Jebusites embrac'd,
> Where Gods were recommended by their taste.
> Such sav'ry Deities must needs be good
> As serv'd at once for Worship and for Food.
> > (*Absalom and Achitophel*, 118-21)

79. Marchand, *Byron*, vol. II, p. 905.

80. 'I so totally disapprove of the mode of Children's treatment in their family . . . the Child shall not quit me again to perish of Starvation, and green fruit or be taught to believe that there is no Deity.' Marchand, *Byron*, vol. II, p. 851.

81. See, for instance, John Keats, *The Complete Poems*, John Barnard (ed.) (Harmondsworth, 1975), p. 655 n. 26.

82. The poem was not published until 1824 and I can find no extrinsic evidence that Byron had read Shelley's poem but it would seem curious if he had not. 'Whether he read *Julian and Maddalo* at this time, we do not know.' John Buxton, *Byron and Shelley* (London, 1968), p. 89.

83. There is no need, for instance, for any annotation to XII, 38, and it does not receive it.

84. J.P. Eckermann, *Goethe*, pp. 413-4.

85. The last line of *Faust*, ed. J.M. Smeed, trans. Bayard Taylor (London, 1969) p. 448.

86. G.M. Ridenour, *The Style of Don Juan* (New Haven, 1960), p. 46 n.9 talks of Byron's 'sentimental Catholicism' in these lines.

87. 'It is important to recall that Juan actively pursues Aurora, and that he does so because he recognises in her that which he was once given but lost.' McGann, *Fiery Dust*, p. 200.

88. I cannot agree therefore with Philip Martin's recent sleight of hand. It may be true that Byron's verse 'was not written with the earnestness of a Shelley or Wordsworth' (Philip W. Martin, *Byron, a poet before his public* (Cambridge, 1982), p. 8) but neither was that of Chaucer or Shakespeare. Dr Martin would have us return to that tone of condescension to Byron's poetry from which American Criticism, at its best, has so signally freed us in the last 25 years. English readers are sometimes more alert to Byron's shifts of tone than North American readers but they scarcely have a monopoly of taste and good sense.

89. 'Romantic Irony' can, of course, be defended in its own right. See, for example, the spirited first chapter of Mellor's *Romantic Irony* (Anne K. Mellor, *English Romantic Irony*, (Cambridge, Massachusetts, 1980)). Dr Mellor writes perceptively about the narrator's desire to outgrow his sceptical understanding in the last cantos of *Don Juan* but sees this as no more than an acknowledgement of Juan, the narrator's opposite. The poem itself cannot grow in her account. I do not agree that the poem is primarily to do with knowledge, whether ironically appropriated or not. Irving Babbit in *Rousseau and Romanticism* (1919, reissued Austin and London, 1977) has a tellingly negative chapter (IV) on Romantic Irony. *Don Juan* is a principal exhibit (p. 207) and Babbit makes much of the convergence of 'irony, paradox and the idea of the infinite' (p. 171) in Romantic literature. Babbit takes too little account of *Don Juan's* solidity and sees it always from the narrator's point of view.

90. Babbit, *Rousseau*, p. 208.

91. In *Epipsychidion*.

92.   Of Newton with his prism and silent face,
        The marble index of a mind for ever
        Voyaging through strange seas of Thought, alone.
                                        (The Prelude, 1850, III, 61-3).

93. 'Lines composed a few miles above Tintern Abbey', 49-50.

94. England, *Don Juan* p. 173. Professor England elswhere has perceptive comments on Aurora and the Duchess (p. 180).

95. *Don Juan*, Steffan, Steffan and Pratt (eds.), p. 740.

96. See note 78 above. When Byron's letter to Moore and these stanzas are compared, the second interpretation is clearly confirmed.

97. 'Sepultus, resurrxit: Certum est, quia impossibile' ('Buried, he rose again: it is certain because it is impossible'). Tertullian, *Liber De Carne Christi* in *Opera Omnia: Patrologiae Cursus Completus*, J.P. Migne (ed.) (1879), p. 806.

98. Stavrou, 'Religion in *Don Juan*', seizes on this feature: 'Two passages often cited as belying Byron's irreligion are the "Ave Maria" verses in Canto III, and the apostrophe to the Gothic pile in Canto XIII. Yet in both passages, the emotion invoked is as much Pagan as Christian' (p. 578). Two pages later, on a different tack altogether, he writes Byron 'perhaps having unconsciously lapsed into piety' (p. 580).

99. It is encouraging that Professor McGann, well aware of Byron's Socinian streak, reads the passage in the second sense: 'Those rationalists skeptical of spiritualism will have to contend with Dr. Johnson, as well as the difficult intransigence of history, tradition, and certain uncomfortable facts.' (*Don Juan*, p. 137). But McGann draws a different conclusion: 'Regarding the worlds of skeptic and believer, Byron's story is, as he says elsewhere, "neither here not [sic] there" (XI, 5).' (ibid.)

100. The maintenance of a tone at odds with what is being recommended whilst at the same time recommending it is a feature of Augustan Verse (e.g. Pope's Imitations of Horace). Byron probably learnt it from Pope and Dryden.

101. Elizabeth Boyd, *Byron's Don Juan* (New Brunswick, 1945), p. 155, comments that Byron's ghost story 'shows under a mask of skepticism, humour and disillusionment, an undeniable will to believe'.

102. McGann, *Don Juan*, p. 186.

103. Aurora is prepared for by Leila who is young and pure 'like a day dawn', fiercely religious in a deliberately comic way (X, 75), and also a gem (X, 51). If Aurora appears sexless in comparison with Fitz-Fulke, she appears womanly after Leila who is wholly dependent on Juan. Leila exists, however, only in so far as she signifies. Her being makes no impression on the reader. Like Dudù, she is quietly disposed of and not later recalled. Leila's religious devotion is linked with Haidée's

('devout as well as fair', II, 93) and Dudù's 'not unholy thoughts' (XI, 54).

104. This insistence is crucial. A.V. Kernan, for instance, describes the comedy of *Don Juan* with relish (*Satire*, pp. 185-99) but nowhere takes account of the anti-comic force of Catharine and the subsequent break in the poem. Hence the ghost-escapade is, for Kernan, simply a typical instance of Life's comic triumph, the landscape of the house is sterile, and the monk is associated with the world of the Amundevilles. There is no sense here of the crux of the poem that Death may be the agency as well as the enemy of comic renewal.

105. Byron perhaps recalled the parodic 'An Ode: Secundum artem' which opens: 'Shall I begin with *Ah!* or *Oh!*' (William Cowper, *Poetical Works*, H. Milford (ed.), 4th edn (London, 1934), p. 289.) The poem is in fact by Robert Lloyd. Cantos VII, VIII and IX begin with 'Oh' and the first stanza of Canto XV elaborates the joke.

106. It is also relevant to posit a third route, that of the religious direction of much Romantic Art. H.G. Schenk, for instance, well known for his lifelong scholarship in this area, wrote in an article published posthumously: ' . . . the simultaneous existence of, and dissonance between the two key notes: namely the quest for religion and the inability to embrace\it whole-heartedly . . . never before was their paradoxical co-existence in man's soul exposed so mercilessly to the glaring light of consciousness'. 'Christianity and European Romanticism' in *The Downside Review*, April 1984, pp. 122-31. James, *Romantic Comedy*, p. 274 declares 'the consummation of the Romantic movement, namely, its rediscovery, in no mere spirit of archaeological zest, of Christian dogma'. James's claim relies heavily on Newman's assertion that Scott, Coleridge, Southey and Wordsworth prepared Men 'for some closer and more practical approximation to Catholic Truth' (ibid., p. 210). Byron cannot simply be slotted into these suggested patterns but *Don Juan* is a major test-case of their validity and places them in a new perspective.

CONCLUSION

I

We began this enquiry with two questions: 'How does *Don Juan* proceed?' and 'What kind of poem is it?' and we have tried to keep to these questions throughout. It should be unnecessary to fashion any conclusive epigrams for the poem's procedure since that has been the subject of continuous enquiry and should now be clear. It should be clear too that *Don Juan* is a comedy but here some threads remain to be gathered in the first part of this conclusion before, in the second part, we take the opportunity to signal the end of our stricter investigation by flying a few kites without any visible support.

The argument of the last chapter claims that *Don Juan* is a comedy not simply because it evidences much of the proper life of comedy but also because it engages in a re-definition of that life which we thus encounter as it were from scratch. What exactly does this mean?

In a very broad sense, Byron readily finds recoverable life in the inherited antitheses of tragedy and comedy. Croker, we recall, saw *Don Juan* as a comedy and *Childe Harold's Pilgrimage* as a tragedy.[1] George Steiner has suggested that, whereas most Romantic writers evaded tragic conclusion by the interposition of remorse or some vista of unearthly victory, Byron holds to a tragic conclusion, for instance, in *Manfred*.[2] In his last years Byron is clearly separating comic works of different kinds such as *Beppo, The Vision of Judgement* and *The Island* from *Cain, Heaven and Earth* and the three historical tragedies. He knew perfectly well that *Don Juan* was the comic counterpart to its unended predecessor, *Childe Harold's Pilgrimage*.

Don Juan, like so many comedies, is concerned with woman, Nature and society. Nature and society are separated in Seville and Haidée's isle but converge in the religiously conceived figure of Aurora Raby who belongs to, and transcends, both. Satire, which often appears to set up an alternative comedy of its own (Ben Jonson versus Shakespeare) and almost does so in *Don Juan*, is reclaimed for the larger vision. It is so in two ways. The satirist's structures tend to enforce his superiority over the common world of men and Nature which comedy finally trusts. Of course, the satirist may serve comic purposes in so far as he criticises would-be angels or would-be animals for departing from Nature and common humanity, but the stance of the satirist tends to isolate him from others and indefinitely widen his contempt. In the early parts of *Don Juan*, the narrative supplies some glowing antitheses to this. When this supply terminates in Catharine the Great, the isolated narrator is saved only by his persistence. Take away all comic connection and satire is the servant of egotism and nihilism but the narrator's enforced persistence in his 'No' puts him within reach of a 'Yes' which emerges as unexpectedly as Aurora Raby herself. Persistence and waiting, though quite uncomic in felt experience, are of the essence of religious faith and comic action. They do not present the spectacle of a slowly transformed experience but somehow make possible an unexpected, sudden and complete reversal. Aurora's exemption from the narrator's direct irony points to this and also to a positive foundation for the sustained satire of the final cantos.

The incidental and larger pattern of *Don Juan* is that of comedy, namely loss and restoration, but Byron's originality consists in making the losses so extreme that they seem to preclude comedy, and he shares with us his poem's exploration of the resources still available for comic restoration. Comedies always rely on presupposed resources, ultimately religious, which are less recognisable or expected in Byron's day or our own than, for instance, the Renaissance. Hence the attempt to found a comedy is now closely tied in with the availability of religious belief. However, comedies must be assured in their conviction of these resources otherwise they do not work as shared presuppositions. *Don Juan* is far more desperate than most comedies but does achieve, via its fraught yet triumphing procedures, a convincing assurance. The appearance of Aurora Raby indicates the depth Byron has finally to reach in order to maintain this assurance. She makes what is implicit already in the Centurion's presence of Canto V into so explicitly religious an authorisation that she could destroy the comic balance which she reinaugurates. Celia's martyrdom in Eliot's *The Cocktail Party* overshadows the comic ending of that play and Evelyn Waugh's fiction, though always deft, does not always interrelate comedy, pessimism and faith in convicing ways. It would have been insuperably difficult for Eliot to continue *Don Juan* as a comedy with Aurora Raby in it but it may even have been an advantage for Byron not to have been a believer in the sense that Evelyn Waugh and T.S. Eliot were. Byron said, of this, according to Medwin: 'No poet should be tied down to a direct profession of faith'.[3] Nowadays too much explicitness may suggest that the author is beleaguered in beliefs which he would like to, but cannot, presuppose and is thus separated from the received opinions of the society to which he would address his comedy. Brian Wilkie informs us that Byron's view of life 'as ultimately without meaning' is a view common amongst 'thinking men' for the last 'two or three hundred years'.[4] Byron was beleaguered certainly by his presumed, and sometimes flaunted, satanism and irreverence but also, I think, by his capacity for reverence in unfashionable forms. The poet who wrote *The Vision of Judgement*, which understands evil, deliberately omits God, and allows George III to creep into heaven at the end, knew more about reverence than the Poet Laureate (Southey) who wrote *A Vision of Judgement* and identified his judgement and his own idea of solemnity with God Himself. Byron was genuinely shocked by Southey's poem but not because he was one of Professor Wilkie's 'thinking men'. Byron was at considerable pains to keep his natural daughter away from this particular elite, for their questions, reason, and assurance were not his own. 'Thinking men' on the whole have not made conspicuously good readers of Byron's poetry.

Byron can nevertheless represent in *Don Juan* a perplexity which he knows that he shares with his contemporaries, however much they wish to put it to one side, yet he is sufficiently close to a Christianity with which he is fully familiar and almost claimed by to give Aurora Raby substance, sweetness and definition. He is sufficiently judicious and inventive as an author to realise her and maintain laughter and balance in his comic word.

We are not concerned, any more than Byron is, with questions of genre in themselves. *Don Juan* is all sorts of things. If it is argued that, in some respects, it is like a novel or a haiku or a bag then, provided that the evidence is carefully marshalled, no one will complain. My argumet has been that the poem does exist and develop as some kind of entity and that the determining life here is comic. The comedy of *Don Juan* contains and uses all the other modes which we find in the poem. Individual picaresque survival, transformation, the overriding concern with a social world satirised for its inability to value Nature, recognise Grace and celebrate an ideal couple, achieve a fine synthesis here. To accomplish this in a long, unfinished poem about a damnable, Spanish hero at a time when Nature is more readily claimed for the Higher Pantheism than the common creed involves a redefinition based on an understanding of tradition[5] and a remarkable capacity both to assimilate and subvert the new conventions of Byron's time.

Byron was more familiar with Regency Theatre than most of his contemporaries but he made no effort to write a comedy for it. 'The days of Comedy are gone, alas!' he claims (XIII, 94), because there is no longer sufficient differentiation in the present, social world. He refers admiringly to Congreve and to Molière whose comedies arise directly out of the societies to which they are addressed. Byron transfers this social comedy to a poem which can itself reveal why the society portrayed in it could not produce a comic theatre. At the same time, he touches much older and deeper resonances than Restoration comedy which surprise us because Byron's art presupposes them and, behold, they work. In a comic drama, the whole society would have to be transformed by the ending. In Byron's endless poem, it is sufficient that the whole society is placed alongside the sources which could renew it and that marriage between Juan and Aurora is understood to be possible. Wordsworth, Blake and Shelley all try to find a basis for affirmation which is not nebulous. Byron does something similar and quite different. We can gauge something of this similarity and difference by instancing M.H. Abram's pronouncement in *Natural Supernaturalism:*

> Whether a man shall live his old life or a new one, in a Universe of death or of life, a state of servitude or of genuine freedom — to the Romantic poet, all depends on his mind as it engages with the world in the act of perceiving.[6]

Even Manfred, who wants to believe something like this, cannot quite manage it and has to learn to wait. The reader of *Don Juan*, who also learns to wait, has not done so in order to celebrate the narrator's mind 'as it engages with the world in the act of perceiving' or to appropriate, so far as he can, some individually generated mythology. Instead, he is confirmed and renewed by what he already knows — that, although Reason may ridicule us for taking things upon trust, we can, should and must do so.

Don Juan is thus a great comedy by a great Romantic poet. It has now found the praise which it so richly deserves but it has been eulogised more for the excellence of its parts and incidental life, or the haphazard inventiveness of its progression, than it has been understood as a whole. When such understanding has been attempted, it has been commonly restricted to a master-theme, image or idea. The purpose of this study has been to make the life and determining form of the whole poem as transparent as possible and, in so doing, to recognise and celebrate Byron's redefinition of modern comedy.

II

Even the strictest sonata form will accept a coda which may or may not pick up the themes whose exposition and recapitulation is already completed. Such serious and playful devices, which mortals rarely 'cavil' at, must afford some relief to those who produce and those who receive them. This is offered as such a coda to the four chapters of this book which are, in intention at any rate, strict in form. This section announces, without preamble, modulation or development, motifs that arise out of but move away from preceding pages.

'Nature' in *Don Juan* is sometimes used with the sublime resonances attached to it by Byron's immediate predecessors as it is in *Childe Harold's Pilgrimage*. In the latter poem, however, interest finally shifts from mountains in Canto III to the art and architecture of European civilisation (Venice and Rome) in Canto IV. The problem in *Childe Harold* is how to celebrate an idealised art which is not merely a comforting fantasy. Byron solves this problem by relating the art which he finally celebrates (St Peter's, Laocoon, etc.) to the endurance of human suffering and to the invulnerability of the human mind. In *Don Juan*, it is other factors which cause our survival, though the stanzas on the ruined architecture of Norman Abbey link the two poems together. Nature is usually associated with Eros in a way that would be anathema to Wordsworth. The awkward 'Vaudracour and Julia' passage, placed in and then withdrawn from *The Prelude*, is an acknowledgement that Eros should (and did) play some part in Nature and Wordsworth's poem but it is weak in itself and without wider connection. In *Don Juan*, Nature fused with Eros is at once a divinity and a dead end. The problem in *Don Juan* is to recover confidence in Eros and Nature by summoning what is, in effect, a religious figure who represents Grace without destroying the former. Byron here enlists the aid of ruins and architecture, vehicles of wasted history and tragic suffering in *Childe Harold*, and makes them support comic ends whilst respecting their sombre austerity. Byron's predicament and purposes are surprisingly close in these respects to those of many medieval and Renaissance poets but their whole supporting framework of concepts and belief, though not extinct, is not readily presupposed in Napoleonic Europe. Norman Abbey sits alongside Nightmare, Northanger and Fonthill but it engages with the substance not merely the Gothic appearance of an older culture. Like Cologne Cathedral, it belongs to the nineteenth century and to a different past.

It is necessary to stress this because, if the argument of this book is accepted, there would still remain the danger that the spiritual life it specifies would be classified indeterminately with other instances of Romantic idealism and religious feeling and thus be quietly disregarded. Of course, Byron is part of his time and it can be helpful to situate him somewhere between Hume and Newman, or Voltaire and Ruskin. What is striking, however, is the distance separating Byron from Goethe and the distinction between the comic solidity of his redefinition of Don Juan Tenorio and the religio-erotic idealism that characterises numerous Continental versions of the story in the nineteenth century after Hoffman. To be sure, Byron's version could not be wholly other than these but the ontological character and explicit evolution of his poem makes it impossible for him to blur, as they do, religious and erotic motifs or to seek out and relish the tensions set up by the pursuit of an enchanting but illusory ideal. Aurora is present not distant, substantial not etherial, grave as well as radiant. She is a realised and intervening vision, not a construct of the narrator's nostalgia or Juan's blurred subjectivity. She has more not less being, more not less knowledge, than the other inhabitants of the Abbey.

Keats moved from his Cynthias and Lamias to the extraordinary conception of Moneta in *The Fall of Hyperion:*

> . . . Then saw I a wan face,
> Not pin'd by human sorrows, but bright-blanch'd
> By an immortal sickness which kills not;
> It works a constant change, which happy death
> Can put no end to; deathwards progressing
> To no doubt was that visage;

> (256-61)

Aurora is Byron's Moneta. There is a fine intensity in Keats's lines which Aurora does not summon. It is probable that neither Aurora nor Moneta would exist if both poets had not read Dante. But Keats, at the very moment when he is most trying to shape something more than an aesthetic impression, fails to do so. Terror, suffering and insight freeze in a magnificent, aesthetic tableau finer far than anything in *Endymion* but not different in kind. The 'awe' which Aurora produces (XV, 47) makes less immediate impression on the reader but it is wholly functional within the poem and reverberates outside it in a way that Moneta does not. Byron chooses a heroine not intensified by the conjunction of imagination and Eros, so typical of nineteenth-century practice, but given a religious solidity. Aurora is, as T.S. Eliot

observes, the most 'real' and the most 'serious' character of Byron's invention.

This may be considered a literary blasphemy for critics, other than
Eliot, usually prefer the intense, quasi-religious delineation of 'this
world's perplexing waste' to that trafficking between the customary
and 'worlds beyond' which marks Aurora. Brian Wilkie tells us that 'the
fact of life's insignificance was something that urgently needed to be
asserted in his day'.[7] Modern thinkers, it appears, have the good for-
tune to take this less urgently. The defence of modern science no longer
seems to require atheists but the defence of modern fictionality more
and more clearly does. Romanticism itself is largely responsible for this.
If, in Coleridge's widely repeated dictum, the imagination is 'a repetition in the finite mind of the eternal act of creation in the infinite I
Am'[8] and if perception and invention are inseparable, then the echo,
having established its identity with the voice, must soon declare that
there is no voice anyway. It will soon maintain that the given character of the environment, from which the echo rebounds, is wholly
shaped by itself: *Don Juan*, like all other fictions, is about itself. If the
past four chapters are right, the poem cannot be read like this.

Do we then need to be religious in Byron's or any other sense in
order to have ears to hear *Don Juan* with? The question is worth
mentioning though it may seem offensive to ears polite.

Our instinctive reply is a firm 'No' with perhaps the rider 'At least
not in any narrow, orthodox sense'. The momentary entertainment of
any other answer would appear to imperil the constitution of the
United States[9] or place our fictional lives in extreme jeopardy, but the
correct answer is in the affirmative. It is not so much a matter of insisting upon a religious attention, however, as of stifling secular pieties or,
in a different sense than usual, of suspending disbelief.

Don Juan is epic in scale though comic in mode. It is addressed to
human beings in society and to human beings as such. In both modes of
address, it is inescapably religious. Any long poem of substance has to
tap, widely and deeply, the inherited resources of the culture to which
it is addressed and whose perennial force it exists to celebrate and continue. These resources, almost by definition, must include the religious.
It is not at all surprising that *The Dunciad*, *The Prelude*, *In Memoriam*
and *Four Quartets* reveal these sources as distinctly as *The Faerie
Queene*, *Paradise Lost* or *The Aeneid*. *The Prelude* is a particularly interesting case because, in what we have come to call its two versions, we
can see Wordsworth gradually allowing the inherited vision of his
culture to claim his own. We should take this at least as seriously as

Wordsworth did but we insist on maintaining, without examination, secular dogmas that discourage any such investigation.[10] *Don Juan* is an English and a European poem, alert to contemporary shifts of thought and feeling, but it relies on and freely exposes historical and perennial sources for its narrative and commentary:

> I say no more than has been said in Dante's
> Verse, and by Solomon and by Cervantes;
>
> (VII, 3)

> I'll therefore take our ancient friend *Don Juan*,
> We all have seen him in the Pantomime
> Sent to the devil, somewhat ere his time.
>
> (I, 1)

The reader of a European poem, whatever his convictions or stance, can locate religious resonances inside as well as outside his presumed experience and should not pretend otherwise. There are no readers anywhere who can step wholly outside their historically received culture in the act of reading. Of course, readers will interpret and place these resonances differently. Some will try to evade them, others to seek them out, but we must avoid two simple errors. It is not a matter of religious readers picking up religious resonances and irreligious ones not doing so for both are equally the inheritors of the same culture and have similar powers of recognition. Nor is it a matter of some readers interpreting x or y in a religious way and others in a political, psychological or purely linguistic one. There is a psychology of political opinion but politics cannot be reduced to it. Religion, for believers and non-believers alike, can be perceived in a variety of ideological classifications but it remains a distinct and irreducible human mode and appears likely to continue as such. Hence the reader of *Don Juan* must see himself included within the outreach of his own culture's habitual resources and recognise them, wanted or unwanted, as his own. This occurs quite naturally in the reading of long poems. No special training or process is called for. However, the cult of fictionality could interpose its own censorship and authorise receptivity only on its own terms. In this sense, we do need to be religious in order to read *Don Juan*.

There is another sense too. *Don Juan* is concerned not only with the character of European and Ottoman social existence but with existence itself. Byron dies simply as a man as well as a great European poet. The poem is filled with English words but they do not fill an English space. Forms of Eros are culturally developed and transmitted but sexual glow is part of human biology and transmits existence itself. The narrator's thoughts are European thoughts but Mind is not European. 'No one', confessed a reviewer of Cantos IX to XI in *The Literary Examiner* for 2nd August, 1823, could so well describe 'the universal condition of being as Lord Byron'. Over and over again, the mental and physical activities of the poem are set against 'a depth of feeling' which embrace thoughts silent and deep as Space. It has been hardest of all to pursue this for it can easily become esoteric and obscurantist,[11] but every good reader of *Don Juan* knows that the lucid vitality of the poem dies into and lives out of a blankness familiar to the reader in the gaps of his experience and as the ground of that experience. Any kind of persistence in the face of this immediate unknown is religious. What else could it be?[12] When this persistence is shaped by comic expectations so that a tragic sense of life or a specifically Stoic indifference (not Aurora's) is made ludicrous, then the religious attention that is provoked is clearly analogous or identical to the Hope of orthodox belief. In so far as we share this comically shaped persistence in *Don Juan* we are, in this other sense too, religious readers.

Indeed, though there are many other legitimate and worth-while modes of enquiry into *Don Juan* than that mounted here, it is pertinent to observe that neither the close reading inaugurated by New Criticism, whose apparent rigour is shaped by a soft and often unexamined consensus, nor Structuralist review of the articulation of relative worlds through writing, will allow us to explicate fully the true bearings of Byron's chiaroscuro. The text of *Don Juan* cannot be relied upon to lie in wait for the earnest exegesis of fresh meanings. To this extent, Structuralist emphasis on gaps, game with conventions, and the manoeuvring of expectations is relevant. *Don Juan* means, but it is undoubtedly concerned with the genesis of meaning. However, Byron's poem is not presented and should not be treated as an *Ecriture* lending temporary and relative stability to an otherwise absurd existence and unknowable world. Nor can its religious character be read off simply as one system of conventions amongst others ('a religious code'). The narrator may well be a proto-structuralist but the poem cannot be merely an instance of the viewpoint which it contains. *Don Juan* is concerned with the genesis of meaning but also with the nature of our ineluctable concern with the genesis of meaning. Forms of language are crucial, indispensable but not constitutive here. It is not so much the constant actualisation of potential meanings but the sustained and unnerving proximity to potentiality itself which *Don Juan* hazards. The risk is not that improvisation might dry up, but that persistence in it might eventually bring us some annihilating sense of the unsayable intelligibility or primal light which is itself disclosed in our potentiality to construct an indefinite series of intelligible structures. The narrator, who is always turned towards the poem which he improvises hears behind his back the muse, hailed so casually, drawing near. Don Juan Tenorio's simpler persistence, similarly, summons and shapes the dreadful intervention whose possibility he denies. In Byron's poem, such an intervention, though reinforcing the mortality of the poet, renews the poem itself and confirms its comic character. Fear, experimental blasphemies and Aurora Raby are the manifestations of this generative anxiety. The reader should be caught up in the process of the last cantos as well as identifying their character.

Byron's music has some 'mystic diapasons' as he ironically acknowledges in another context (XIV, 22) but he does not play on them all the time. Enquiries into Byron's own religious views invariably confine themselves to specific statements of belief or non-belief together with some allusion to Byron's mobility of temperament. We do not, however, confine Chaucer's or Dante's or Ben Jonson's or Tolstoy's religion solely to their explicitly religious declarations. The vivid and comprehensive humanity of these writers and their sure grasp of familiar life is not seen as something quite distinct from their religious consciousness. Byron changes his mind and is in touch with more aspects of human experience than his readers or critics are likely to be, but he always tries to see things as a whole and his comic art convinces us that this is possible, though we cannot separately see the foundations of this unity. Zoe's famous fried eggs and coffee intrude upon Haidée's glorious, selfish exaltation; Aurora's peace infiltrates the sterile bustle of the Amundevilles. At any moment in *Don Juan* we will be aware of bewildering interactions of all kinds, held in a lucid attentiveness which nevertheless suggests an enigmatic containment. Such containment, to the narrator's exasperation, can neither be separately named nor resolved away, but the procedures of the poem itself depend upon its presupposition.

We cannot say then, and have not argued, that *Don Juan* is a religious poem because it exhibits a religious code which exists despite or apart from its worldliness any more than Ben Jonson's *Bartholomew Fair* suspends a religious vision discernible elsewhere in his work. Professor McGann makes a similar point but with a different emphasis:

God and all transcendentals are meaningless answers to human problems unless they are held firmly within the restricted (and hence absurd) limits of human understanding. For this reason does Byron leave God out of his poem, except as He is a matter of various human speculations, beliefs, or experiences narrated in the stories — except as He is a part of history, tradition, and facts. In this way Byron "naturalises the supernatural", he does not, however, "humanize the divine". God and all transcendentals remain for him in their defined (and hence proper) positions: beyond the world. We are left only with our definitions of them, their fictional presences.[13]

Professor McGann insists, in all his writings on Byron, on the poet's fidelity to his experience of uncertainty. He is quite right to do so and Aurora cannot be more than a 'fictional presence' for the transcendent. But *Don Juan* is not quite as detached from its knowledge as McGann implies throughout *Don Juan in Context*. The process of the poem involves it in a testing, trusting and evolving relationship with the mysterious given as well as a clarifying hold on it. Similarly, Aurora's fictional presence is lost in the silent spaces of Pascal's fearful intimation[14] and the awe she excites is directed not towards that fictional presence but towards unknown modes of being 'beyond this world's perplexing waste'.

Religion is, of course, to be found in the devotional verse of isolated sensibilities and it can be examined in the public products of 'ages of faith'. We may trust it not to bite us. Be that as it may, literary study, though it has its own appropriate methods and concern, will always encounter and have to admit religious forms of awareness profoundly diffused in all manner of literary texts. Neither economics, linguistics or end-stopped fictionality will eradicate sacred places from secular citadels for secular citadels are founded on sacred places. Byron, according to Medwin, asked, 'Will men never learn that every great poet is necessarily a religious man — so at least Coleridge says?'[15] There is thus some food for critical thought in Byron's lines on St Peter's:

Enter: its grandeur overwhelms thee not;
And why? it is not lessened; but thy mind
Expanded by the genius of the spot,
Has grown colossal and can only find
A fit abode wherein appear enshrined
Thy hopes of immortality; and thou

Shalt one day, if found worthy, so defined
See thy God face to face, as thou dost now
His Holy of Holies, nor be blasted by his brow.

(*Childe Harold's Pilgrimage*, IV, 155)

Eros has an analogous effect to art here, for Haidée finds in the presence of Juan 'such/Enlargement of existence' (II, 173). Byron's *Don Juan* should excite an answering largeness in its readers and critics.

Notes

1. See Chapter 4, note 56. |
2. G. Steiner, *The Death of Tragedy* (London, 1961, paperback, 1963), p. 202. Steiner elsewhere calls Byron's mystery plays 'pageants of the religious imagination' (p. 209).
3. *Medwin's Conversations of Lord Byron*, Ernest J. Lovell, Jr. (ed.) (Princeton, 1966), p. 77.
4. Brian Wilkie, *Romantic Poets and Epic Tradition* (Madison and Milwaukee, 1965), p. 211.
5. Leo Weinstein, in his invaluable survey *The Metamorphoses of Don Juan*, maintains that Byron's *Don Juan* is so odd an instance of the genre that Byron has complete 'lack of respect for tradition'. This is understandable, given Weinstein's panoramic view of Don Juan versions, but mistaken. Byron's is the only version to modify the tradition substantially but recover its original existential *frisson*.
G.B. Shaw in *Man and Superman* (1903) copies Byron's inversion of Juan's role, derides Byron, and concludes his play with the marriage of John Tanner (Juan Tenorio). However, he deflates and talks out the dread inherent in Tirso's and Byron's conceptions by his unfortunate 'Don Juan in Hell' scene. Instead there is much talk of the 'Life Force' raising men to a higher existence in the manner of Goethe's Faust (though that play too is ridiculed by Shaw). Shaw's play is far too explicit about the sources of comedy for it to work as a whole. It refuses to be superficial and fails to be profound. See also Candace Tate, 'Byron's *Don Juan*: Myth as Psychodrama', *Keats-Shelley* Journal, vol. XXIX, 1980, pp. 131-50. Tate sees Byron's re-working of the Don Juan story but his emphasis is psychological.
6. M.H. Abrams, |*Natural Supernaturalism* (New York, 1971), p. 395.
7. Wilkie, *Romantic Poets*, p. 211. Professor Wilkie nowhere mentions Aurora. Byron claims to reassert not 'Life's insignificance' but 'the Nothingness of life' as confessed 'By saint, by sage, by preacher, and by poet' (VII, 6). This is something else.
8. S.T. Coleridge, *Biographia Literaria* (1817, reprinted Scholar Press, Menston, 1971), vol. I, chapter xiii, p. 296.
9. In *The Liberal Imagination* (London, 1951) Lionel Trilling argues that it is not necessary to share the beliefs of an author in order to understand and enjoy his work. This is certainly the case but not the end of the matter. We may, for example, be able to imagine or to know something whilst remaining detached and unaffected by our exercise of knowledge and imagination. It is quite a different thing to relinquish or gainsay kinds of recognition. Literature cannot be assessed simply in so far as it is the expression of our preferred opinions but it may strengthen, modify or diminish the character and capacities of our assent. It would be odd if our beliefs were in no way implicated or affected by our reading of

literature.

10. D.G. James writes of Wordsworth after 1805: 'But from then on his imagination . . . found adequate conveyance in Christian dogma, a change which . . . was in accordance with all that was fundamental in his earlier imaginative life' (p. 209). 'Wordsworth bowed to what he came to feel was the superior expressiveness of Christian dogma' (p. 211). *Scepticism and Poetry* (London, 1937).

11. For an attempt of a parallel kind see Bruce F. Kawin, *The Mind of the Novel: Reflexive Fiction and the Ineffable* (Guildford, N.J. 1984).

12. Byron is fascinated by kinds of human persistence and associates them, as Wordsworth does, with extra-human orders of consciousness. Manfred's persistence, for instance, is clearly religious in character. He rejects the Abbot's remedy but seems to accept his diagnosis. Like the narrator he will submit to no one, but his death represents his acquiescence to waiting itself.

13. J.J. McGann, *Don Juan in Context* (London, 1976), p. 139.

14. Blaise Pascal, *Pensées*, p. 206. The intimation is Pascal's; the terror is probably imputed to the imagined unbeliever not to Pascal himself.

15. *Medwin's Conversations*, p. 198.

INDEX

Works by writers other than Byron are only selectively specified with the remaining references being entered tacitly under the authors' names.